For my parents and my grandparents

Raising Royalty

CAROLYN HARRIS

RAISING
Royalty

1000 Years of Royal Parenting

DUNDURN
TORONTO

Cover image: Wikimedia Commons/ Franz Xaver Winterhalter
Printer: Friesens

Library and Archives Canada Cataloguing in Publication

Harris, Carolyn, 1984-, author
     Raising royalty : 1000 years of royal parenting / Carolyn Harris.

Includes bibliographical references and index.
Issued in print and electronic formats.
ISBN 978-1-4597-3569-9 (hardcover).--ISBN 978-1-4597-3570-5
(PDF).--ISBN 978-1-4597-3571-2 (EPUB)

     1. Kings and rulers--Children--History. 2. Parent and child--
History. 3. Royal houses--History. I. Title.

D226.7.H37 2017   305.5'220922   C2016-907272-X
                                               C2016-907273-8

1 2 3 4 5   21 20 19 18 17

Conseil des Arts du Canada Canada Council for the Arts Canadä ONTARIO ARTS COUNCIL CONSEIL DES ARTS DE L'ONTARIO an Ontario government agency un organisme du gouvernement de l'Ontario

We acknowledge the support of the **Canada Council for the Arts** and the **Ontario Arts Council** for our publishing program. We also acknowledge the financial support of the **Government of Ontario**, through the **Ontario Book Publishing Tax Credit** and the **Ontario Media Development Corporation**, and the **Government of Canada**.

Care has been taken to trace the ownership of copyright material used in this book. The author and the publisher welcome any information enabling them to rectify any references or credits in subsequent editions.
                                                            — *J. Kirk Howard, President*

The publisher is not responsible for websites or their content unless they are owned by the publisher.

Printed and bound in Canada.

VISIT US AT

 dundurn.com | @dundurnpress | dundurnpress | dundurnpress

Dundurn
3 Church Street, Suite 500
Toronto, Ontario, Canada
M5E 1M2

Contents

Introduction   Raising a Royal Child   9

1   Edgar "the Peaceable" (c. 943–75) and   17
     Elfrida of Northampton (c. 945–1001)

2   William I "the Conqueror" (c. 1028–87) and   25
     Matilda of Flanders (c. 1031–83)

3   Henry II (1133–89) and Eleanor of Aquitaine   33
     (c. 1124–1204)

4   Henry III (1207–72) and Eleanor of Provence   44
     (c. 1223–91)

5   Edward III (1312–77) and Philippa of Hainault   52
     (1314–69)

6   Richard III (1452–85) and Anne Neville (1456–85)   65

7   Ferdinand II of Aragon (1452–1516) and   75
     Isabella I of Castile (1451–1504)

8   Henry VIII (1491–1547) and   84
     Catherine of Aragon (1485–1536)

9	Frederick V, Elector Palatine, (1596–1632) and Elizabeth of England and Scotland (1596–1662)	93
10	Charles I (1600–49) and Henrietta Maria of France (1609–69)	104
11	Peter I "the Great" of Russia (1672–1725) and Catherine I (1684–1727)	114
12	Anne (1665–1714) and George of Denmark (1653–1708)	123
13	George II (1683–1760) and Caroline of Ansbach (1683–1737)	132
14	Louis XVI of France (1754–93) and Marie Antoinette of Austria (1755–93)	141
15	Victoria (1819–1901) and Albert of Saxe-Coburg-Gotha (1819–61)	150
16	Nicholas II of Russia (1868–1918) and Alexandra of Hesse-Darmstadt (1872–1918)	165
17	Juliana of the Netherlands (1909–2004) and Bernhard of Lippe-Biesterfeld (1911–2004)	176
18	Elizabeth II (1926–) and Philip of Greece and Denmark (1921–)	184
19	Prince Charles (1948–) and Diana Spencer (1961–97)	193
20	Prince William (1982–) and Catherine Middleton (1982–)	201
Epilogue	The Future of the Royal Nursery	213
Acknowledgements		219
Notes		221
Further Reading		239
Index		249

INTRODUCTION

Raising a Royal Child

Prince William made his first parenting mistake in the eyes of the world on the day that his son, Prince George, left hospital in July 2013. There had been journalists and photographers camped around the maternity wing of St. Mary's hospital in London for weeks leading up to the birth, waiting for the moment when William and his wife Catherine — nicknamed Kate by the media — the Duke and Duchess of Cambridge, would emerge from the hospital to present their newborn child to the world. Every moment of baby George's first public appearance was captured on camera to be scrutinized by people around the world on their television screens and online streams. The royal parents received a great deal of praise. William had his sleeves rolled up as though he had just changed a diaper, and Kate wore a fitted dress that did not attempt to disguise her post-pregnancy figure. Even little George appeared to be waving to the crowds from his swaddling clothes.

The criticism came when it was time for William to strap George into his car seat. In previous generations, this kind of task would have been left to a member of the royal household, but William was determined to strap his son into the car and drive his family home like any other new father. Knowing the world's press would be watching him closely, William reputedly practised assembling the car seat in the privacy of Kensington Palace during the weeks leading up to the birth. Despite these careful preparations, not everything went perfectly on the big day. Within moments of the royal couple and their baby leaving hospital and returning to the palace, parents from all walks of life were posting on internet forums that George had not been properly strapped into his car seat.

On the British childcare blog "Baby Centre," an irate commenter posted, "If you scroll down to the photos of the baby in the carseat [*sic*] you will see he is not properly strapped in AT ALL!! Very disappointed! I'm sure they were in a hurry, and I hope that Kate will fix it once they are in the vehicle as it appeared she was sitting in back with the baby." The commenter included guidelines from the website ChildCarSeats.co.uk to back up her comments. Over at iVillage, online commenters questioned whether a swaddled baby should be in a car seat at all. By the time George's younger sister, Princess Charlotte, was born in 2015, William seemed to have mastered the car seat — but there was a new complaint: the baby princess's bonnet appeared to be on backwards for her first public appearance!

The debate over William and the car seat continued for years after George's birth. In May 2016, one of the United Kingdom's most prominent etiquette experts, William Hanson, complained that Prince William's approach to fatherhood was undermining the traditional grandeur, and therefore the future, of the monarchy, writing in the *Daily Mail*, "I want a well-waxed chauffeured Bentley, not Prince William driving mother and latest child home from the hospital in their family car like a regular bloke."

Commentary of this kind is almost unknown in the Commonwealth realms, including Canada, where William and Kate were praised for touring with a small entourage in 2011 and spending time with their children in 2016. When the Canadian edition of *Hello!* published photographs of William holding George at a garden party at Government House in Victoria, British Columbia, in the autumn of 2016, the coverage included praise of William's close relationship with his son. *Hello!* reported that "Royal watchers will never forget how he expertly fastened Prince George into the back seat of the car when the tot was just one day old and leaving the hospital." William's decision to strap his newborn son into a car seat and drive his family home from hospital had transcended popular debates over the nature of good parenting to encompass the public image of the monarchy as an institution.

The monarchy has always been a family affair. *Raising Royalty* is the story of how twenty royal couples over the past thousand years have navigated the unique challenges of parenting in the public eye. From fending off Vikings to fending off paparazzi, royal mothers and fathers have made decisions for royal children that encompassed their own personal ambitions and the stability of the throne as well as the timeless needs of young children. Over the past ten centuries, royal children have been parented both in country palaces with well-appointed nurseries and in exile far from their birthplaces. As royal parents, William and Kate are following in the footsteps of centuries of kings and queens, princes and princesses, who were mothers and fathers as well as royalty.

The length and definition of childhood has changed over the centuries, shaping the experiences of royal children. Before the Norman Conquest of 1066, a boy was old enough to swear allegiance to the king at the age of twelve, but Richard III's nephew, Edward V, was considered too young to rule as king in his own right at that age in 1483. Until the nineteenth century, royal children were often betrothed before they were twelve and married in their early teens to seal diplomatic alliances. The business of ruling was conducted in person by kings and queens who were often away from their children for long periods of time. Even the most devoted royal parents paid little attention to the emotional needs of their children, expecting the obedience of a subject to a sovereign as well as a child to a parent. At a time of high infant mortality, royal parents often expressed their attachment to their children through concern for their health instead of their happiness.

By the late eighteenth century, a new emphasis on "natural" childrearing resulted in royal mothers such as Queen Marie Antoinette of France creating parenting philosophies that took the individual personalities and emotional needs of their children into account. Older methods of royal parenting, however, proved remarkably resilient. Well into the twentieth century, generations of royal children complained that they saw little of their parents and were expected to obey them without question, even as adults. The public viewed the open displays of affection between Diana, Princess of Wales, and her sons, captured by photographers, as a break from royal tradition. Today, William and Kate emphasize that their children will receive as normal an upbringing as possible, demonstrating that the youngest generation of royal parents recognizes the differences between royal tradition and modern parenting trends.

The intense public scrutiny William and Kate experience as parents seems like a modern phenomenon fuelled by the 24-hour news cycle and ubiquity of online message boards, but for as long as there has been royalty, there has been public scrutiny of royal parenting. For centuries, observers from diverse social backgrounds have expressed advice intended for royal parents. Critiquing royal parenting has also been a way of expressing political dissent. Until the twentieth century, high politics was the preserve of a tiny, predominantly male elite, but everyone had ideas about marriage and childrearing from their own experiences and observations. A royal couple whose marriage and family did not meet popular expectations might find themselves the target of satire in popular verse and pamphlets. If relations between monarchs and their people completely broke down, royalty might find themselves having to defend their parenting as well as their political decisions before parliament or a revolutionary tribunal.

Satisfying public opinion is just one of the many challenges royal parents have faced over the centuries. Parenting advice manuals written for commoners — even wealthy commoners — had little to say that addressed the unique circumstances in the royal nursery. Seventeenth-century Protestant clergymen urged fathers to take charge of their children's training and education, as mothers might be inclined to spare the rod and therefore spoil the child, but King Charles I of England and Scotland had signed a marriage contract that guaranteed his French wife Henrietta Maria control of their children until they turned thirteen. Eighteenth-century French philosophers encouraged mothers to breastfeed and allow their children to explore freely, but when Marie Antoinette tried to follow this advice, she found herself at odds with the strict court etiquette of Versailles. The parenting experts of the 1950s urged parents to teach their children self-reliance, but Queen Elizabeth II's children were surrounded by servants charged with making their beds and preparing their meals.

For centuries, one of the biggest differences between royalty and everyone else was whom they married. While most people found partners within their own communities, kings and queens, princes and princesses married foreign royalty to cement diplomatic alliances. Until the First World War, royalty was expected to marry other royalty, and that sometimes meant co-parenting with a spouse who did not speak the same language let alone share the same culture and parenting philosophy. In medieval and Renaissance times, English kings often married princesses from regions that are now part of France or Spain, popularizing new baby names such as Eleanor, Isabelle and even Alphonso. In the eighteenth and nineteenth centuries, a series of German royal consorts brought their own traditions to England, including, most famously, the Christmas tree.

When British princesses married foreign princes, they brought their own customs with them, often in the face of considerable opposition. In the nineteenth and early twentieth centuries, Queen Victoria's granddaughters and great-granddaughters found that their traditions, parenting techniques, and British nannies were not always appreciated in Germany, Russia, Romania, Greece, or Spain. After the First World War, British royalty married into the English and Scottish aristocracy, who were accustomed to more privacy for their families than royalty usually experienced. William is the first direct heir to the British and Commonwealth thrones to marry a woman from a middle-class background since 1660, and Kate's upbringing was very different from his own. Of all the royal parents discussed in this book, only one couple — Richard III and his queen, Anne Neville — were raised in the same castle with a similar outlook on life.

William is involved in the upbringing of his children and enjoys a close relationship with his father, Prince Charles, but in past centuries, raising a son often meant raising a rival for European royal fathers. William the Conqueror's queen, Matilda of Flanders, interceded with her husband on behalf of her eldest son Robert, who led an army against his father. Henry II went to war against his three elder sons; his queen, Eleanor of Aquitaine, backed her children against her husband. These conflicts had the potential to turn deadly — Czar Peter the Great of Russia sentenced his son and heir to death — but by the eighteenth century, conflict between royal parents and children had been absorbed into the political system. The origins of opposition parties date from the political factions that surrounded the sons of George I and George II, who were in constant conflict with their fathers. Among the royal fathers who had the most success as parents were those who bonded with their children during periods of war and revolution that threatened their thrones.

For a royal mother, the vast responsibilities of being a queen consort, including witnessing legal charters, ruling the kingdom while the king was at war, and acting as a patron of artists and musicians, often took priority over day-to-day childrearing. The result was generations of royal children raised by grandmothers, governesses, and nannies. Those queens who expected to raise and educate their children themselves, such as Eleanor of Provence, Catherine of Aragon, and Marie Antoinette, left themselves open to accusations of bringing foreign ideas into the nursery and acting beneath the dignity of a queen. A royal mother's distance from the nursery, however, did not mean disinterest. The relatives and servants charged with day-to-day childrearing received constant instructions and requests for news. Royal mothers were often extremely ambitious for their children and willing to go to great lengths to ensure their future. The first crowned English queen consort, Elfrida of Northampton, was accused of orchestrating a murder to ensure her son became king.

Regardless of who raised a royal child, a decision had to be made about where they would be raised. In the fourteenth century, the ideal home for a growing English prince or princess was a country palace, far from the Black Death plague that spread so quickly in crowded towns. By Victorian times, royal palaces throughout Europe had nursery wings where children had their own routines separate from those of their parents, including simple food, open windows for plenty of fresh air, and regular walks. There were plenty of royal children, however, who grew up far from home because their kingdoms were at war. King Ferdinand of Aragon and Queen Isabella of Castile spent much of their reigns on military campaign, and their children accompanied them as they waged war against the Emir of Granada to unite all of Spain under their rule. King Frederick and Queen Elizabeth of Bohemia had to leave Prague so quickly during the Thirty Years' War that they nearly left their baby son on the castle floor. The future Queen Juliana of the Netherlands spent the Second World War in Canada, raising her young daughters in Ottawa. When deposed monarchs such as Charles I, Louis XVI of France, and Nicholas II of Russia were imprisoned by their former subjects, their children also lost their liberty, and sometimes their lives.

Even monarchs in peacetime feared for the health and safety of their children. Until the twentieth century, infant mortality in Europe was high, and royalty was not spared the loss of infants and children to illness and accidents. Royal parents were often devastated by the loss of their young children. Grieving kings and queens commissioned memorials and ordered days of mourning when their children died. These family tragedies had lasting political consequences. The death of Ferdinand and Isabella's only son as a young man threatened the unity of Spain. The death of their grandson as a toddler ended any hope of a lasting union between Spain and Portugal. The hemophilia of Nicholas II's only son, which threatened the child's life on numerous occasions, undermined the Russian monarchy in the years leading up to the Russian Revolutions of 1917. Of Queen Anne's seventeen pregnancies, her only child to survive infancy died at the age of eleven, resulting in the end of Stuart rule of Britain and the accession of the German House of Hanover.

For children who survived infancy, there was the question of how they should be educated. Until the mid-eighteenth century, English kings led troops into battle themselves, so the sons of medieval rulers usually spent their formative years in the tiltyard, learning how to ride a horse or wield a sword. Even the future Richard III, who suffered from scoliosis, was trained to be a formidable warrior. Younger sons sometimes received more academic training, as the church was a suitable vocation for princes who were unlikely to succeed to the throne. When second sons, such as Henry VIII or Charles I, unexpectedly became king, they raised education standards for all their children. Lessons varied for princesses. A medieval princess often had to manage her families' castles and lands while her husband was at war. Renaissance princesses received a classical education, as the sixteenth century was a period of unprecedented female rule in Europe. In the seventeenth and eighteenth centuries, the curriculum focused on so-called feminine accomplishments such as dancing, deportment, painting, and religious instruction. Today, both princes and princesses attend university, experiencing a period of relative anonymity before assuming a full-time schedule of public engagements.

In the past, before many princes and princesses completed their education, it was already time to leave home. Medieval heirs to the English throne were sent to Wales as teenagers to preside over their own royal households and learn the business of ruling. Edward III placed his dozen children in the households of prominent members of the nobility, a practice followed by numerous other medieval monarchs. Charles I's and Henrietta Maria's eldest daughter Mary was only ten when she left England with her mother to reside with her future husband's family in the Netherlands, and other princesses of the period were not much older when they travelled abroad in preparation for marriage. Royal parents found many ways to keep in touch with their children from far away, including correspondence, gifts, and the occasional visit. Even in the twentieth century, both Prince Charles and Prince William attended boarding school from an early age, completing their educations far from their parents.

For William and Kate's children, the biggest difference between their upbringing and that of previous royal children will be close proximity to their parents throughout their childhoods. There is speculation that George and Charlotte will attend a day school for their elementary education, allowing them to spend evenings and weekends at home. William and George are unlikely ever to be locked in a struggle for the throne like previous royal fathers and sons, and Charlotte will have the same educational opportunities as her brother. Public scrutiny of royal parenting, however, has remained a constant theme over the past thousand years. For as long as there has been royalty, everybody has had an opinion on royal parenting. George's car seat and Charlotte's bonnet are only the beginning of a lifetime of parenting in the public eye for William and Kate, following in the footsteps of more than a millennium of royal parents.

ONE

Edgar "the Peaceable" (c. 943-75) and Elfrida of Northampton (c. 945-1001)

Around the year 968, King Edgar of England and his queen, Elfrida, presented their newborn son Ethelred to the public for the first time. It was Ethelred's christening day, an important occasion for a royal couple with a shared interest in the reform of monasteries and convents. In common with the christening of Prince George in 2013, the Archbishop of Canterbury performed the ceremony. From 960 to 988, the Archbishop was Dunstan, who implemented the royal couple's program of religious reform. Edgar and Elfrida were accustomed to ceremonies of this kind; their elder son, Edmund, had made his first public appearance in a similar ceremony just a few years before, and both Edgar and Elfrida had children from previous marriages.

Unfortunately, the infant Ethelred did not make a good first impression on the assembled nobles and clergymen. During the ceremony, the newborn prince "interrupted the sacrament by opening his bowels." Archbishop Dunstan was horrified and declared to the assembled congregation, "By God and His Mother, he will be a wastrel when he is a man."[1] Future chroniclers interpreted the incident at the christening as an omen of Ethelred's disastrous reign. In her determination to see her son crowned king, however, Elfrida would appear to have placed her maternal ambitions above the will of God. She would go down in history as the ultimate wicked stepmother, willing to resort to any means, including murder, to advance Ethelred's interests and her own.

Anglo-Saxon kings, who first governed seven distinct English kingdoms from the sixth century and then an England united under the House of Wessex from the reign of King Athelstan (927–39), had long resisted the idea of a royal family with a recognizable public profile. Roman emperors, who governed Britain from 43 to 410, had empresses consort whose statues appeared in public forums — and whose conduct enhanced or undermined the legitimacy of the ruler. In contrast, Anglo-Saxon rulers kept their families firmly in the background. Asser, the biographer of Athelstan's grandfather, Alfred the Great (r. 871–99), explained:

> For the nation of the West Saxons do[es] not allow a queen to sit beside the king, nor to be called a queen, but only the king's wife; which stigma the elders of that land say arose from a certain obstinate and malevolent queen of the same nation, who did all things so contrary to her lord, and to all the people that she not only earned for herself exclusion from the royal seat, but also entailed the same stigma upon those who came after her; for in consequence of the wickedness of that queen, all the nobles of that land swore together that they would never let any king reign over them, who should attempt to place a queen on the throne by his side.[2]

The complicated personal lives of Anglo-Saxon kings contributed to the absence of a defined royal family. Christianity had come to the British Isles with the conversion of King Ethelbert of Kent around the year 600, but the Christian conception of marriage as an indissoluble sacrament did not become standard practice among the Anglo-Saxon kings. Instead, kings married successive women "according to the Danish custom," in handfast ceremonies, reserving Christian rites for a final marriage to a particularly wealthy noblewoman or foreign princess. Edgar's three marriages followed this pattern, prompting the *Anglo-Saxon Chronicle* to observe, "He loved evil foreign customs and brought too firmly heathen manners within this land."[3] During the late 950s, before succeeding his brother Eadwig as King of England, Edgar married Ethelflaed, "the white duck," the daughter of a high-ranking royal official, who may have died giving birth to their son Edward in 960. A second marriage to a well-born woman named Wulfthyrth was dissolved around 963, soon after the birth of a daughter, the future St. Edith of Wilton. Wulfthyrth's retirement to a convent, along with her daughter, allowed Edgar to marry Elfrida according to Christian rites in 964.

There is evidence that Edgar maintained an interest in the upbringing of his children long after his relationships with their mothers had ended. Edward appears to have been absorbed into his father's household, appearing as a witness to royal charters from early childhood. St. Edith's hagiography emphasizes her close relationship with Edgar, stating that he appointed two foreign tutors for her education and readily granted her petitions. Both Edward and Edith were clearly acknowledged as the king's children, and gained prestige from their relationship with their ruling father.

During the early years of Edgar's reign, there was no predictable line of succession. All sons recognized by a king were considered *atheling* — throne-worthy — and the claims of women and children were often disregarded in favour of leadership by an adult male who was an experienced military leader. Anglo-Saxon England experienced frequent Viking invasions and a deceased king's adult brother or grown son from a hand-fast marriage could command far more support than young "legitimate" sons like Ethelred or his elder brother Edmund.

The reign of King Edgar saw the emergence of a clearly identifiable royal family, as Elfrida was determined to ensure that her sons were the only royal children viewed as throne-worthy by the Witan, the council of earls and bishops who would acclaim the next king. The 966 founding charter for the New Minster at Winchester, a royal Benedictine abbey, made clear who was considered part of the royal family after the marriage of Edgar and Elfrida. In the charter, the infant Edmund was described as the king's "legitimate heir," and his mother Elfrida was "she who is legitimately at the king's side." In contrast, Edward appeared as the king's "procreated heir."[4] The symbols on the charter reinforced this definition of a legitimate royal family: Edgar, Elfrida, Edmund, and Edgar's grandmother, Eadgifu of Kent, all had gold crosses beside their names, while Edward received only the outline of a cross. Despite Edgar's care for his elder children, a clear transition was underway from anonymous royal wives and equally throne-worthy sons to a queen consort who was the mother of legitimate heirs.

In 973, Elfrida became England's first consecrated queen consort when she was crowned alongside Edgar in a lavish coronation ceremony at Bath Abbey. The ceremony, composed by Archbishop Dunstan, set precedents for all future English (then British) royal coronations. Dunstan's choice of Biblical verse from the Book of Kings, the anointing of King Solomon (set to music as "Zadok the Priest" by George Frideric Handel for the coronation of King George II in 1737), has remained part of the consecration of successive monarchs, including Queen Elizabeth II in 1953. For Elfrida in 973, the coronation affirmed her legitimacy as queen and her prominence in religion as well as politics. As an anointed queen, Elfrida was expected to act as protector and patron of convents, the places where the daughters of Anglo-Saxon kings were often educated to become abbesses or the consorts of foreign rulers. The monasteries and convents began to offer prayers not just for the king but for the entire royal family.

Ethelred's birthplace is not recorded, and there is little evidence of how he and Edmund spent their early childhood. There were precedents in the House of Wessex for royal children to be raised in close proximity to their parents and by foster parents in separate households. Alfred the Great, the youngest of five surviving brothers, appears to have received a great deal of personal attention from his parents. Asser states that he went on a pilgrimage to Rome with his father, King Ethelwulf of Wessex, and was taught to read by his mother, Osburga. In contrast, Edgar spent his childhood in the care of a foster father, known as Athelstan "the half king" because of his wealth and political influence. Foster parentage of this kind was not evidence of neglect of royal children by their parents, but rather an opportunity to develop relationships with powerful figures who would pass on their knowledge and connections. Edgar and Elfrida probably met through Athelstan, since Elfrida's first husband was the half-king's son, Ethelwald. Marriage between Edgar and the widowed Elfrida brought the king the support of her powerful noble family in Northampton in addition to reinforcing his connection to the half-king's family.

Regardless of where an Anglo-Saxon royal child grew up, childhood was comparatively short. A young man was considered old enough to swear allegiance to the king and answer for a crime at the age of twelve, and daughters were often wives or nuns by their early teens. Evidence of childhood pastimes is fragmentary. Pre-Christian Anglo-Saxon burial sites contained possessions belonging to the deceased, but few toys survive. One child was buried with a dog, which may have been his beloved pet, and there are numerous surviving examples of board games, suggesting they were a popular pastime for children and adults. *Beowulf,* the earliest surviving long poem in Old English, dates from the Anglo-Saxon period, and listening to tales of heroic deeds and legendary figures was probably part of Ethelred's childhood. Elfrida may have raised her sons herself to ensure that there was no doubt regarding her significance as mother of legitimate heirs. She certainly played a key role in the upbringing of her grandchildren. The will of Ethelred's son, Athelstan, provides a bequest for prayers for "the soul of [Elfrida], my grandmother, who brought me up," a description that suggests a family matriarch who paid close attention to the care and education of the royal children.[5]

While Athelstan remembered Elfrida fondly, there is evidence that she was harsher toward her sons than her grandsons. The chronicler William of Malmesbury recounted that Ethelred "so irritated his furious mother by his weeping, that, not having a whip at hand, she beat the little innocent with some candles she had snatched up."[6] While William's claim that Ethelred was beaten until he was "nearly lifeless" and left with a lifelong fear of candles is probably exaggerated because his survival was essential to Elfrida's position, it's certainly possible that she administered corporal punishment. According to Pope Gregory the Great, whose *Regula Pastoralis* was translated into Old English during the reign of Alfred the Great, "Young people are to be admonished in one way, old people in another, because the former are for the most part guided to make progress by severe admonition, while the latter are disposed to better deeds by gentle remonstrance."[7] The parenting advice available in eleventh-century England supported physical punishments for children to ensure that they made the necessary "progress" to adulthood.

Ethelred's emergence as a political figure occurred at a particularly early age because his father, Edgar, died suddenly in 975 at the age of only thirty-two. Despite Elfrida's efforts to promote Ethelred's position as a legitimate heir (Edmund had died in early childhood), her teenaged stepson Edward was acclaimed king. At first, relations between Elfrida and Edward appeared cordial. Since Edward was childless, his half-brother Ethelred was granted the lands and income suitable to a king's heir. When Edward was murdered in 978, he was on his way to visit Elfrida's residence, a Saxon hall on the site of the later Corfe Castle, "the house where his much loved brother dwelt with the queen, desiring the consolation of brotherly love."[8] During the journey or upon his arrival, Edward was stabbed to death.

Elfrida benefited from the murder almost immediately. Despite his youth, Ethelred was the senior male claimant, and he became king. Elfrida became one of the most powerful figures in England, acting as regent for her son along with one of her key supporters in the church, Ethelwold, Bishop of Winchester. Elfrida attended meetings of the royal council and witnessed charters as *mater regis* — "the king's mother." Elfrida's coronation alongside Edgar in 973 had been contentious because the House of Wessex did not have a tradition of consecrated queens. Elfrida already had a reputation for ambition during Edgar's lifetime, and her assumption of power during Ethelred's minority fueled rumours that she was responsible for the murder of her stepson, who quickly became known as Edward the Martyr.

Elfrida's reputation as a wicked stepmother grew as tales of Edward's sanctity spread. The villainous stepmother was a stock figure in folklore at a time when the average life expectancy was around thirty-five and the experience of being under the care of a step-parent was widespread for children. Accounts of the lives of saints who lived and died in Anglo-Saxon England contained frequent references to murderous stepmothers. The death of St. Juthwara of Dorset, a sixth-century martyr whose relics were transferred to Sherbourne during Ethelred's reign, was reportedly orchestrated by her stepmother; other well-known Anglo-Saxon saints, including Sidwell of Exeter and Urith of Chittlehampton, met similar fates.[9]

In an environment in which fear of wicked stepmothers was part of both popular culture and religious tradition, the degree of Elfrida's involvement in her stepson's murder grew in the popular imagination in the decades following Edward's death. The earliest accounts of the murder simply describe Edward as having been murdered or martyred, without further elaboration. The Life of St. Edith, a chronicle dating from Ethelred's reign, described the murderers as "noble and chief men, who stayed with the queen."[10] By the time William of Malmesbury was writing in the early twelfth century, Elfrida was believed to have orchestrated the murder personally. William wrote, "The woman, however, with a stepmother's hatred, began to mediate a subtle stratagem, in order that not even the title of king might be wanting to her child, and to lay a treacherous snare for her [stepson]...."[11]

According to William, Elfrida ordered one of her attendants to stab Edward while she welcomed him to her home at Corfe Castle, violating the conventions of hospitality as well as morality. Corfe Castle was built in the eleventh century, decades after Elfrida's death, but this forbidding Norman fortress where later kings would house noble prisoners became part of the popular image of the murder. More than a thousand years after the event, it is impossible to answer the question of whether Elfrida arranged her stepson's murder or simply seized the opportunity to establish herself as *mater regis* after the deed was committed by Edward's enemies. Regardless of her actual role in the murder, Elfrida entered the popular imagination as the archetypal wicked stepmother. The establishment of a recognizable royal family during Edgar's reign created the conditions for the public to judge how monarchs, their consorts, and their children treated each other, setting precedents that last to the present day.

When Ethelred came of age, Elfrida temporarily lost her political influence and experienced a period of obscurity. She returned to public life as the guardian of her grandsons from Ethelred's first marriage, witnessing charters alongside them in the 990s. Ethelred's first wife, Elfgifu of York, was completely eclipsed by her mother-in-law, who assumed her position as a royal mother in addition to the religious patronage allotted to the queen by the coronation service of 973. Only after Elfrida's death would her son Ethelred enter into a Christian marriage with Emma of Normandy, a foreign princess who followed in the footsteps of her mother-in-law by becoming a consecrated queen. Elfrida died around the year 1001 in her mid-fifties, and therefore did not live to see Ethelred's authority break down during the invasion of Sweyn Forkbeard of Denmark in 1013. The successful Viking invasion of Anglo-Saxon England earned the king his famous nickname, Ethelred the Unready.

Elfrida's controversial activities as a mother and a grandmother had two lasting consequences for future royal parents: the emergence of an identifiable royal family that attracted public comment, and the expectation by future royal heirs that their mothers would do everything possible to advance their interests. Ethelred's son, King Edward the Confessor, would complain that his mother, Emma of Normandy, "did less for him than he would have wished, before he was king and after."[12] The children of Emma's grandnephew, William the Conqueror, would not have any reason for similar complaints; William's queen, Matilda of Flanders, would act as her children's champion and intercessor even when they came into conflict with their own father, the king.

TWO

William I "the Conqueror" (c. 1028-87) and Matilda of Flanders (c. 1031-83)

In 1080, Matilda of Flanders, queen consort of England since the Norman Conquest of 1066, was fearful that her eldest son, twenty-nine-year-old Robert, would lose his wealth, status, and perhaps his life. During the Easter celebrations that year, she defended his conduct from her position as a mother and queen. In an impassioned speech delivered on her knees, she declared:

> Do not wonder that I love my first-born child with such tender affection. By the power of the Most High, if my son Robert were dead and buried seven feet deep in the earth, hid from the eyes of the living and I could bring him back to life with my own blood, I would shed my life-blood for him and suffer more anguish for his sake than, weak woman that I am, I dare to promise. How do you imagine that I can find any joy in possessing great wealth if I allow my son to be burdened by dire poverty?[1]

Matilda had been negotiating terms with rebellious noblemen and hostile foreign rulers for years, and knew how to project royal authority. During her husband William's invasion of England, she served as his regent in Normandy, the duchy in what is now northwest France that he had inherited as a child. Her crucial leadership role in Normandy meant that she was not crowned Queen of England until 1068, nearly two years after her husband had been crowned at Westminster Abbey in the aftermath of the Battle of Hastings. In her pleas for Robert, however, Matilda was in a very different position than the one she had faced as a regent representing William as ruler of Normandy. Robert was not in conflict with another nobleman or the ruler of a neighbouring territory; instead, Matilda was making a case for her son to her own husband, the king. Robert had raised troops in a rebellion against William. Father and son had faced each other on the battlefield, where William had been wounded and unhorsed. The king was furious, and there was every sign that Robert would be punished severely. As William's queen and Robert's mother, Matilda was the only person in a position to intercede for her son.

In her pleas for Robert, Matilda was defending not only her son but also the importance of motherhood over all of a queen's other roles. William expected his queen to be loyal to him over all other considerations, including the ambitions of their children. Throughout their marriage, William had cultivated a close personal relationship with Matilda in addition to their political partnership. Unusually for a medieval ruler, William did not have any known mistresses or illegitimate children. Matilda was viewed as a calming influence on the fierce-tempered king. The chronicler Orderic Vitalis wrote that after the Norman Conquest, "King William, by the advice of Matilda, treated the English kindly."[2] That claim was overstated, but William's harshness toward his Anglo-Saxon subjects increased after the death of his queen, suggesting that she did exercise some degree of moderating influence.

Matilda's feelings toward William are more difficult to discern. As the daughter of the powerful Baldwin V, Count of Flanders, and the granddaughter of King Robert II of France, Matilda grew up with a keen sense of her royal lineage, and there is evidence that she resisted marrying William, the illegitimate son of Duke Robert I of Normandy and Herleve, a tanner's daughter from Falaise. In the centuries following the wedding, which took place around 1051, legends would develop of a rough courtship in which William beat Matilda or dragged her around her bedchamber by her braids until she acquiesced to the marriage. Once the marriage took place, however, there was little public evidence of marital tension until Robert's rebellion. William's reign in England brought Matilda increased authority in Normandy, and her coronation as Queen of England brought her an enhanced status as his consort that had not existed in Anglo-Saxon times. While Elfrida's coronation had affirmed that she was Edgar's legitimate wife and protector of convents, Matilda's coronation service included three new definitions of queenship: "The Queen is placed by God among the people," "the Queen shares royal power," and "the English people are blessed to be ruled by the power and virtue of the Queen."[3] Following this ceremony, Matilda had a status suitable to her illustrious lineage, but as in Elfrida's time, the mother of a reigning monarch had the potential to be even more influential than a queen consort. Robert's succession to the Duchy of Normandy would place Matilda in a powerful position as mother of the reigning duke.

Matilda's dramatic intercession on Robert's behalf was prompted by William's fury over her conduct during their son's rebellion. According to Orderic Vitalis, Matilda "often used to send [Robert] large sums of silver and gold and other valuables without the king's knowledge."[4] In contrast to most other married women of the period, queens consort controlled lands and wealth independently, enabling them to support their children against their own father. William was outraged by Matilda's conduct, and in the aftermath of Robert's rebellion, he confronted her in the presence of his entire court. The rebellion had unfolded in the public eye, and its aftermath would also take place in front of an audience. William declared:

> How very true here and now is the maxim of a certain sage, "A faithless wife brings ruin to the state." After this who in this world shall ever find himself a trustworthy helpmate? The wife of my bosom, whom I love as my own soul, whom I have set over my whole kingdom and entrusted with all authority and riches, this wife, I say, supports the enemies who plot against my life, enriches them with my money, zealously arms and succours and strengthens them to my grave peril.[5]

Matilda's pleas as a mother failed to calm the king's wrath. He declared that the messenger who had maintained contact between Matilda and Robert should have his eyes gouged out. (Matilda managed to smuggle a warning to her servant and he fled the court before the sentence was carried out.) In the longer term, however, William recognized an opportunity to use Matilda's intercession to bring peace to Normandy without losing face. In April 1080, William and Robert were reconciled officially before an assembly of Norman barons and clergymen: "The queen and representatives of the king of France, with noble neighbours and friends, all combined to restore peace."[6] The rebellion came to an end.

The precise thoughts of the witnesses to the public confrontation between William and Matilda and its eventual resolution are unknown, but "noble neighbours and friends" supported peace, and it is possible that there was quiet sympathy for Matilda's devotion to her son. The religious climate and popular culture of the late eleventh century supported Matilda's conception of herself as a mother first and foremost. The Virgin Mary was a popular figure for religious devotions, which reinforced the image of mothers as intercessors. French epic poetry contained examples of heroes seeking the support of their mothers. William and Matilda had four sons who survived to adulthood, and at least five daughters. As Duchess of Normandy, then Queen of England, Matilda commanded a large household with servants who could assume day-to-day childrearing duties. The practices of sending royal sons to be fostered in noble or ecclesiastical households and royal daughters to be educated in convents, which existed in Anglo-Saxon England, continued during William's reign. Two of the royal couple's younger sons, the future kings William II — nicknamed Rufus because of his red-faced complexion — and Henry I, may have spent time in the household of Langfranc, Archbishop of Canterbury, and two of their daughters were educated at the Holy Trinity Convent in Caen, Normandy, which had been established by the royal couple. Nevertheless, the queen was expected to take an active interest in the development of her children. If the royal children were properly educated and well-behaved, the queen received praise for her conduct as a mother.

The hagiography of Matilda's contemporary, St. Margaret, Queen of Scotland, after her marriage to King Malcolm III in 1070, demonstrates the popular approval received by attentive royal mothers in the mid-eleventh century. Bishop Turgot of St. Andrews wrote of Margaret's parenting:

> Nor was she less careful about her children than she was about herself. She took all heed that they should be well brought up and especially that they should be trained in virtue.... Thanks to their mother's religious care, her children surpassed in good behaviour many who were their elders; they were always affectionate and peaceable among themselves, and everywhere the younger paid due respect to the elder.[7]

Margaret's parenting was considered praiseworthy by the standards of her time and milieu, but it was strict compared to modern royal households. Like Elfrida, Margaret imposed corporal punishment, but unlike the Anglo-Saxon queen, she did not strike her children herself, but instead "charged the Governor who had care of the nursery ... to whip them whenever they were naughty, as frolicsome childhood often will be." At the same time, Turgot's account of Margaret's parenting demonstrates that she called them "my dear ones" and tailored their lessons to their level of understanding. When she gave them religious instruction, "she frequently called them to her, and carefully instructed them about Christ and the things of Christ as far as their age would permit."[8] The Scottish royal children were expected to be well-behaved and obedient, but allowances were made for their young age.

Margaret's example of piety ensured that her children would continue her tradition of religious patronage. The deference the younger children showed for the elder children raised hopes that Scotland would be spared the violent succession disputes of the previous generations. Before Malcolm's reign, the Scottish succession had been even more uncertain than the Anglo-Saxon tradition. While all the sons of an Anglo-Saxon king were considered throne-worthy, grandsons and great-grandsons of Scottish kings could also fight for the crown. Malcolm had come to the throne in a bloody struggle against his kinsman Mac Bethad, events that would be dramatized in William Shakespeare's play, *Macbeth*, centuries later. Margaret's attention to the upbringing of her children promised not only personal fulfillment but also political stability for Scotland.

Matilda took the same interest in the development of her children at a time when the level of learning expected of kings was steadily rising. There is little evidence that William the Conqueror received an education beyond the training in sword fighting and horsemanship required of a military leader, and he did not become a patron of writers or artists as king. In contrast, Matilda had grown up in the more intellectual atmosphere of Flanders and could read Latin. The difference in education between the members of the royal family was common in Western Europe at that time. When William's contemporary, King Henri I of France, married Anna of Kiev, the bride signed the marriage contract "Anna Regina" while her new husband merely marked an *x*. In Scotland, Malcolm was a talented military leader, but the clergy were impressed by the learning Margaret had acquired at the court of her granduncle, Edward the Confessor, for "just as no one among them possessed a deeper intellect than herself, so none had the power of clearer expression."[9]

In these royal households, the queen naturally took charge of the education of the next generation. Matilda's three elder sons appear to have received similar training to their father, but the youngest, Henry, who may have been intended by his parents for a career in the church during his youth, learned to read Latin like his mother and received a grounding in the liberal arts. As King Henry I, he would be known as Henry Beauclerc, because he was the first English monarch since Alfred the Great known to have been a proficient reader. As king, Henry I would declare that "an unlettered king was but a crowned ass,"[10] and the standards Matilda set for the education of her children would continue for future generations. Matilda's daughters shared her erudition. Cecily and Adeliza became nuns, while Adela, the mother of the future King Stephen of England, became a respected literary patron after her marriage to the Count of Blois.

Unlike the Scottish royal children, William and Matilda's sons were never "affectionate and peaceable among themselves," and a fierce rivalry developed as they grew older, fueled by the tense relationship between Robert and his father; William thought little of his eldest son, nicknaming him "Curthose" or "short-stockings" because of his diminutive height.

While Robert enjoyed a close relationship with Matilda, the younger sons — Rufus, Richard, and Henry — remained loyal to their father and shared his contempt for their elder brother. After Richard's death in a hunting accident in the 1070s, the surviving brothers provoked Robert into a fight. Rufus and Henry dumped the contents of a chamber pot over Robert's head, sending their elder brother into a "towering rage," and William had to intervene in the brawl that followed between the brothers and their entourages.

For the Norman elite observing the conflict within the royal family, William's estrangement from Robert and favour toward Rufus and Henry were cause for alarm. The Norman magnates who had fought alongside William at the Battle of Hastings were rewarded with English lands, resulting in a nobility with property on both sides of the English Channel. In exchange for their landholdings, landed barons were expected to provide financial and military support for the king's wars. If the same heir inherited both England and Normandy, these barons would owe their allegiance to a single overlord; if William left Normandy to one son and England to another, loyalties would be divided. William's sons had faced each other on the battlefield during Robert's rebellion, and there was every indication that the brothers would continue to fight each other for supremacy after the death of their father. Conflict between royal parents and children promised political instability, and the queen's intercessions would therefore have been welcomed by the elites, who benefited from unity within the royal family.

The uneasy truce brokered between William and Robert in 1080 came to an abrupt end when Matilda died in 1083. At war with his heir once more, William decided to reward his younger sons for their loyalty. Inheritance law in Normandy varied by region, and there was little reason for William to favour succession based on primogeniture, which would reward Robert with all his father's lands, or equal division of land, which would give the brothers comparable resources to continue the conflict into the next generation. On the advice of Norman barons who argued that Robert should not be disinherited entirely, William bequeathed Normandy to Robert, England to Rufus, and £5,000 in silver to Henry, enough to make him one of the richest barons on either side of the English Channel. William died alone in

1087 as his sons hurried from his deathbed to claim their inheritance. After Rufus's death in 1100, Henry seized both England and Normandy, defeating Robert on the battlefield and imprisoning him for life.

The experiences of William and Matilda as parents demonstrated that for a reigning monarch, raising an heir also meant raising a potential rival. Royal heirs expected increased authority when they came of age, which often brought them into conflict with the monarch, whose goal was usually to maintain centralized authority. Younger sons joined these conflicts, hoping to gain lands, wealth, and power by siding with either their father or elder brother. In these circumstances, the queen had the potential to act as a peacemaker, using her authority as a royal wife and mother to allow reconciliation without any side losing face. The balance within the royal family, however, changed if the queen had political interests that were threatened by the king's authority. Only the kind of unity within a royal family fostered from childhood by a mother like St. Margaret of Scotland could promise lasting harmony and political stability. In 1100, William and Matilda's son, King Henry I, married Malcolm and Margaret's daughter Edith, who assumed the name of her late mother-in-law. Their grandson, King Henry II, would face a rebellion instigated by his three elder sons and his queen, Eleanor of Aquitaine.

THREE

Henry II (1133-89) and Eleanor of Aquitaine (c. 1124-1204)

For Eleanor, Duchess of Aquitaine (now part of southwestern France) and queen consort of England, the knowledge that she was pregnant with a tenth child in 1166 would have come as a surprise, perhaps an unwelcome one. Childbirth was dangerous, even for the most powerful woman in twelfth-century Europe. Eleanor was in her mid-forties, and her first grandchild was due to arrive that same year. Her marriage to King Henry II of England was in crisis. While Henry viewed his vast Anglo-French empire, which included England, Normandy, Anjou, and Aquitaine, as his personal holdings to be governed as he saw fit, Eleanor wanted to govern Aquitaine herself, and her sons were eager to come into lands of their own.

The conflict within the royal family was personal as well as political. Like his grandfather, Henry I, Henry II had numerous mistresses over the course of his reign, but his conflicts with Eleanor over the administration of her lands coincided with a long relationship with Rosamond Clifford that was rumoured to provide the emotional solace that did not exist in his marriage. Henry and Eleanor's youngest child, the future King John of England, was born into this rapidly deteriorating royal marriage on Christmas Eve of 1166 at Beaumont Palace in Oxford. Henry is reputed to have nicknamed his youngest son "Sans-Terre" because he already planned to divide his lands among his three elder sons: England, Normandy, and Anjou for the young Henry, Aquitaine for Richard, and Brittany for Geoffrey through an advantageous marriage to the duchy's heiress, Constance.

Henry and Eleanor made decisions about John's upbringing according to his position as the youngest and presumably least significant member of his family. Along with his youngest sister, Joanna, John was sent for his early education to the royal abbey of Our Lady of Fontevraud, a religious community in Anjou that enjoyed royal patronage. His seclusion at the abbey meant that he had little opportunity to spend time with either of his parents as a young child. John outlived his brothers to become one of the most unpopular monarchs in English history, the first to have limits on his power imposed by his subjects in the form of a charter of liberties better known today as Magna Carta. For centuries after Magna Carta, John's critics looked for reasons why his reign had been a failure, and one possible conclusion they reached was that his character was the result of bad parenting.

Neither Eleanor nor Henry viewed the rearing and education of their children as their personal responsibilities. Throughout her tumultuous life, Eleanor had appointed guardians for her children and arranged for their education while involving herself little in their day-to-day lives. Her surviving sons received tutors and households of their own, and her daughters made dynastic marriages before reaching their teens. Eleanor's approach to royal parenting changed when her children grew up and acquired positions of political power. She became a powerful advocate for her sons, enabling both Richard and John to acquire and maintain power. At a time when dynastic marriage often permanently separated royal parents from their female children, she visited her adult daughters and became an influential figure in the lives of their children. Her remarkable longevity allowed her to assume a key role in the upbringing of a number of her grandchildren, arranging their marriages and determining their political prospects.

In contrast to Eleanor, whose relationships with her children became stronger as they grew older, Henry was not able to maintain a successful bond with his adult sons. Like William I, Henry discovered that raising heirs meant raising rivals, and his relations with his daughters were more harmonious. In contrast to Matilda of Flanders, who acted as an intercessor between her husband William and her eldest son, Robert, Eleanor inflamed the conflicts between her husband and sons, participating in a rebellion against Henry in support of young Henry, Richard, and Geoffrey. The discord within the royal family entered popular culture, ensuring that Henry, Eleanor, and their sons Richard "the Lionheart" and John "Lackland" remain among the best-known medieval royal personages to the present day.

For both Henry and Eleanor, childhood was short, and they assumed prominent adult roles in society from an early age. Henry led his first military campaign at the age of fourteen, and Eleanor succeeded her father as ruler of Aquitaine and married King Louis VII of France when she was around the same age. Henry's parents were Matilda, the widowed consort of Holy Roman Emperor Henry V, and her second husband Geoffrey, Count of Anjou, whose lands bordered Normandy. Geoffrey was nicknamed "Plantagenet" because he wore the flower of the broom plant, or *planta genesta*, in his cap. The name came to be associated with his descendants until the death of Richard III in 1485. Henry was named for his maternal grandfather, King Henry I of England. Matilda was Henry I's only surviving legitimate child, and there was speculation that the king intended to leave the throne to his grandson. Henry I, however, died suddenly in 1135 when the future Henry II was just three years old. Matilda's cousin Stephen seized the throne, beginning nearly two decades of warfare that became known as "The Anarchy." Henry identified strongly with his mother's cause, calling himself "fitzEmpress." His first campaign was unsuccessful, but the attempt demonstrated Henry's potential for the military leadership necessary for a medieval monarch. At nineteen, Henry contracted an advantageous marriage to the thirty-year-old Eleanor, Duchess of Aquitaine, just weeks after the annulment of her union with Louis VII. Eleanor was already a mother at the time of her second marriage; her first marriage had produced two daughters, Marie and Alix, and the absence of a male heir precipitated the formal annulment.

Eleanor was the first Queen of England since the Norman Conquest to become a controversial public figure over the course of her marriage and tenure as queen consort. The previous four queens had displayed very different personalities, but all received praise for their conduct as wives and mothers in historical chronicles written by clergymen. Matilda of Flanders's devotion to her son Robert was considered natural for a loving mother, and was the only source of conflict in an otherwise harmonious marriage to William I. Edith of Scotland shared her mother St. Margaret's reputation for piety and engaged in joint religious and cultural patronage with Henry I. Adeliza of Louvain, Henry I's second wife, also shared his cultural interests and was a supportive stepmother to Henry and Edith's daughter, Empress Matilda. Stephen's queen, Matilda of Boulogne, was a wealthy heiress in her own right who raised troops in support of her husband's long war with his cousin. All four of these eleventh- and twelfth-century queens married young and established their reputations over the course of their marriages. In contrast, Eleanor had already established a controversial reputation as Louis's queen. Her decision to accompany Louis on the Second Crusade attracted widespread criticism, and she was rumoured to have committed adultery in the Holy Land.

When Eleanor embarked on the Second Crusade, she left her daughter Marie in France. When her first marriage was annulled, Louis retained custody of both their daughters. After her marriage to the Count of Champagne, Marie may have visited Eleanor in Aquitaine, and mother and daughter shared a common interest in troubadour culture, but the queen was almost entirely absent from the upbringing of her two eldest daughters. Eleanor's absence from the daily lives of her young children continued during her marriage to Henry. The royal family came together for important religious festivals, such as Christmas, and Eleanor often travelled with one or two of her children, particularly her son Richard and daughter Eleanor, but the siblings were rarely brought together in the company of their parents.

Eleanor's parenting choices were criticized by her contemporaries, who accused her of placing her own ambitions above her responsibilities as a wife and mother. When she encouraged her teenage sons to rebel against their father, Peter of Blois, secretary to the Archbishop of Rouen, wrote her a letter stating, "You should return with your sons to your husband whom you are obliged to obey and live with."[1] Eleanor's comparative distance from the daily care of her young children contributed to the perception, popular to the present day, that she was a disinterested mother, more concerned with the governance of Aquitaine and patronage of musicians and authors in "the courts of love" in Poitiers than with her children. As adults, however, all of Eleanor's children displayed a fierce loyalty to their mother that contrasted with Henry's difficulties with his sons, suggesting that the queen had spent enough time with her children to forge lasting bonds that continued for the rest of her long life.

While twelfth-century observers expected Eleanor to make arrangements for the daily care of her young children and prepare her daughters for marriage, Henry was supposed to make sure that his sons received training suitable to their future roles. The *chansons de geste* (songs of heroic deeds) popular at Henry's court contain glimpses of noble fatherhood as kings, barons, and knights arranged for their sons to acquire military training, often in the households of prominent members of the nobility. In *The Song of Aiol*, composed between 1160 and 1170 — the decade in which Henry's three youngest legitimate children were born — Aiol's impoverished and exiled father, a king's brother-in-law, laments the effect that the isolation of his household will have on the character and education of his son, exclaiming, "Ah! Dear son Aiol! I know not what to do with you!/ Dwelling in these woods is never going to make you wise./ You'll grow completely childish, foolish and uncivilized./ I don't see who will teach you about steeds and weapons."[2] In ordinary circumstances, a boy of Aiol's lineage would have been fostered in a noble household, but his exiled father does his best to pass along the necessary martial skills. The poem makes clear, however, that an isolated upbringing in which children spent time solely with their parents was less beneficial than being surrounded by other children and the example of accomplished adults outside the family. When Aiol leaves home at fourteen, his mother laments, "His replies will make no sense, for he knows so little," and he rapidly matures once he has the opportunity to learn from others.[3] As king, Henry ensured that his elder sons left home at an early age and were well-placed in the households of accomplished barons and church leaders.

The king paid particular attention to the training of his eldest son, young Henry. The heir spent his early years in the household of Thomas Becket, Archbishop of Canterbury, where he would have received a thorough grounding in Latin, the language of diplomacy, and Norman French, the language of the court. At fifteen, young Henry completed his military training in the household of William Marshall, 1st Earl of Pembroke, one of the most renowned knights of the late twelfth and early thirteenth centuries. In an effort to prevent another succession crisis like the Anarchy that followed the death of Henry I, Henry II had his eldest son crowned in his lifetime, following precedents established by French monarchs. The heir to the throne became known as "Henry, the Young King." The coronation increased young Henry's stature and expectations of political influence during his father's lifetime. In an attempt to avoid conflict after his death, Henry II contributed to a crisis within his own family during his lifetime by giving his eldest son the title of king without the power to act independently of his father. Subsequent English monarchs did not crown their heirs, ensuring a clear hierarchy within the royal family.

Twelfth-century chroniclers expected there to be conflict between royal fathers and sons as the children grew to maturity. *Chansons de geste* often included young men who had to choose between loyalty to their fathers and other powerful men. In *The Song of Aoil*, one of Aoil's knights discovers that his father is plotting against Aoil. When the knight seeks advice from his mother, she reminds him of his duty to Aoil, stating, "Since he gave you arms, you must be loyal to him / And serve and honour him above all men; / And your father is going to betray and trap him!"[4] The knight follows his mother's advice and disowns his father for treachery. The poem demonstrated that there were examples within the popular culture of the period of sons being justified in their rebellion against their fathers and of mothers supporting their children against their husbands. Family conflict occurred within elite households, and the popular culture of the twelfth century explored the dramatic possibilities of disagreements between husbands and wives and fathers and sons.

Henry II's contemporaries viewed him as unusually autocratic in his dealings with his sons, especially young Henry, Richard, and Geoffrey. Henry II's clerk, Gerald of Wales, explained how relations between the king and his sons broke down as the younger generation grew to adolescence, writing,

> On his legitimate children [the king] lavished in their
> childhood more than a father's affection, but in his more
> advanced years he looked askance at them after the manner
> of a stepfather; and although his sons were so renowned
> and illustrious, he pursued his successors with a hatred
> which perhaps they deserved, but which nonetheless
> impaired his own happiness. And because man's prosper-
> ity is neither enduring nor perfect, through the outrageous
> malice of fortune he incurred a sword when he ought to
> have obtained joy.[5]

Gerald made his criticism of Henry's parenting clear by describing him as having the manner of a stepfather toward his sons. Just as medieval stepmothers had a cultural reputation for malicious behaviour toward the children of their husbands, the presence of a stepfather was thought to disadvantage his stepchildren. The Coronation Charter issued by Henry I in 1100 granted noble widows the freedom to choose whether to enter into a second marriage, reflecting concerns about how the children of first marriages would be treated by their stepfathers. The nobility opposed attempts by successive monarchs to arrange marriages for wealthy noble widows, and the right of these women to decline a second husband would be upheld by Magna Carta in 1215. For Henry to be compared to a stepfather was an indictment of his parenting and relationship with his grown sons. Gerald made clear that children were supposed to bring joy to a father's life, and the strife within Henry's family cast a shadow over his entire reign.

The tensions within the family erupted into open warfare in 1173 when eighteen-year-old young Henry, sixteen-year-old Richard, and fourteen-year-old Geoffrey rebelled against their father in what became known as the Revolt of the Eaglets. The catalyst for the rebellion was the king's decision to confiscate castles granted to young Henry to create an inheritance for John. As Henry's relations with his elder sons deteriorated, the king became determined to ensure that his youngest son would receive lands of his own. Henry considered his authority over his family and vast Anglo-French empire to be absolute, but by the time of the revolt, his queen and sons were not reliant upon him for their status. Eleanor was Duchess of Aquitaine in her own right, with Richard as her heir; young Henry was crowned during his father's lifetime; and Geoffrey would be Count of Brittany through his marriage. Henry's decision to make changes to the distribution of his lands without consulting his family fueled open rebellion. Eleanor supported her sons against their father. The king ultimately prevailed in the hostilities and forgave his sons, but Eleanor was confined to a series of castles for the remainder of her husband's reign. The deaths of young Henry from dysentery in 1183 and Geoffrey in an 1186 tournament accident led to further hostilities between Henry and Richard, as the king expected his new heir to cede Aquitaine to John. Henry spent his last years at war with Richard. Father and son publicly reconciled, but Henry whispered privately to his son, "May God let me live until I can have my revenge upon you."[6] John showed little appreciation for his father's efforts on his behalf, and joined Richard's forces during the last weeks of Henry's life.

Speculation regarding Henry and Eleanor's marriage and their tempestuous relations with their sons long outlasted their own lifetimes, becoming part of popular culture to the present day. Gerald of Wales made clear that he considered the breakdown of their marriage central to the conflict between the king and his sons, writing, "Whether by some breach of the marriage tie or as punishment for some crime of the parent, it befell that there was never true affection felt by the father towards his sons, nor by the sons towards their father, nor harmony among the brothers themselves."[7] Other contemporaries of Henry and Eleanor argued that there was a curse on the House of Anjou that made Henry's sons "the Devil's brood." By the late sixteenth century, during the reign of Elizabeth I, the blame for the family strife had been placed on Eleanor's shoulders. In his play *King John*, William Shakespeare presented the queen as "a canker'd grandam" and imagined her daughter-in-law Constance blaming her own son Arthur's troubles on "Being but the second generation/ Removed from thy sin-conceiving womb."[8]

Twentieth-century playwrights and filmmakers took a more expansive view of the family conflict, emphasizing the ambitions and failings of Henry, Eleanor, and all of their sons. The plot of James Goldman's 1966 play *The*

Lion in Winter, which was adapted into an Academy Award–winning 1968 film of the same name starring Peter O'Toole and Katharine Hepburn, revived the rumours that swirled about the unhappy royal family in the twelfth century. The play and film depicted Henry pursuing an affair with his son Richard's fiancée, Alais of France, which was the publicly stated reason why Richard considered himself free to abandon the betrothal and marry elsewhere. Since Henry and Alais were rarely in the same place at the same time, it is possible that the rumours of an affair were unfounded but provided Richard with a convenient pretext to contract a more politically advantageous marriage. The salacious speculation about Henry and Eleanor as parents did not dissipate after their deaths, but instead is part of their popular image to the present day.

Eleanor was certainly not considered "a canker'd grandam" in her lifetime. Like Henry II's mother, Matilda, Eleanor's reputation improved once she became an elder stateswoman, furthering the political interests of her sons. After Henry died in 1189, one of the first decisions made by the new King Richard was to release Eleanor from confinement. The chronicler Roger of Howden observed Eleanor's re-emergence as a powerful figure in her son's reign, writing that in the early weeks of Richard's reign she "circulat[ed] with a queenly court: she set out from city to city and castle to castle just as it pleased her," ensuring that pledges of allegiance were sworn to Richard and outstanding legal cases from Henry's reign were resolved.[9] When Richard was taken captive on his way home from the Third Crusade, Eleanor was instrumental in raising the ransom necessary for his release. In a letter to Pope Celestine III requesting his assistance in securing Richard's freedom, she expressed her grief for the sons she had lost, declaring, "My posterity has been snatched from me.... [Henry] the young king and [Geoffrey], the Count of Brittany, sleep in the dust. Their unhappy mother is forced to live on, ceaselessly tormented by their memory."[10]

After Richard's death, Eleanor made her last significant decision as a both a parent and a political figure. She decided to support her youngest son, John, an adult with military experience, over Arthur, the twelve-year-old son of her late son Geoffrey. When Eleanor died in 1204, the vast Anglo-French empire that she had created with Henry II was still intact under the leadership of a single ruler — John.

In the last decades of her life, Eleanor was also an influential figure in the lives of her daughters' children. Eleanor and her sons Richard and John had supported the future Holy Roman Emperor Otto IV in his ambition to become King of the Germans. Otto was the son of Henry and Eleanor's eldest daughter, Matilda, and he had spent extended periods in Aquitaine with his mother's family. As emperor, Otto remained John's ally, and supported him in his wars with King Philip II of France. Eleanor personally selected her granddaughter, Blanche of Castile, as queen to the future King Louis IX of France, travelling to the court of her son-in-law and daughter, King Alfonso VIII and Queen Eleanor of Castile, to select one of their daughters for the prestigious French match. These examples of family solidarity among Henry and Eleanor's descendants demonstrate that they did not simply cause conflict in their roles as parents and grandparents, but helped to solidify lasting personal and diplomatic bonds that stretched across western Europe. Eleanor's descendants did not all fit the stereotype of "The Devil's Brood." Her daughters' children gained personal and political support from their connection to their Plantagenet grandmother and uncles.

Richard and John benefitted from the political power wielded by their mother, but they kept their own queens firmly in the background, even within the domestic circle. Once Richard was released from captivity, he avoided spending time with his queen, Berengaria of Navarre, and only returned to her bed and fulfilled such public duties as escorting her to church after being criticized for his neglect of his queen by Pope Celestine III. Richard and Berengaria were childless. John had his first marriage to Hawisa of Gloucester annulled, and outraged his barons by marrying twelve-year-old Isabelle of Angoulême, the fiancée of one of his vassals, in 1200. John's second marriage did not affect Eleanor's position as the most prominent woman in the royal family. Eleanor retained lands and income that traditionally supported the king's consort. When Eleanor died in 1204, John withheld the traditional "queen's gold" and dower lands from Isabelle, leaving her financially dependent on his good will. Although John would become more unpopular than his father Henry over the course of his reign, Isabelle was never in a position to support his adversaries in a rebellion against him. Isabelle also appears to have been marginalized from major decisions concerning the upbringing of her five children with John, a pattern that continued during her widowhood. Despite the unfortunate precedents set by his parents and grandparents, John and Isabelle's eldest son Henry III became the first English monarch from the House of Plantagenet to find contentment in marriage and fatherhood. The upbringing of Henry III's queen, Eleanor of Provence, demonstrated that family harmony was possible for medieval royalty, and she brought her experience of domestic tranquility to the tumultuous House of Plantagenet.

FOUR

Henry III (1207-72) and Eleanor of Provence (c. 1223-91)

Katherine, the youngest child of King Henry III of England and his queen, Eleanor of Provence, was different from her four elder siblings. According to the chronicler Matthew of Paris, Katherine was "mute and useless, though a most beautiful face."[1] Her precise condition remains unknown. Possibilities include deafness or autism. The most widely accepted diagnosis is Rett syndrome, a rare neurological disorder characterized by an inability to speak, stunted growth, and repetitive hand movements.

From her earliest childhood, it was clear that Katherine would never play the traditional role of a king's daughter at the English court. Nevertheless, both Henry and Eleanor cared deeply for their youngest daughter, and did everything in their power to ensure her health and contentment. Henry's reign saw efforts to ensure that heirs and heiresses with intellectual disabilities had their needs met and were not turned off their lands. The King decreed in 1255, "The King shall have custody of the lands of natural fools taking the profits of them without waste or destruction and shall find them their necessaries...."[2] Within his own family, Henry III recognized that the "necessaries" of life included companionship as well as physical care. Katherine's condition made friendships with other children difficult, so Henry ensured that she had a variety of pets, including a tame goat from the Windsor Castle park.

When Katherine died in 1257 at the age of just three, her devastated parents publicly mourned her passing. The same chronicler who pronounced Katherine "mute and useless" recorded that "the queen, her mother, as a result of her anguish, was seized of a grievous illness that neither physician nor human consolation could alleviate."[3] Henry III's health also suffered as he developed a life-threatening tertian fever as a result of being "plunged into such sorrow that he fell ill."[4] In their grief, Henry and Eleanor commissioned an elaborate tomb monument for their daughter at Westminster Abbey that included a wooden effigy of the little girl with silver plating adorned with pearls and amethysts.[5] Katherine was the first member of the royal family to be buried in Westminster Abbey, which Henry III ordered to be rebuilt during his reign in the gothic style of architecture fashionable in the thirteenth century, setting precedents for future royal burials there.

The tender care that Henry and Eleanor displayed for Katherine both during her short life and after her death had little in common with the tumultuous circumstances of Henry's youth. Henry's parents, King John and Isabelle of Angoulême, took little interest in the upbringing of their five children and were instead preoccupied with the political upheaval of early thirteenth-century England that culminated in the sealing of Magna Carta in 1215. The charter provides evidence of how the barons and clergy defined and perceived the royal family. Magna Carta is best known today for its contribution to the development of principles of common law in the English-speaking world, including equality before the law and trial by peers; but it also contained clauses that regularized inheritance law and the amount of financial support the public would provide for royal children. Both clauses would have profound implications for Henry and his successors down to the present day.

Magna Carta decreed that "if the heir of [any earl, baron, or other person that directly holds lands of the Crown] is under age and a ward, when he comes of age he shall have his inheritance without relief or fine."[6] When Henry succeeded his father in 1216 at the age of nine, there had not been a child monarch in England since Ethelred the Unready. The primary duty of a king was to lead troops into battle, which meant that the succession claims of women and children had been set aside in the past to allow adult males with military experience to ascend the English throne. This disregard for the rights of underage heirs affected the entire noble class, which derived its status from military service. Magna Carta's regularization of inheritance rights for child heirs of barons and knights had profound implications for succession to the throne. The days of the royal succession being settled by battles between throne-worthy heirs and treaties at the end of military conflicts were being replaced by a regular system of primogeniture. After Magna Carta, the eldest surviving son could expect to inherit the entire kingdom regardless of his age at the time of his father's death. An orderly royal succession increased popular interest in the upbringing and education of the eldest royal son as it became clear that, if he survived childhood, he would become king regardless of the abilities of his siblings.

Magna Carta also codified how much financial support monarchs could expect from their subjects for the maintenance of royal children, creating another clear distinction between older and younger members of the royal family. Henry II and Eleanor of Aquitaine attempted to ensure that all four of their surviving sons controlled lands of their own and all three of their daughters sealed diplomatic alliances by marrying wealthy and powerful European sovereigns. Magna Carta made clear that future monarchs could only expect public support for the financial position of their eldest children, stating, "In future we will allow no one to levy an 'aid' from his free men, except to ransom his person, to make his eldest son a knight, and (once) to marry his eldest daughter."[7] Since Magna Carta established that not even the king was above the law, this provision was one of the earliest attempts by the monarch's subjects to streamline the royal family, defining the eldest royal children as the responsibility of the state and their younger siblings as the personal responsibility of the king and queen.

From the time Henry III ascended to the throne at the age of nine, the parental figures in his life would be guardians and tutors appointed by a series of noble regents. There was no further parental involvement in his upbringing. After John's death, Isabelle returned to Angoulême, where she remarried and raised a second family. As Henry grew older, he assumed a parental role in the lives of his siblings and half-siblings, including them in his household and ensuring that they were well cared for and financially secure. In 1236, twenty-eight-year-old Henry married twelve-year-old Eleanor of Provence. The young queen's upbringing could not have differed more from Henry's experiences. While Henry had lost his father and been abandoned by his mother at an early age, Eleanor spent her early life in a close family circle with her parents, Ramon Berenguer IV, Count of Provence, and Beatrice of Savoy, and her three sisters, Marguerite, Sanchia, and Beatrice, who became queens consort of France, the German states, and Sicily respectively. Beatrice of Savoy took her role as a mother seriously, reading the parenting literature of the time and commissioning works of her own.

In 1256, Beatrice commissioned the *Régime du corps* by Aldobrandino of Siena, which contained a chapter about the health needs of pregnant women followed by a section on the care of young children after birth. The text was written in vernacular French rather than Latin, allowing elite women with varying degrees of education to access this medical advice. Beatrice's interest in childrearing advice was shared by her daughters. As Queen of France, Marguerite commissioned a treatise from a Dominican friar, Vincent of Beauvais, on the proper education of children, emphasizing mental discipline and moral improvement in addition to intellectual accomplishments. The treatise included a chapter advocating education for girls, stating, "They should be instructed in letters ... because often they will carefully shun harmful thoughts to follow this honourable occupation, and avoid carnal lusts and vanities."[8] This advice was progressive compared to the view that literacy had the potential to corrupt the morals of young women by allowing them to correspond with suitors. Beatrice occasionally referred to her four daughters as "sons," a practice that chroniclers of the time found objectionable, but which demonstrated her pride in her daughters and refusal to consider them less important than boys.

The age difference between Henry and Eleanor meant that the king initially assumed the same paternal role toward his queen that he did in his dealings with his younger siblings, ensuring that she was comfortable in her new role. Henry had a keen interest in architecture and landscape design, and his marriage was an opportunity to commission gardens "in the Provençal style" to complement his new castle in Winchester. Once the royal children arrived, however, Eleanor became the dominant influence over the family, ensuring that they were raised in the close family circle that mirrored her own childhood, with careful attention to their development, rather than in the lonely circumstances of Henry's youth. Eleanor remained close to her family. Her mother visited England in 1243 for the wedding of Eleanor's sister Sanchia to Henry's brother Richard, bonding with her young grandchildren.

Henry and Eleanor first demonstrated their distinctive approach to royal parenting when they established new traditions in choosing names for their children. Since the Norman conquest of 1066, there had been a defined set of names for royal children, particularly sons. William I, Henry I, and Henry II all had sons named William. Other popular names for the sons of Norman kings were Henry and Richard. These names are still used by the royal family today. For women, there was more variety, as foreign princesses married into the royal family and named their daughters after themselves. Eleanor of Aquitaine's numerous descendants spread her name throughout modern-day England, France, and Spain, while Isabelle of Angoulême gave her own name — a variant of Elizabeth popular in numerous European ruling families of the time — to one of her daughters. Even for royal women, however, there were established Norman name traditions. William I, Henry I, and Henry II all had daughters named Matilda. The names popular with the royal family spread to the rest of the Anglo-Norman elite. An 1185 record of the lands held by noble widows and wards of the crown reveals that the most popular name for English noblewomen in the late twelfth century was Matilda.[9]

Henry III and Eleanor of Provence revived royal naming traditions that predated the Norman Conquest and introduced new names that continue to be popular in the royal family to the present day. Instead of giving his eldest son a traditional Norman name, Henry chose to honour his favourite saint, the second-last Anglo-Saxon king, Edward the Confessor. Edward had been the name of three Anglo-Saxon kings, but had fallen out of favour completely in royal circles after the Norman Conquest until Henry III reintroduced it for his eldest son, the future Edward I. Henry's younger son, Edmund, also received a Saxon name rather than a Norman one. Eleanor named her two elder daughters Margaret and Beatrice, after her sister and mother, rather than the women of Henry's family. Since Eleanor's sisters were all married to other European rulers, these choices of names reflected sound diplomatic policy as well as family feeling. The youngest daughter, Katherine, was born on the feast day of St. Catherine of Alexandria. Like another youngest royal child, the future King John, who was born close to the feast day of St. John the Baptist, she was named according to the ecclesiastical calendar.

Henry and Eleanor also broke with general royal precedent regarding the amount of personal attention they gave to their children both as young children and as adults. In contrast to Henry II and Eleanor of Aquitaine, they did not have a vast Anglo-French empire under their personal control and were therefore based in England throughout much of their marriage. The sons and daughters of Henry III and Eleanor of Provence were fostered in the households of noble families in the manner of previous royal children, but the king and queen were close at hand and their expenditure suggests a close relationship with their growing family. Eleanor purchased matching hawking gloves for herself and her daughter Beatrice, demonstrating that she viewed falconry as an opportunity to spend time with her children. Eleanor also passed on her love of fashion and royal pageantry to her children, ordering gowns for Beatrice and a silk tabard (sleeveless short coat) for Edward. When Edward married, Eleanor was concerned that her daughter-in-law's wardrobe was too plain for her official entry into London and sent her new clothes to wear upon her arrival.

There is evidence, in addition to their attention to Katherine's needs, that Henry and Eleanor were concerned with the health of all the young people in their family, even after they married and left home. When Edward fell ill while visiting Beaulieu Abbey in the New Forest in Hampshire, Eleanor disregarded the strictures against women residing in the monastery and spent three weeks nursing her son back to health. After fifteen-year-old Edward married thirteen-year-old Eleanor of Castile in Burgos in 1254, Henry encouraged the couple to live apart for a time, circumstances that would reduce the risk of an early pregnancy. Henry may have been giving advice from his own experience, as Eleanor of Provence was just twelve when they married, but sixteen when Edward was born, suggesting a period of abstinence early in the marriage. Eleanor of Castile may have suffered a miscarriage in the first year of her marriage, indicating that that the new-lyweds did not follow this advice, and Henry III and Eleanor of Provence remained concerned about their daughter-in-law's health and that of their children. When Henry and Eleanor's elder daughter Margaret married ten-year-old King Alexander III of Scotland in 1251, at the age of eleven, her parents maintained a close interest in her welfare and were dismayed when Alexander's regents refused permission for Margaret to visit England the following year with her husband. When Margaret wrote to her parents that she was unhappy, Henry and Eleanor travelled north with an armed escort to ensure that they would be permitted to see their daughter. A family reunion took place in Northumberland in 1255, and Alexander and Margaret visited Windsor Castle in 1261, where Eleanor was present for the birth of the Scottish royal couple's eldest child.

Henry and Eleanor's care for their children was rewarded with the loyalty of their eldest son. While both William I and Henry II faced their sons on the battlefield, Edward won military victories for his father during the Second Barons' War of 1264–67. Edward's loyalty was not a foregone conclusion. The leader of the rebel barons was Simon de Montfort, Earl of Leicester, who was both the husband of Henry's youngest sister Eleanor and Edward's godfather. In addition to the family connection, Edward may have shared some of Montfort's attitudes toward political reform. The parliament of 1265, known as "de Montfort's parliament," established the framework for modern parliamentary democracy, and as king, Edward I continued the practice of summoning parliaments consisting of representatives of the nobility, landed gentry, clergy, and wealthy townspeople. Edward did not accept Montfort as the leader of the rebellion against his father, however, and rallied opponents to Montfort's increasing power to win a decisive victory at the Battle of Evesham in 1265.

Edward was on his way back to England from the Ninth Crusade when he received news of the death of both his father, Henry III, and one of his own sons, John, in 1272. In contrast to Henry III and Eleanor of Provence, Edward and his queen, Eleanor of Castile, spent little time with their young children, and did not have a sentimental attitude toward them. Like their mutual ancestor Eleanor of Aquitaine, Edward and Eleanor of Castile went on crusade without their children. John and his siblings were left in the care of their granduncle, Richard, Duke of Cornwall, and their doting paternal grandparents. Edward reportedly greeted the news of the deaths in his family with the words, "It was easy to beget sons but the loss of a father was irredeemable."[10] Edward's reaction heralded a return to the royal parenting of the time of Henry II and Eleanor of Aquitaine, when the daily childrearing was left to others and royal fathers had little personal attachment to their sons. Edward would quarrel publicly with at least one of his daughters as well as his youngest and only surviving son, the future Edward II.

Edward I's fond memories of his childhood and relationship with his own father, however, demonstrated that warm relations between parents and children were possible within the royal family. Eleanor of Provence had brought her family traditions with her when she married into the House of Plantagenet, and fostered a close relationship with her husband and children. Future kings and queens would also attempt to create harmony within the royal family. During the fourteenth century, Henry III and Eleanor of Provence's great-grandson, Edward III, would make lasting changes to royal finances to ensure that his numerous sons all became the ancestors of wealthy families. Instead of putting an end to sibling rivalry among royal sons, however, Edward III's determination to provide for all his children would ultimately create the conditions for the Wars of the Roses.

FIVE

Edward III (1312-77) and Philippa of Hainault (1314-69)

King Edward III of England spent most of his fifty-year reign fighting the Hundred Years' War with France, a conflict that would be inherited by four generations of his descendants. Like his grandfather, Edward I, Edward III was accompanied by his wife during military campaigns. The presence of his queen, Philippa of Hainault (a region that overlaps with modern-day Belgium), was not only a personal comfort but a political asset. As a king at war, Edward III had to project a ruthless image that would intimidate his adversaries into surrendering. The intercession of the queen, however, allowed the king to perform occasional acts of mercy without undermining his position as a military leader.

Philippa's motherhood was key to her role as intercessor, and influenced Edward's conduct during the siege of the French town of Calais in 1347. The town was a strategic port on the English Channel, and King Philip VI of France ordered its inhabitants to resist the English siege. Calais's refusal to surrender gave Edward's forces the right to pillage the town and massacre its citizens if his siege was successful, according to the accepted rules of war in the fourteenth century. As the besieged townspeople began to succumb to starvation, Edward proposed an end to the standoff: if six residents of

Calais offered him the keys to the city and agreed to be executed for the intransigence of the whole town, the rest of the town would be spared. The calm resignation of the six "Burghers of Calais" in the face of death was eventually immortalized in an 1889 sculpture by Auguste Rodin that still stands in the centre of the town.

According to Philippa's clerk, Jean Froissart, the six townspeople were about to be executed on Edward's orders when the queen intervened:

> Then the noble queen of England, who was heavily pregnant, humbled herself greatly and wept so tenderly that none could bear it. The valiant and good lady threw herself before her lord the king and said, "Ah, my dear lord, since I came across the [English Channel] in great peril, as you well know, I have asked nothing of you nor required any favour. Now I humbly pray and request of you favour, that for the Son of Holy Mary and the love of me, you shall wish to have mercy on these six men." The king waited a little before he spoke and he looked upon the good lady his wife, who wept so tenderly on her knees before him. A change of heart came over him as she knelt there before him; and when he spoke, he said, "Ah, lady, I would have much preferred you were anywhere but here. You have prayed so strongly that I dare not refuse the favour you ask of me."[1]

Froissart's account of Edward granting his queen's request for mercy combines the historical circumstances of the Siege of Calais with a popular perception of Philippa as a mother first and foremost that persisted throughout her time as queen consort of England. When Calais fell to the English, Philippa had ten children, and the eleventh would not be born until nearly nine months after Edward spared the lives of the Burghers of Calais. At the time of the siege, Philippa may have been aware that she was once again expecting a child, but she would not have appeared "very pregnant" to onlookers. As far as the public was concerned, however, Philippa was always pregnant and surrounded by her children, as well as by orphaned children of knights, who were raised under her supervision.

The queen's fertility prompted speculation that Edward had chosen her as his bride because of her childbearing hips. A fifteenth-century chronicler claimed that Edward agreed to marry Philippa with the words, "We will have her with her good hips, I wean / for she will bear good sons at mine intent / To which they all accorded with one assent / And chose Philippa that was full feminine."[2] Like Froissart's account of the "very pregnant" queen at the Siege of Calais, the description of Edward's attraction to Philippa says more about her popular image after the births of numerous children than the circumstances of her betrothal. For Philippa, becoming the mother of a large family gave her influence over her husband and popularity with his subjects, setting an example for future generations of royal mothers. Edward also set key precedents as a father. His efforts to provide for their numerous children created the framework for the private income that the British royal family enjoys today. Edward and Philippa became a model royal couple whom subsequent kings and queens were expected by their subjects to emulate.

Like Henry III and Eleanor of Provence, Edward and Philippa had very different upbringings, with Edward spending his adolescence amid political turmoil while Philippa enjoyed stability. The marriage of Edward's parents, King Edward II and the French princess Isabelle of Valois, was never close, as the king preferred to spend time with his male favourites, but they appear to have maintained a functional royal union until Edward II fell under the influence of a particularly ambitious courtier, Hugh Despenser. Like past generations of royal children, Edward II's two sons and two daughters were placed in the households of noble guardians, but Isabelle recognized that she needed control of her eldest son to challenge Despenser's influence over her husband. She saw an opportunity in 1325 when her brother, King Charles IV of France, seized Gascony in Aquitaine. That spring, Isabelle and her thirteen-year-old son, the future Edward III, travelled to the French court to represent Edward II in negotiations for the return of Gascony with ostensible plans to return to England by the summer.

The young heir to the throne's presence was crucial to the success of this diplomatic mission as he would do homage to his uncle the King of France on behalf of his father, satisfying French demands for lordship over Gascony but allowing Edward II to avoid humbling himself personally before another sovereign. Having completed his first major diplomatic mission, the future Edward III faced an even greater crisis: the breakdown of his parents' marriage. Isabelle remained in France with her son, where she rallied rebel barons who shared her dismay at the influence of Despenser at Edward II's court. Edward II recognized the danger of his heir being in the company of an entire faction led by his discontented queen and appealed to the young Edward as his father and his king to return home, even if departing France meant defying his mother. Edward II wrote in December 1325, "Very dear son as you are young and of tender age, we would remind you of that which we charged and commanded you when we left you at Dover, and you answered then, as we know, with good will, that you would not trespass or disobey our injunctions … return to us with all speed in the company of your mother … if she will not come, come you without further delay."[3] At the French court, the young Edward was treated as an adult capable of representing the English ruling house, but his father clearly regarded him as a boy susceptible to being manipulated by his mother and her faction.

The young Edward decided to remain with his mother, disregarding subsequent letters in which his father chastised him for his loyalty to Isabelle and ordered him to return to England. Isabelle's goal eventually changed from removing Despenser from a position of influence to an audacious plan to overthrow her husband and rule as regent for her son. She already had the support of her French royal relatives in addition to that of barons who commanded the loyalty of knights and foot soldiers, but a successful invasion of England would require ships. Isabelle made use of her network of dynastic connections, meeting with her cousin Joan of Valois, Countess of Hainault, Avesnes, Holland, and Zeeland over the winter of 1325–26. Joan and her husband, the reigning Count William, had the necessary ships, and five daughters — Margaret, Philippa, Agnes, Joanna, and Isabelle — available for a possible dynastic marriage to the young Edward.

The relations between the Count and Countess of Hainault and their daughters appear to have been harmonious. Bishop Stapledon of Exeter described one of the elder daughters, either Margaret or Philippa, as "well taught in all that becometh her rank, and highly esteemed and well beloved of her father and mother."[4] The young Edward may have observed the contrast to his own worsening family life. Isabelle had begun to dress as a widow on the grounds that Despenser had come between her and her husband, while Edward II wrote further letters censuring his son for disloyalty and his queen for adultery with Roger Mortimer, 1st Earl of March. In these circumstances, the young Edward's interest in marrying Philippa, who reputedly cried when it was time for them to part after their first meeting, may have reflected his personal inclinations as well as Isabelle's political ambitions.

Isabelle, the young Edward, and their faction invaded England in 1326. The coup attracted popular support, as the queen was careful to emphasize her role as a suffering mother interested only in securing her son's inheritance. Her faction achieved military victories and the execution of the hated Despenser. In January 1327, parliament affirmed Edward III's succession, having persuaded Edward II to abdicate. The deposed king was most likely murdered at Berkeley Castle in September of that year. Despite his complicity in his father's loss of kingship, the teenaged Edward III attended the funeral at Gloucester Abbey in October and publicly mourned his passing.

Edward's relations with his mother were becoming strained by this time. He and Philippa were married in York Minster Cathedral in 1328, a rite of passage that appeared to demonstrate that the fifteen-year-old king was an adult capable of ruling in his own right. Nevertheless, Isabelle and Mortimer continued to rule on his behalf. Philippa was kept in the background as Isabelle continued to hold the income and lands traditionally bestowed upon a queen consort. Philippa only received a coronation ceremony of her own in March 1330, during her pregnancy with her first child, circumstances that may have informed the public's perception of her as a queen who appeared in public and gained influence through motherhood. For Edward, the birth of an heir in June 1330 emboldened him to seize control of the government in the autumn of that year. Mortimer was executed for treason, including the murder of Edward II, and Isabelle was given a pension and sent to Castle Rising in Norfolk. For both Edward III and Philippa, becoming parents themselves affirmed their adulthood and contributed to their control of the full power and wealth of a king and queen.

Following the removal of Isabelle and Mortimer from power, Edward and Philippa were determined to create a family atmosphere that resembled the harmony of the queen's childhood instead of the turmoil of the king's adolescence. They were indulgent parents who allowed their children far more personal autonomy than previous generations of medieval royal children had experienced. Their five surviving sons — Edward (called the Black Prince because of his dark-coloured armour), Lionel, John, Edmund, and Thomas — and four surviving daughters — Isabella, Joan, Mary, and Margaret — enjoyed a secure childhood and adolescence that contrasted with the difficult choices faced by their father in his youth. They were frequently brought together in the company of their parents and grandmother, Isabelle, who emerged from retirement to help care for her grandchildren. The royal children were integrated into the lives of their parents from an early age. As heir to the throne, the Black Prince received his own household, but his younger siblings spent much of their childhoods in the company of their mother. When the royal family was under the same roof, Edward took meals with his young children, and as they grew older, his sons joined him in his pastimes, which included gambling and participating in tournaments.

The autonomy of Edward and Philippa's children extended to one of the key roles for the sons and daughters of reigning monarchs: dynastic marriages. The daughters of Henry II and Eleanor of Aquitaine — and then Henry III and Eleanor of Provence — had been betrothed and married as children to foreign princes. In contrast, Edward and Philippa allowed their eldest daughter Isabella to remain in England until well into adulthood and to refuse to marry eligible princes. Edward described her as "our very dear eldest daughter whom we have loved with a special affection."[5]

The king's affection for Isabella remained constant even after she caused a diplomatic incident in 1351, at the age of nineteen, by refusing to board the ship intended to carry her across the English Channel for a prestigious marriage. Edward granted her an independent income, which increased when she was twenty-six, and paid her debts, including the wages of her servants. The unwillingness to accept an unwanted dynastic marriage was not confined to Isabella. As heir to the throne, the Black Prince was expected to marry a foreign princess and there were negotiations for a wedding to Margaret of Flanders. Instead, he married his cousin once removed and childhood friend Joan, nicknamed "the Fair Maid of Kent" for her beauty. As a descendant of Edward I, Joan's lineage was impeccable, but she had been married twice (having been widowed once and having had another marriage annulled), and was the mother of four children. The couple may have married secretly in 1360 to circumvent the displeasure of the king and queen. Edward and Philippa ultimately accepted their son's choice of bride. The king supported the papal dispensation required for a marriage between close relatives. The Black Prince and the Fair Maid of Kent solemnized their union in 1361.

At first glance, Edward and Philippa's willingness to allow their children to arrange their own marriages and otherwise assert their wishes over those of their parents appears contrary to all fourteenth-century parenting advice. Prescriptive and literary sources alike emphasized the importance of obedience to parental dictates at any age. In his 1303 treatise *Handlyng Synne*, Gilbertine monk Robert Mannyng (or Robert of Brunne) reminded his readers, *"The fourþe comaundment ys, oure Fadyr & modyr we shal honoure."*[6] According to Mannyng, it was a grave sin to refuse to act according to one's parents' wishes, and it was sinful even to argue with them or obey them only grudgingly. Edward's reign, however, saw parents of all social backgrounds experience an unexpected and terrifying bereavement that may have encouraged them to draw closer to their surviving children, even those who were disobedient or willful.

In 1348, the Black Death arrived in England, killing 30 to 50 percent of the population. Subsequent fourteenth-century outbreaks of plague caused less mortality but still left thousands of grieving parents to mourn the loss of their children. The 1361–62 outbreak killed 23 percent of the heirs to landed estates.[7] Edward and Philippa shared the experience of bereavement with their subjects. In 1348, their two youngest sons, the toddler William of Windsor and the infant Thomas of Windsor, died in the first outbreak of plague in England. That same year, their second daughter, Joan, died of the plague in Bayonne, near the border between France and Spain, on her way to marry the future King Pedro the Cruel of Castile. A devastated Edward wrote to Pedro's father, King Alfonso XI: "Destructive

Death (who seizes young and old alike, sparing no one and reducing rich and poor to the same level) has lamentably snatched from both of us our dearest daughter, whom we loved best of all, as her virtues demanded."[8] Edward consoled himself with the image of his daughter in heaven surrounded by choirs of angels. Isabella's refusal to cross the English Channel for a dynastic marriage occurred just three years after the death of her sister from the plague, which may have informed the king's decision to overlook her disobedience and continue to act as an indulgent father.

The independence of Edward and Philippa's children may have also been influenced by the sheer number of young people in the royal household as Philippa's responsibilities as a mother extended beyond supervising the care of her own children. The queen took charge of the orphaned children of knights, making arrangements for their care and employment within her household or those of her children and organizing their marriages. The queen's patronage allowed otherwise obscure children of the landed gentry to advance socially. Among the most famous of the queen's wards were Philippa and Katherine de Roet, the daughters of Sir Gilles de Roet, one of the knights from Hainault who had accompanied the queen to England at the time of her marriage. The queen found a place for the teenaged Philippa de Roet as mistress of the pantry in the household of her daughter-in-law, Elizabeth de Burgh, an Irish heiress married to the queen's second son Lionel. There, Philippa de Roet met and married one of Elizabeth's pages, Geoffrey Chaucer. The couple received an annuity from the queen and spent their entire lives in royal service. Chaucer ultimately became Edward's court poet, rewarded in 1374 with "a gallon of wine daily for the rest of his life,"[9] and the author of numerous pioneering works in Middle English, including the famous *Canterbury Tales*.

Katherine de Roet made an even more prestigious marriage. She served as governess to the children of Edward and Philippa's third son, John of Gaunt, from his first marriage to Blanche of Lancaster, and became John's mistress during his second marriage to Constance of Castile. After Constance's death, John married Katherine and their children were ultimately legitimized during the reign of Henry IV and given the name Beaufort. One of John and Katherine's descendants was the first Tudor king, Henry VII. Queen Philippa's patronage of the de Roet sisters, an example of her maternal attitude toward all the children in the care of her household, changed the course of English royal history.

As a doting father, Edward III was concerned for the future of his large family. Magna Carta, whose provisions were expanded during Edward's reign to apply to men of all social backgrounds, made it clear that the king could expect the public to provide financial support only for the knighting of his eldest son, the Black Prince, and the dowry of his eldest daughter Isabella, who finally married a French nobleman, Enguerrand VII de Coucy, at the age of thirty-three. His immediate predecessors had comparatively small numbers of surviving younger children to support, and their eldest sons succeeded to the throne as young men. Edward, however, had nine children who survived to adulthood. The king was determined to ensure that the Black Prince had a reliable income as heir to the throne and that the younger sons were independently wealthy. The arrangements Edward made for his sons shaped the financial futures of all English and then British royal children to the present day.

Before Edward III's reign, there were no distinctive titles for an English monarch's daughters and younger sons. Instead, they were distinguished from one another by their birthplaces. Edward's younger siblings were known as John of Eltham (Eltham Palace in Kent), Eleanor of Woodstock (Woodstock Palace in Oxfordshire) and Joan of the Tower (the Tower of London). When Edward I conquered Wales in the late thirteenth century, he revived the title of Prince of Wales, previously held by Welsh princes from the House of Gwynedd, bestowing it on his eldest surviving son, the future Edward II, in 1301.

The new title appeared to reflect the unique circumstances of the Welsh campaign. Edward II was born in Caernarfon during the construction of the English castle there, and a legend developed that Edward I promised the Welsh people a prince who could speak no English, fulfilling his vow with his infant son, who could not yet speak any language. Edward II did not, however, bestow the title on the future Edward III, who was known during his childhood as Edward of Windsor, distinguished only by his birthplace (Windsor Castle) like his younger siblings.

In contrast to his own experience, Edward III did more to ensure the status and financial security of his eldest son than any previous king since Henry II crowned his eldest son during his lifetime. Edward not only conferred the title of Prince of Wales on the Black Prince, but bestowed upon him the Duchy of Cornwall, which enabled him, and subsequent eldest sons of the monarch, to be financially independent of their subjects and the rest of the royal family. Edward also began the practice of bestowing dukedoms on younger sons of the monarch, and ensured that his sons married heiresses who would allow them the same financial independence as their eldest brother. Edward and Philippa's second son, Lionel of Antwerp, became Duke of Clarence and married Elizabeth de Burgh, fourth Countess of Ulster. The third son, John of Gaunt, married Blanche of Lancaster, daughter of Henry of Grosmont, first Duke of Lancaster, the wealthiest peer in England. Blanche inherited her father's lands and Edward recreated the title of Duke of Lancaster for John. The Duchy of Lancaster remains the main source of the British monarch's private income to the present day. The process of conferring dukedoms on younger sons of the monarch continued into the next reign, when Edward's fourth son, Edmund of Langley, became Duke of York and his youngest surviving son, Thomas of Woodstock, became Duke of Gloucester.

The premature death of the Black Prince in 1376, from dysentery contracted on a military campaign, had the potential to create a crisis in the royal succession: the Prince of Wales had left a single male heir, his nine-year-old son, Richard of Bordeaux. Lionel had predeceased his elder brother, and his only child was an adult daughter, Philippa, fifth Countess of Ulster, who was married to Edmund Mortimer, third Earl of March, and had young sons of her own. In past centuries, the claims of Richard, Philippa, and her sons — a woman and small children — would have been easily swept aside by John of Gaunt. As Duke of Lancaster, John was the wealthiest nobleman in England and he had acquired extensive military experience in campaigns against French and Spanish incursions into Gascony. His ambition, leadership abilities, and financial resources, in addition to his status as the son of a reigning monarch, were all the qualifications that would have been required to make him King of England both before the Norman Conquest and immediately after. The Black Prince recognized that John was a threat to young Richard's succession prospects, and insisted on his deathbed that his brother swear to support the boy's claim to the throne. John upheld his oath to his brother, but he looked for other opportunities to raise his place in the line of succession.

By Edward III's reign, parliament had become involved in determining who was eligible to succeed to the throne, regulating a line of succession that had once been shaped as much by warfare and proximity to the centre of power as by hereditary right. A statute passed in 1351 stated, "the law of the Crown of England is, and always hath been such, that the children of the kings of England, in whatsoever parts they be born, in England or elsewhere, be able and ought to bear the inheritance after the death of their ancestors."[10] The statute made clear that parliament considered a royal child born outside England to be just as eligible to succeed to the throne as any other member of the dynasty, a ruling that was especially relevant during the Hundred Years' War, when Philippa, and later her daughters-in-law, accompanied their husbands on campaign to France. Richard's birth in Bordeaux took place while his father, the Black Prince, was representing Edward III in Gascony, accompanied by his young family. Richard's place in the succession was therefore difficult to challenge, but John saw an opportunity to sponsor parliamentary statutes that would support his own position.

At the "Good Parliament" of 1376, John petitioned parliament to "make a law on the pattern of the French that no woman be heir to the kingdom."[11] If successful, this petition would have removed Philippa, Countess of March, and her sons from the succession. John's petition proved controversial. There were precedents in English common law for a noble estate to be entailed to the male line, prohibiting female succession, but previous kings had considered their daughters eligible to become the next monarch. In 1290, Edward I decreed that in the event of an absence of male heirs, the eldest of his five surviving daughters was entitled to succeed to the throne. The decree had been necessary at the time as Edward had only one surviving son and English common law allowed for noble estates to be divided among co-heiresses in the absence of a male heir. Edward I's decree made clear that the kingdom was not divisible among sisters, but women could succeed to the throne in their own right. The circumstances of the Hundred

Years' War, during which Edward III claimed to be the rightful King of France through the French royal lineage of his mother, made the exclusion of female heirs seem even more out-of-place in the English monarchy. John's petition was rejected by parliament under the leadership of the first recorded Speaker of the House, Sir Peter de la Mare, a steward of Philippa's husband. Although the ailing Edward III appears to have supported his son John's position and prepared a document that treated the crown as an estate entailed to the male line, the Good Parliament's acceptance of female succession set important precedents for future claims to the throne and the upbringing of subsequent female royal children.

The succession dispute demonstrated the fragility of the family harmony that existed among Edward III's children during his lifetime. Richard of Bordeaux succeeded his grandfather as King Richard II at the age of ten in 1377. Instead of a single regent, the king was advised by a council whose members initially included both his uncle John of Gaunt and his cousin Philippa's husband, the Earl of March. For Richard's forebear Henry III, kingship had brought an abrupt end to childhood within a conventional family circle as his mother left England and remarried; in contrast, Richard maintained a close relationship with his widowed mother, Joan, who remained a close adviser during his adolescence. During the Peasants' Revolt of 1381, Joan was one of the most popular members of the royal family because of her perceived moderating influence over the fourteen-year-old king. Just like Richard's grandmother, Philippa of Hainault, Joan appeared to have the ability to intercede with the king through the authority conferred by her status as a royal mother.

Richard's relations with the rest of his family were less harmonious. He distrusted both John of Gaunt and John's eldest son, Henry Bolingbroke, who was almost exactly Richard's age. The king never had children of his own, and seemed to prefer to keep the matter of the succession ambiguous, treating his cousin Philippa's son and then grandson as his heirs without giving them the same titles and honours that he bestowed on his relatives through the male line. In 1399, Richard was overthrown by Henry, who had been exiled and forbidden from inheriting the lands accumulated by his parents, John of Gaunt and Blanche of Lancaster. The new king, Henry IV, founded the ruling House of Lancaster, but the parenting decisions and succession disputes from the time of his grandparents, Edward III and Philippa of Hainault, would contribute to the political turmoil faced by his descendants. During the Wars of the Roses (1455–85), junior members of the royal family would further their own interests independent of the monarch's wishes, and a rival dynasty, the House of York, would emerge to challenge the House of Lancaster. The political upheaval allowed one of the most controversial monarchs in English history to seize power in 1483: King Richard III.

SIX

Richard III (1452-85) and Anne Neville (1456-85)

In 1484, King Richard III of England and his queen, Anne Neville, suffered the most grievous blow possible as both parents and as the monarch and consort of a ruling house: their only son, Edward of Middleham, died at the age of ten. Richard's character, actions, and motives have been debated by historians and the general public for more than five hundred years, but the king's admirers and detractors agree that the loss of his only legitimate child was devastating for the royal couple.

One of Richard's contemporaries, possibly John Russell, the Bishop of Lincoln, provided a vivid account of Richard and Anne's grief in the *Croyland Chronicle*: "This only son of his, in whom all the hopes of the royal succession, fortified with so many oaths, were centred, was seized with an illness of but short duration, and died at Middleham Castle.... On hearing the news of this, at Nottingham, where they were then residing, you might have seen his father and mother in a state almost bordering on madness, by reason of their sudden grief."[1] Richard and Anne were not the first royal couple to have their grief described in these terms. The physical and mental health of Henry III and Eleanor of Provence was reported to have suffered when they lost their youngest child, Katherine, in 1257.

The parenting advice of the fifteenth century acknowledged that the loss of a child was a destabilizing event for parents of any background. The instructive poem "How the Goode Wife Taught Hyr Doughter," which dates from the reign of Henry VI (1422–61 and 1470–71), warns readers against losing their faith in God in the face of great adversity, including the deaths of friends and children. The poem warned that grief-stricken parents could be undone by their loss of faith:

> And if it thus thee betyde,
> That frendes falle thee fro on every syde,
> And God fro thee thi child take,
> They wreke one God do thou not take,
> For thyselve it wyll undo.[2]

By the time Richard and Anne lost their son Edward, they had already lost numerous friends and family members. Both of their fathers had died in battle fighting for opposite factions during the Wars of the Roses. Richard outlived all three of his brothers. The eldest, King Edward IV, died suddenly in 1483, precipitating the political crisis that brought Richard to the throne. Edmund died with their father at the Battle of Wakefield in 1460. George was executed in 1478 for plotting against Edward, reputedly by being drowned in a barrel of malmsey wine. Anne's sister (and George's wife), Isabel, died of a fever following childbirth in 1476. Other elite families in late-fifteenth-century England suffered similar losses from the unique political and military circumstances of the Wars of the Roses or the age-old causes of premature death such as childbirth or disease. Richard and Anne's bereavement as parents, after all their other losses, should have brought them popular sympathy.

The difference for Richard and Anne was that the death of their son had political as well as personal dimensions. Richard had come to the throne in unusual circumstances in 1483 and it was not clear which one of his numerous relatives would assume the position of heir to throne in the event that he did not father any further legitimate children. The *Croyland Chronicle* also implied that there was an element of divine retribution for Richard's ambitions in his son Edward's death. Before describing Richard and Anne's grief, the chronicler explained that when Edward died, "It was fully seen how vain are the thoughts of a man who desires to establish his interests without the aid of God."[3] At the time of his son's death, Richard's reign was already the focus of opposition. Public opinion would ultimately judge the king as a parental figure, guardian, and monarch not by his attachment to his own son but by the disappearance of his nephews, King Edward V and Richard, better known as the Princes in the Tower.

As the youngest surviving son of a non-reigning branch of the Plantagenet dynasty, Richard III was not born to be king. His father, Richard, Duke of York, inherited his title through descent from Edward III's fourth son, Edmund of Langley. The elder Richard, however, was also the son of Anne Mortimer, a granddaughter of Philippa, Countess of March, whose succession rights had sparked a parliamentary debate during the last years of Edward III's reign. Henry VI, grandson of Henry IV and king at the time of the future Richard III's birth, was descended from the third son of Edward III, but Richard, Duke of York, was descended from Edward's second and fourth sons. The titles, fortunes, and prominent public roles that Edward provided for his younger sons meant that their descendants remained important figures in subsequent reigns. When Henry VI, who was also a grandson of King Charles VI ("the Mad") of France through his mother Katherine of Valois, went into a catatonic state in 1453 after learning of England's final defeat in the Hundred Years' War, Richard, Duke of York, acted as regent, against the wishes of Henry VI's queen, Margaret of Anjou. When Henry became responsive again in 1454, he acted under the influence of Margaret and her adviser, the Duke of Somerset, marginalizing the Duke of York and his supporters. Military hostilities broke out in 1455, with a Yorkist victory at the Battle of St. Albans, beginning the Wars of the Roses between the supporters of the Houses of Lancaster and York that would continue until Henry Tudor defeated Richard III at the Battle of Bosworth Field in 1485.

Richard III's predecessors had to negotiate parenting with consorts who were foreign or came from a different social background than they did. In contrast, Richard and his wife Anne were raised in the same residences and each had experienced multiple sudden changes in fortune due to the circumstances of the Wars of the Roses before they reached adulthood. Anne's father,

Richard Neville, Earl of Warwick, nicknamed "The Kingmaker," was one of the most powerful men in England with the wealth and ability to shape the royal succession. He supported Richard, Duke of York, who was the husband of his cousin, Cecily Neville, and then their son, Edward IV, who sent his younger brother Richard to Warwick's household to gain additional training as a knight. Richard would have spent most of his time in military training with other young noblemen, but his education also included training in courtly manners, which were practised in conversation with the Countess of Warwick and her daughters, Isabel and Anne.

Richard's time in Warwick's household was a rare period of stability during his youth, contrasting with his forced flight abroad following the deaths of his father and brother Edmund. This calm adolescence came to an end when Warwick rebelled against Edward IV, who had married Elizabeth Woodville, the widow of a Lancastrian knight, without consulting him. Richard remained loyal to his brother, while Warwick first backed his son-in-law George, Edward's younger brother, as a possible replacement king and then supported the exiled Lancastrians, arranging a marriage between his daughter Anne and Edward of Westminster, the son born to Margaret of Anjou while Henry VI was unresponsive. Edward IV regained his throne, defeating and killing both Warwick and Edward of Westminster on the battlefield. Richard married the widowed Anne. The marriage created conflict between Richard and his brother George because the Neville inheritance was divided between them. George hoped to keep Anne unmarried so that all the Neville lands and income would remain under his control as the husband of her elder sister Isabel. For the newly restored Edward, however, Richard's marriage to Anne and acquisition of her half of the Neville inheritance provided a useful counterweight to George's ambitions. Neither George nor Richard would be able to command the resources that had been available to their late father-in-law, "The Kingmaker."

After their wedding in 1472, Richard and Anne, Duke and Duchess of Gloucester, attempted to recreate the peaceful time in their lives when they had both resided in Warwick's household. They settled at Middleham Castle in Wensleydale, north Yorkshire, one of the Warwick landholdings. Richard acted as his brother Edward IV's deputy in the north of England, administering justice, collecting revenues, and repelling a Scottish invasion.

There are few sources concerning his family life, and the precise birthdate of their only son, Edward of Middleham, Earl of Salisbury, is unknown. The similarities between Richard and Anne in upbringing, experiences, and interests may have contributed to her comparatively low profile in the chronicles of the period. William I and Matilda of Flanders, Henry II and Eleanor of Aquitaine, and Edward II and Isabelle of Valois attracted scrutiny because of discord in their marriages, which included struggles for the loyalty of their children. In contrast, Richard and Anne appear to have shared a common interest in maintaining their wealth, power, and influence in the north of England, following precedents set by their fathers.

Edward IV's death in 1483 appeared to threaten Richard and Anne's position. The new king was Edward's son, twelve-year-old Edward V, who had been raised under the influence of his Woodville relatives. Edward IV's marriage to Elizabeth Woodville had prompted Warwick's rebellion, and Richard appears to have disapproved of the influence of Elizabeth and her family at Edward's court. Neither Richard nor Anne would have welcomed the possibility of greater influence for the Woodvilles during the reign of a child monarch. Richard marched southward, intercepted his nephew, and arrested the king's uncle, Anthony Woodville. Instead of becoming Lord Protector for Edward V, Richard claimed the throne in London for himself, presenting evidence that Edward IV had drawn up a marriage contract with another noblewoman, Eleanor Butler, before marrying Elizabeth Woodville, and that the royal children were therefore illegitimate. Edward IV's children experienced the same abrupt change in fortune that had characterized Richard's and Anne's childhoods. Edward IV's five surviving daughters and younger son resided with their mother in sanctuary in Westminster Abbey. The former Edward V remained in the Tower of London, where medieval English monarchs traditionally lodged before their coronations. Richard then removed Edward IV's younger son, also named Richard, Duke of York, from his mother's care and placed him with Edward V in the Tower.

On July 6, 1483, Richard was crowned King of England. Anne was present for their coronation, but their son remained at Middleham Castle. Edward V and Richard, Duke of York, "The Princes in the Tower," disappeared from public view in 1483. The diplomat Dominic Mancini wrote in December 1483, "I have seen many men burst forth into tears and lamentations when mention was made of [Edward V] after his removal from men's sight; and already there was a suspicion that he had been done away with. Whether, however, he has been done away with and by what manner of death, so far I have not at all discovered."[4] There were rumours of a murder and suspicion of the new King Richard's involvement, but the precise circumstances of the princes' fate remains a mystery to the present day. After the disappearance of the princes, Henry Tudor, a descendant of the House of Lancaster through his mother, Margaret Beaufort, became the centre of opposition to Richard III's rule. Henry publicly swore to marry Elizabeth of York, the eldest sister of the Princes in the Tower, a match that would unite the Houses of Lancaster and York.

Richard was the first monarch to be crowned King of England after the introduction of the printing press in London, which allowed new ideas to disseminate to a wider audience, particularly in urban areas where literacy was more prevalent. The German publisher Johannes Gutenberg introduced mechanical moving-type printing to Europe around 1450 and the English merchant William Caxton set up a press in London in 1476. Even though print was accessible to a wider audience than manuscripts, Caxton still sought royal patronage, and dedicated a book about chivalry to Richard III. Caxton's press published a diverse array of literature and philosophy including Chaucer's *Canterbury Tales,* but his audience was also interested in reading prescriptive literature, such as parenting advice.

One of Caxton's publications, *The Book of the Knight of the Tower*, printed in 1484, provided advice for raising daughters in the form of instructions provided by a widower to his children. The treatise emphasized manners and morals shaped through physical discipline. The author encouraged young women to fast on bread and water regularly to temper lustful thoughts, writing, "my dear daughter you ought to fast as long as you are single, three days in the week, the better to mortify the flesh, that it was not wanton, and you may dedicate yourself, more chastely and holily, to the service of God."[5] Fasting was part of the upbringing of royal children as well because it was part of key ceremonies in the lives of monarchs and their families. Monarchs fasted before their coronations and their sons fasted before receiving their knighthoods. Richard displayed ruthlessness in his seizure of the throne, but his public image and that of his family included conventional displays of piety.

The rituals of Richard's reign demonstrated his determination to assert the legitimacy of his family's place at the apex of English society in addition to his own right to rule. The creation of Edward of Middleham as Prince of Wales demonstrated both Richard's status as king and his pride as a father in his ten-year-old son. Richard declared at the investiture in York Minister cathedral: "We therefore, following the footsteps of our ancestors and with the assent and advice of the said prelates, dukes and barons of our realm of England, we have determined to honour our dearest first born son Edward, whose outstanding qualities, with which he is singularly endowed for his age, give great and, by the favour of God, undoubted hope of future uprightness, as prince [of Wales] and earl [of Chester]."[6]

The speech is the only surviving evidence of Richard's personal relationship with his son. In contrast to other young noblemen of the period, including his own father, Edward of Middleham spent his childhood with his parents instead of being fostered in another noble household. When Richard spoke of his son's fine qualities, he may have been drawing upon his own observations in addition to the conventional expressions of confidence in his heir.

As king, Richard also looked after the interests of his two known illegitimate children, John and Katherine. Their precise dates of birth are unknown, but the responsibilities that they were granted during Richard's reign suggest that they were in their teens by the mid-1480s and were therefore conceived before the marriage of Richard and Anne in 1472. The identities of their mothers are unknown. Richard knighted his son John during the festivities surrounding the investiture of Edward as Prince of Wales and appointed him Captain of Calais in 1485 on what may have been his seventeenth birthday. At the same time, Richard arranged the marriage of his daughter Katherine to William Herbert, Earl of Huntingdon. Katherine's marriage contract arranged for her to have independent control of lands and incomes, stating, "by God's grace he shall take to wife Dame Katherine Plantagenet, daughter to our said sovereign lord; and before their marriage to make or cause to be made to her behalf a sure, sufficient, and lawful estate of certain [of] his manors, lordships, lands and tenements in England to the yearly value of two hundred pounds."[7] The arrangements Richard made for the future of his illegitimate children were dependent on his position as king and the stability of his dynasty. After Richard's death in 1485, John lost his position as Captain of Calais, and Katherine may have been repudiated by her husband.

After the loss of his son Edward, Richard was forced to contemplate the succession and the future of his dynasty. He appears to have treated his sister Elizabeth's son, John de la Pole, Earl of Lincoln, as heir to the throne after Edward's death, conferring upon his nephew the position of Lord Lieutenant of Ireland and expanding his landholdings. The death of Richard's queen soon after the loss of her son in 1484, however, meant that it was possible for Richard to remarry and have another legitimate heir. There was speculation that he intended to seek a papal dispensation to marry his niece, Elizabeth of York, a choice of bride that would have called into question Richard's own claim that his nieces and nephews were illegitimate. According to the *Croyland Chronicle*, Richard publicly denied the rumours "in the presence of the mayor and the citizens of London, in the great hall of the Hospital of Saint John, by making the said denial in a loud and distinct voice."[8] The chronicler implied that the Londoners were not entirely convinced by Richard's denial, attributing it to his advisers instead of his own convictions. During the last months of his reign, Richard entered into negotiations for a marriage to Joanna of Portugal, planning a reciprocal union between Elizabeth of York and Joanna's cousin Manuel, Duke of Beja. Richard, however, never had the opportunity to remarry and father another heir, as he was defeated and killed by Henry Tudor at the Battle of Bosworth Field in 1485.

After his death, Richard entered popular culture to a degree unknown to any of his predecessors with the possible exception of Henry II and Eleanor of Aquitaine. For centuries, the most famous depiction of the king's reign was William Shakespeare's play *Richard III*, written around 1592, during the reign of Henry VII's granddaughter, Elizabeth I. Shakespeare ignored Richard's role as a father and instead portrayed him as a wicked uncle who was willing to murder his relatives to advance his own political ambitions. Favourable interpretations of Richard's reign emerged in the nineteenth century with greater attention given to other possible suspects in the murder of the Princes in the Tower, including Edward Stafford, Duke of Buckingham, and Henry VII. The Richard III Society was founded in 1924 and its membership exploded in the 1950s with the publication of Josephine Tey's detective novel *Daughter of Time* and a film adaptation of Shakespeare's *Richard III* starring Laurence Olivier. The society, under the patronage of Queen Elizabeth II's cousin Prince Richard, Duke of Gloucester, has published new research concerning Richard III's reign, including analysis of whether Edward of Middleham had a brother who died in infancy.[9]

The Richard III Society was also instrumental in the excavation and identification of Richard's remains in a parking lot near the University of Leicester in 2012. The ensuing debate concerning Richard's final resting place revived interest in his relationship with his son, Edward. The *Press* newspaper in York argued for Richard to be interred at York Minster, where Edward became Prince of Wales, or the Norman church of St. Helen and the Holy Cross at Sheriff Hutton, where Edward is probably buried in the Neville family chapel. The paper stated that "British soldiers killed fighting overseas are repatriated home to their loved ones. We should do no less for the last Plantagenet king."[10] The question of Richard's burial place was settled by a judicial ruling, and his funeral took place at Leicester Cathedral in 2015.

The death of Richard III and the establishment of the new Tudor dynasty had profound implications for Richard III's nieces and nephews. With the exception of Edward IV's eldest daughter, Elizabeth of York, who became Henry VII's queen, uniting the succession claims of the Houses of Lancaster and York, the youngest generation of Plantagenets could no longer expect to be treated as senior members of the royal family as they had been during their childhoods. Henry affirmed the legitimacy of Edward IV's daughters, but he did not arrange dynastic marriages for his sisters-in-law or provide them with dowries commensurate with their status as daughters of a king. Instead, Cecily, Anne, and Katherine of York, and their cousin Margaret, Countess of Salisbury, were married to members of the nobility to bolster support for the new dynasty. The youngest York sister, Bridget, became a nun. The surviving male Plantagenets represented a threat to the legitimacy of the Tudors. Henry imprisoned the young Edward, Earl of Warwick, son of Richard III's brother George, in the Tower of London, and ultimately ordered his execution. John de la Pole died at the Battle of Stoke in 1487. Henry VIII would inherit his father's suspicion of the surviving Plantagenets, and his reign would see the execution of numerous descendants of Edward III.

While Henry VII was marginalizing or eliminating the royal children of the previous dynasty, he was also emphasizing his own children's status. The most powerful symbol of the new Tudor dynasty's legitimacy would be for Henry's sons and daughters to make dynastic marriages with the established ruling families of continental Europe. In search of a prestigious royal bride for his eldest son, Arthur, Henry VII entered into negotiations with the monarchs whose own marriage united Spain: King Fernando II of Aragon and Queen Isabel I of Castile. The Spanish royal couple, better known in the English-speaking world as Ferdinand and Isabella, had four daughters. Henry secured the youngest, Catherine of Aragon, for his heir.

SEVEN

Ferdinand II of Aragon (1452-1516) and Isabella I of Castile (1451-1504)

On October 19, 1469, seventeen-year-old Ferdinand, the only surviving son of King Juan II "the Faithless" of Aragon, and eighteen-year-old Isabella, younger half-sister and legal heir of King Enrique IV "the Impotent" of Castile, married in secret in the Palacio de los Vivero in Valladolid. The young couple married on the day they met because Isabella's brother disapproved of the match, and the terms of the treaty that made her heir to the throne forbade her from marrying without her brother's permission. Ferdinand and Isabella were determined to marry before Enrique became aware of their intention to wed and intervened to prevent the union.

Isabella's place in the Castilian succession was tenuous. Her half-brother Enrique's queen, Juana of Portugal, had given birth to a daughter in 1462, but the child's paternity was widely disputed. Nevertheless, there was always the possibility that Enrique would marry Isabella off to a distant prince and make the child his heir instead of her. Over the course of Isabella's childhood, Enrique had considered a variety of foreign royal husbands for her, including the future kings Edward IV and Richard III of England. A marriage to Ferdinand of Aragon, one of Castile's neighbours on the Iberian Peninsula, would keep Isabella close to home and give her additional resources to maintain her senior place in the Castilian succession.

Despite Isabella's status as a future queen, Ferdinand may have expected to be in charge of their family after the marriage — and, once they succeeded to their respective thrones, their kingdoms as well. In the late fifteenth century, even women entitled to wield power in their own right usually became subject to the authority of their husbands. Just eight years after Ferdinand married Isabella, Archduke Maximilian of Austria married Mary, Duchess of Burgundy (a territory that overlaps with modern-day Belgium and the Netherlands), protecting her lands from annexation by the King of France. Maximilian officially became Mary's co-ruler, but he effectively assumed control of Burgundy. Since Mary died in a riding accident when her children were still young, Maximilian was also the parent with the most influence over their children's upbringing. Following the Battle of Bosworth Field, Henry Tudor was careful to ensure that he was crowned King Henry VII by right of conquest before marrying Elizabeth of York, whose claim to the throne was far superior to his own once her legitimacy was restored. Elizabeth became closely involved in the day-to-day upbringing of her children, but the conditions of her confinements were dictated by Henry's mother, Margaret Beaufort, and Henry made the key decisions regarding where the children would live and whom they would marry. Maximilian and Mary, as well as Henry and Elizabeth, were Ferdinand and Isabella's contemporaries, and the children of these three royal couples would marry one another.

Isabella, however, was determined to maintain her authority in both Castile and the family she intended to create with Ferdinand. Before she agreed to marry Ferdinand, she insisted that he accept a list of marriage concessions, which would ensure their equal partnership in public and private. The majority of the concessions were political: Isabella insisted that Ferdinand provide financial support for her plan to conquer the Emirate of Granada, the last Muslim-controlled region in the Iberian Peninsula, and that she be involved in the negotiation of all diplomatic treaties. There were other concessions, however, that demonstrated Isabella's commitment to sharing authority within the domestic sphere. She expected Ferdinand to agree that "if God should grant us offspring, either sons or daughters as we hope, I will never remove them from her, nor will I remove them from those kingdoms...."[1] The concessions also dictated that Ferdinand was not to travel in Aragon and Castile without the knowledge and permission of his wife. Isabella would be an equal partner in her marriage and make childrearing decisions jointly with her husband instead of being subject to his authority.

Isabella's concern for her role in her children's upbringing reflected the values of her time. Spanish humanists and priests writing about family life during the century after the reigns of Ferdinand and Isabella made it clear that all mothers, even those who could afford to employ numerous servants, should take an active role in childrearing. In a 1583 treatise entitled *The Perfect Wife*, Augustinian friar Luis de León advised Lady Maria Varelia Orosio that marriage meant "serving one's husband, governing one's family and raising one's children," criticizing women who "think that in having a child from time to time and then handing it over to the arms of a governess they are complete and perfect women."[2] León encouraged mothers to breastfeed their infants for twenty-four months. Humanist scholar Pedro de Luxán emphasized the feelings of personal fulfillment for a mother "when she sees her infant break into a laugh, or make a face as though to cry, or to ask for his gruel, or run his hand over her breast and even pull at her coif, running his hands over his parents' chins and saying a thousand funny little things."[3]

Spanish parenting tracts had less to say about the role of fathers in the upbringing of their children, as it was assumed that once children were old enough to leave the continuous care of their mothers, the instruction and spiritual development of well-born children would be shaped by a variety of adults, including priests, tutors, and noble foster parents. Nevertheless, Luxán made it clear that an attentive father took an interest in the education and morals of his children and encouraged "everyone [to] gather around the fireplace," where the boys could read aloud and the girls could do their needlework.[4] Spanish parents maintained the ability to make decisions about a son or daughter's marriage partner and contributions to the household economy. The legal age of majority in Castile was twenty-five, ensuring that young people remained under the authority of their parents even after they had begun their adult lives.

For Ferdinand and Isabella, the unique circumstances of their marriage and position precluded the ability to create the ideal household conditions for raising children. Isabella's brother Enrique immediately challenged the validity of their marriage and her succession rights. After Enrique died in 1474, Isabella spent five years embroiled in the War of the Castilian succession against his disputed daughter, who enjoyed Portuguese support. Ferdinand did not succeed his father until 1479, and Catalan demands for independence threatened the cohesion of Aragon during his time as heir to the throne. This political uncertainty may have delayed the expansion of Ferdinand and Isabella's family. Their eldest child, Isabel, was born just a year after their marriage in 1470, but there were no further children until their only son Juan was born in 1478. Three more daughters followed in quick succession: Juana in 1479, Maria (born with a stillborn twin sister) in 1482, and Catalina (Catherine of Aragon) in 1485.

Ferdinand and Isabella arranged for trusted guardians to care for their children during times of war, but the hostilities sometimes directly threatened the security of the royal nursery. The turmoil surrounding the Castilian succession threatened Isabella's eldest daughter, Isabel, on at least one occasion: when the inhabitants of the town of Segovia rebelled in 1477, Isabella rode to the city with a small entourage to negotiate the safe release of her daughter, who was trapped in a castle tower with her guardians. Even when Ferdinand and Isabella were together with their children, the royal household was always on the move; Madrid would not emerge as a capital city until 1561, and there was no primary residence for the royal family. The king and queen were expected to dispense justice in person, and constant progresses around their kingdoms were vital to ensuring the loyalty of their subjects. The travelling court also doubled as military camp during the royal couple's ten-year war with Granada, which ended with their victory in 1492.

Despite the demands of her position, Isabella paid close attention to the education and upbringing of her children. Her own childhood had been comparatively isolated. Enrique had viewed his half-siblings as a political threat, and Isabella had therefore spent her early childhood in the remote town of Arévalo with her widowed, reclusive mother. Her only friend was Beatriz de Bobadilla, the daughter of the Arévalo castle's governor, who eventually became Isabella's daughter Isabel's guardian during the war of the Castilian succession. In contrast, Isabella fostered dozens of young people at her court, ensuring that the royal children shared their lessons and games with companions. The queen also arranged for her daughters to receive a more comprehensive education than she had experienced in Arévalo. Isabella struggled with Latin, the language of diplomacy, as queen, but her daughters learned the language from childhood, ensuring that they would be able to assume prominent roles in the courts of their husbands once they made dynastic marriages to foreign rulers. Isabella also passed on her devotion to the Roman Catholic Church, which had a particular impact on the lives of her two youngest children, Maria and Catherine, and Catherine's daughter, Queen Mary I of England. As queen consort of Portugal, Maria would co-found the Jerónimos Monastery in Lisbon, and Catherine would oppose the establishment of royal supremacy over the Church of England during the breakdown of her marriage to Henry VIII.

Ferdinand assumed a greater role in the education of Juan. The heir to the throne turned twelve, the traditional age for Spanish knighthood, in 1490, during the war with Granada. Ferdinand knighted his son himself at a public ceremony within view of the Alhambra fortress. Once knighted, Juan accompanied his father on military campaigns, along with the other young men of the royal household who shared his military training. In his later years, Ferdinand acted as a father figure in the life of his namesake grandson, Ferdinand of Austria, the son of Ferdinand and Isabella's daughter Juana "the Mad" and her husband Philip "the Handsome" of Flanders (son of Maximilian and Mary). The younger Ferdinand was born in Alcalá de Henares in Castile in 1503 and spent his youth in his grandfather's household. Ferdinand of Aragon also involved himself in the advancement of his illegitimate children, who were highly placed in ecclesiastical careers. His son Alonzo became Archbishop of Zaragoza at the age of eight, while a daughter, Isabella, became Abbess of the royal convent of Our Lady Mother of Grace at Avila.

Within the splendour and ritual of her court, Isabella attempted to maintain a comparatively simple domestic sphere. She sewed Ferdinand's shirts herself, a practice that her daughter Catherine would adopt during her marriage to Henry VIII. In private, the royal couple and their children dressed comparatively simply and attempted to create an intimate family circle. Isabella's care for her children and simple domesticity attracted the admiration of her subjects, and the popular memory of her ability to manage a household endured long after her death. In *The Perfect Wife*, León wrote, "In the time of our grandparents, we find clear examples of this virtue [of domestic management], as in the case of the Catholic queen, Lady Isabella."[5] *The Perfect Wife* was a frequent wedding gift for Spanish brides into the twentieth century, ensuring that Isabella's reputation for domestic virtue remained constant throughout Spain's history.

Ferdinand and Isabella were not concerned only with the upbringing of their own children and the other young people who travelled with their household. They also had strong views about the domestic lives of their subjects, and attempted to change existing childrearing practices, particularly those favoured by religious and cultural minorities within their kingdoms. For parents of all social backgrounds, the arrival of a healthy baby was cause for rejoicing at a time when nearly half of all children failed to survive to adulthood. The birth chamber was a strictly female space where women came together to encourage the mother-to-be in her labour. Once the child arrived, the women joined the men for days of feasting and dancing. In kingdoms as fragmented by geography and culture as Castile and Aragon, the gathering of neighbours and extended family to celebrate a birth could bring discontented subjects together in rebellion. In 1493, Ferdinand and Isabella banned the multiday feasts that followed births in Galicia. Since Galicia and the neighbouring Basque country enjoyed autonomy within Castile and were far from the travelling royal court, it is unknown how effective these new laws were in curbing traditional celebrations.

There was far more surveillance of how recent converts to Christianity from Judaism or Islam celebrated the births of children or made decisions regarding childrearing. Medieval Spain had been renowned for *La Convivencia*, an arrangement through which Christians, Jews, and Muslims coexisted in relative harmony. In 1480, Ferdinand and Isabella established the Spanish Inquisition through a "Letter of Commission to Carry Out Inquiries into Bad Christians" with the power to investigate heresy among *conversos* (converts from Judaism) and *moriscos* (converts from Islam). Their subjects were encouraged to report parents who were secretly passing along their traditional religious beliefs and practices to their children. An edict that was still in use in the seventeenth century encouraged people to report, "[i]f you know or have heard of anyone … placing their hands on the heads of their children without making the sign of the cross or saying anything but 'Be blessed by God and me'… or if they circumcise their children or give them Jewish names." The traditional hierarchy of the family was challenged, as children were encouraged to report the behaviour of their parents, and the testimony of minors, even those under the age of fourteen, far below the Castilian age of majority, was accepted in Inquisition courts.[6]

The careful arrangements Ferdinand and Isabella made for the future of their own children and their kingdoms were destroyed by a series of deaths within the family. The chronicler Andrés Bernaldez explained, "The first knife of grief that stabbed the spirit of La Reyna Doña [Isabella] was the death of the Prince [Juan], the second was the death of Isabel, her firstborn child, queen of Portugal; the third stab of grief was the death of Miguel, her grandson, with whom she consoled herself. From these times on, [she] … lived without pleasure, her life and health foreshortened."[7]

Juan, Prince of Asturias, was Ferdinand and Isabella's only surviving son, and his succession was crucial to ensuring that the dynastic union of Aragon and Castile would continue beyond the reign of his parents. Although the king and queen worked together in foreign policy and ensured a common value for the coinage used throughout their kingdoms, they did not combine their territories into a single political entity. Spain remained a geographical term rather than the name of a centralized state. Juan's death in 1497, just months after his marriage to Margaret of Austria (daughter of Maximilian and Mary), exposed the fragilities of the union of Castile and Aragon. The grieving Isabella expected both Aragon and Castile to accept her eldest daughter, Isabel, queen consort to King Manuel I of Portugal, as the new heir, but while Castile was a centralized kingdom that accepted female succession, Aragon was a federation of five regions that expected a male sovereign. As Isabel became pregnant with her first child within months of Juan's death, the final decision regarding the succession was delayed in the hope of a male heir who would be acceptable to both Aragon and Castile. Isabel died giving birth to her son Miguel in 1498.

Ferdinand and Isabella took charge of the upbringing of their grandson, who became heir to Castile, Aragon, and Portugal and therefore seemed destined to unite the entire Iberian Peninsula under his rule. But the young Miguel died in Isabella's arms in 1500. The deaths of Ferdinand and Isabella's two eldest children and their Portuguese grandson in close succession meant that the succession passed to their daughter Juana. Her eldest son, the future Holy Roman Emperor Charles V, would inherit kingdoms from each of his four grandparents — Maximilian, Mary, Ferdinand, and Isabella — becoming the ruler of most of Europe, including modern-day Spain, Belgium, the Netherlands, Germany, Austria, Hungary, and the Czech Republic in addition to the Spanish colonies in Latin America.

The death of Isabella in 1504 was a political blow to her surviving children as well as a profound personal loss to them. Without Isabella, the dynastic union of Aragon and Castile temporarily came to an end, as Ferdinand remained King of Aragon while Juana succeeded her mother as Queen of Castile. Isabella's testament specified that Ferdinand was to assume the regency of Castile if Juana were unable to exercise her prerogatives as sovereign. Juana's reputation for mental instability, displayed through an obsessive attachment to her unfaithful husband, Philip of Flanders, threatened her ability to wield power as successfully as her mother had done. In England, Catherine's desirability as a marriage partner for the future King Henry VIII declined after her mother's death, as she was now only the daughter of the King of Aragon instead of the sovereigns of a united Spain.

Juana and Catherine could expect little support in their changed circumstances from their father. Niccolò Machiavelli praised Ferdinand in *The Prince* for his dissimulation; Ferdinand displayed the same ruthlessness in his dealings with his adult daughters, placing politics over parental sentiment. Ferdinand and his son-in-law, Philip, agreed between them that Juana was mentally unfit to rule, and she was confined to a convent for the rest of her life, arrangements confirmed by her own son Charles upon Ferdinand's death in 1516. Catherine endured years of uncertainty and financial hardship in England after the death of her first husband, Arthur, Prince of Wales, in 1502, as Ferdinand and Henry VII argued over her dowry, status, and diplomatic role.

Ferdinand lived to see his youngest daughter become Queen of England. In 1509, Henry VII died and his seventeen-year-old son, the new King Henry VIII, was eager to prove that he did not need Margaret Beaufort, "My Lady, the King's Grandam," to govern on his behalf. An immediate marriage was the most public way for the new king to proclaim that he was an adult man capable of ruling instead of a youth in need of guidance from his grandmother. Catherine, now twenty-three and already resident in England, married Henry VIII less than two months after his accession to the English throne. There were strong political and personal arguments in favour of the match. Henry had known Catherine since he was ten years old, and throughout his life he made it clear that he was uncomfortable choosing any bride whom he would not meet before the marriage negotiations were concluded, as many of his predecessors had done. Henry also romanticized the Hundred Years' War (1337–1453), and was eager to regain the lands that England had won, then lost, during this conflict. Henry knew that his new father-in-law, Ferdinand, was also eager to contain French interests, and hoped they would become military allies in a renewed war with France.

In 1509, the marriage of Henry VIII and Catherine of Aragon appeared to have every chance of success. By the late 1520s, however, Henry was seeking an annulment, and his determination to end his first marriage would lead to the establishment of the monarch as Supreme Governor of the Church of England. The breakdown of Henry and Catherine's marriage, however, did not originate in the church, but in the nursery. The royal couple had one surviving child, a daughter named Mary. Henry and Catherine would be driven apart by the question of whether Mary could be raised to rule as Queen of England in her own right.

EIGHT

Henry VIII (1491-1547) and Catherine of Aragon (1485-1536)

Until recently, the birth of a daughter to a royal couple without living sons was usually greeted with disappointment by both the parents and the public. Daughters were useful to seal diplomatic agreements through dynastic marriages, but a son was the best hope of an uncontested royal succession. The birth of Princess Mary, daughter of Henry VIII and Catherine of Aragon, in 1516, however, was greeted with widespread rejoicing. In seven years of marriage, the king and queen had lost at least four children: a stillborn daughter and three successive sons who died at birth or in infancy. During Catherine's pregnancies, the king had discreet affairs with ladies at court, but there would be no acknowledged children born from these relationships until 1519. At twenty-five, Henry did not have a single acknowledged surviving child — an alarming circumstance for any reigning monarch, particularly one who emphasized his personal virility through his military campaigns and active pastimes such as jousting, hunting, tennis, and wrestling.

The arrival of Mary demonstrated that the king was capable of fathering healthy children. A delighted Henry announced to the Venetian ambassador, "We are both young; if it was a daughter this time, by the Grace of God, sons will follow."[1] The newborn princess received a lavish christening worthy of a king's heir. Henry proudly displayed his daughter to visiting ambassadors, boasting to the French envoy, "This child never cries."[2] For Catherine, the arrival of a healthy child was the answer to her prayers. The loss of successive infants had strained her marriage to the king. Mary had the potential to bring the king and queen together through the common bond of parenthood. For the first decade of Mary's life, the royal family achieved a measure of domestic harmony. The sons Henry anticipated, however, never followed. In his pursuit of male heirs, Henry would seek an annulment of his marriage to Catherine, bringing an abrupt end to Mary's secure childhood.

At the time of Henry's accession and marriage to Catherine in 1509, the Tudors were a newly established royal dynasty that faced rival claimants for the English throne. Successive Tudor monarchs therefore established new precedents and ceremonies that differentiated them from the English nobility. These new customs shaped the upbringing of a new generation of royal children from the time of their birth.

The first formal protocol concerning the births of royal children was introduced by Margaret Beaufort, for the birth of her first grandson, Arthur, in 1486, just one year after the Battle of Bosworth Field. The circumstances surrounding the births of previous royal children were varied. While most heirs were born in royal residences, Edward IV and Elizabeth Woodville's eldest son, the future Edward V, was born while his mother and sisters were first in sanctuary in Westminster Abbey during the brief restoration of Henry VI. Margaret's ordinances were intended to ensure that all royal births followed a similar pattern, right down to the furnishings. Margaret's daughter-in-law Elizabeth of York was permitted to choose the room where she would give birth, but the chamber would be decorated according to Margaret's dictates. The ordinances stated, "Her Highnes [Elizabeth of York] Pleasure beinge understoode in what Chamber she will be delivered in, the same must be hanged with riche Clothe of Arras, Sydes, rowffe, Windowes and all, excepte one Windowe, which must be hanged so as she may have light when it pleasethe her. Then must there be set a Royall Bedde, and the Flore layed all over and over with Carpets."[3] Any tapestries decorating the room were to show only pleasant scenes to ensure the royal mother's serenity during childbirth. Margaret's ordinances appear to reflect a desire to proclaim the legitimacy of the new Tudor dynasty and manage every aspect of the arrival of her grandchildren, but her careful instructions may have also have reflected a desire for Elizabeth to give birth in comforting surroundings.

When Margaret gave birth to the future Henry VII in 1457, she was the thirteen-year-old widow of Henry VI's half-brother, Edmund Tudor, becoming a mother amid the turmoil of the Wars of the Roses. The difficult birth left Margaret unable to bear subsequent children. Margaret's ordinances ensured that Elizabeth knew what to expect in the birth chamber and that she would be shielded from any political turmoil unfolding at court during the weeks prior to the arrivals of her children.

Margaret's prominence at her son's court, which included the cultural patronage and intercessions traditionally practised by queens consort, allowed her daughter-in-law Elizabeth to assume a more domestic role within her family. As Prince of Wales, Arthur had his own household, but the younger children — Margaret, the future Henry VIII, and Mary — were raised together. The inscription in Elizabeth's *Book of Hours*, "Elysabeth ye queen" bears a close resemblance to the handwriting of her three younger children, suggesting that she helped teach them to read and write.[4] Elizabeth also shared her love of Arthurian romances with her children; as king, Henry VIII would romanticize the medieval ideal of chivalry. As the young Henry and his siblings grew older, Margaret Beaufort and Elizabeth combined their influence over Henry VII to ensure the best interests of the children. Henry VII negotiated the betrothal of the young Margaret to King James IV of Scotland when she was just eleven, but the bride's mother and grandmother successfully persuaded the king to delay her departure until she reached the age of fourteen. Elizabeth extended her motherly care to Catherine when she arrived in England in 1501 to marry Arthur, writing to Isabella to assure her that her daughter would be welcomed into her new family.

The practice of dynastic marriage, which had determined the upbringing of generations of princesses, was critiqued in Henry's lifetime. After Catherine's niece, Isabella of Austria, married King Christian II "The Tyrant" of Denmark, a union arranged by Isabella's brother, Holy Roman Emperor Charles V, she wrote to their elder sister Eleanor: "It is hard enough to marry a man ... whom you do not know or love, and worse still to be required to leave home and kindred, and follow a stranger to the ends of the earth, without even being able to speak his language."[5] Isabella's sentiments were undoubtedly shared by other princesses of her generation. While medieval royal women had often been educated at the courts of their future husbands, sixteenth-century princesses were more likely to spend their early childhoods in the kingdoms of their birth, developing closer bonds with their parents and siblings.

The princesses whose futures were determined by dynastic marriage were not the only critics of the practice. The philosopher Desiderius Erasmus sympathized with the young women who travelled far from their homes to seal diplomatic alliances through their marriages, writing that these princesses "would be happier if they could live among their own people, even though with less pompous display."[6] Erasmus also argued that the alliances sealed by dynastic marriages rarely lasted, using the warfare between Henry VIII and his brother-in-law King James IV of Scotland as an example of historic enmity that transcended the numerous marriages between the English and Scottish royal houses. Henry and his sisters Margaret and Mary all contracted dynastic marriages in their youths, but chose non-royal commoners as second spouses following annulment or widowhood, suggesting that they also had doubts about how royalty traditionally chose their spouses and the parents of their children.

Henry and Catherine were the first English king and queen to contemplate the education of a female heir to the throne. When Henry I, Edward I, and Edward III supported the possibility of female succession, they were considering the prospects of their adult daughters after the untimely deaths of male heirs. In contrast, Catherine's last known pregnancy occurred in 1518, when Mary was only three years old. There was a strong possibility that she would be an only child. Decisions concerning Mary's education therefore took into account the possibility that she would succeed to the throne. Henry and Catherine had different views of female rule informed by their own childhoods. While Catherine's mother Isabella of Castile had been a reigning female monarch, Henry's mother Elizabeth of York had been the consort of a reigning king. While male monarchs had claimed the English throne through the royal descent of their mothers since the accession of Stephen, then Henry II, in the twelfth century, an uncontested female monarch had never ruled England in her own right.

Mary's education unfolded amid a wider debate among Europe's elite about how women should be educated within the new climate of Renaissance humanism. The fifteenth century saw the emergence of female scholars who made a strong case for women's potential to succeed as both intellectuals and political figures. In her 1405 treatise *The Treasure of the City of Ladies*, French author Christine de Pisan argued that royal women had a duty to intervene in European wars and counsel their husbands to find peaceful solutions. de Pisan also questioned France's Salic law, which prevented women from ruling in their own right. In Verona, humanist scholar Isotta Nogarola challenged biblical justifications for the subordinate status of women in society, composing her "Dialogue on The Equal or Unequal Sin of Eve and Adam" in 1451.

Interest in women's education and status in society spread from continental Europe to England. The philosopher Thomas More, who enjoyed the patronage of both Henry and Catherine, and became Lord Chancellor in 1529, ensured that his daughters received a thorough classical education. Erasmus praised the accomplishments of More's daughters in Greek, Latin, and music.

Catherine commissioned Spanish humanist Juan Luis Vives to compose a treatise on suitable principles for Mary's education, entitled *The Education of a Christian Woman*. Vives's ideas demonstrated the tension among traditional domestic roles for women, new expectations that elite women would participate in the revival of classical education, and Mary's unique role as Henry VIII's only legitimate child. Vives favoured education for women because of its ability to shape their character and morals rather than their suitability to assume public roles. He wrote that "the mind, set upon learning and wisdom, shall not only abhor from foul lust, that is to say the most white thing from soot, and the most pure from spots. But she shall leave all such light and trifling pleasures, wherein the light fantasies of maids have delight, as songs, dances and other such wanton and peevish plays. A woman, saith Plutarch, given unto learning, will never delight in dancing."[7] Catherine applied Vives's advice selectively. Whether Mary became a reigning queen or the wife of a king, music and dancing were key elements of court display. Mary received a thorough classical education, but she also learned to dance and play the virginals, interests that would continue throughout her life. Vives's disapproval of dancing and other forms of public merriment did not preclude Mary's participation in court entertainments.

Henry and Catherine were more closely involved in the upbringing and education of their daughter Mary than their contemporaries among the English nobility. The Bishop of Durham remarked, "See how [Mary] jumps forward in her nurse's lap when she catches sight of her father."[8] Henry and Catherine included Mary in state occasions from the age of four, and she often entertained visiting envoys with her abilities in music and dancing. While other royal children were sent to separate households from infancy, Mary remained close to her mother in early childhood, and both Henry and Catherine selected her attendants personally from among their most trusted courtiers. Catherine corrected Mary's Latin exercises and nursed her through her childhood illnesses. Mother and daughter forged a strong bond that would endure through the breakdown of Catherine's marriage to Henry.

Despite his close relationship with Mary during her early childhood, Henry was never entirely comfortable with the prospect of a female heir, and pursued other possibilities for the succession. In 1525, Henry elevated his six-year-old illegitimate son Henry Fitzroy to the peerage and invested him with the titles of Duke of Richmond and Somerset. There were numerous past examples of English monarchs conferring honours and incomes on their illegitimate children, but Henry VIII's decision to grant his son a dukedom and the title of Richmond, which had belonged to Henry VII prior to his accession to the throne, appeared to indicate that Fitzroy was being groomed for the succession. Mary spent time at Ludlow Castle, the traditional residence of Princes of Wales, suggesting that she was being trained as heir to the throne. In the late 1520s, however, Henry decided a new course for the succession: he would seek an annulment from Catherine on the grounds that she had been his brother's wife, and marry Anne Boleyn in the hope of fathering sons in a second marriage.

Catherine, however, was unwilling to relinquish her position and jeopardize Mary's place in the succession, and as her nephew Charles V had sacked Rome in 1527, he was in a position to exert political pressure on the

Pope. In her public plea to Henry before the papal legate in 1529, Catherine reminded him of the children they had lost, stating, "These twenty years or more I have been your true wife and by me ye have had divers children, although it hath pleased God to call them out of this world."[9] In 1531, Catherine was banished from court and forbidden to see her daughter. Catherine's close relationship with Mary appeared to pose a political threat to Henry's rule: if she had custody of Mary, Catherine would be in a stronger position to oppose the king.

Unable to secure a papal dispensation for the annulment, Henry declared himself Supreme Head of the Church of England and had his marriage to Catherine annulled by the Archbishop of Canterbury. These religious and political changes were highly controversial. More was beheaded for his refusal to accept the Act of Supremacy, which affirmed Henry's position as Head of the Church of England, and made Henry's daughter with Anne Boleyn, Elizabeth, heir to throne.

Throughout the breakdown of her parents' marriage, Mary displayed steadfast support for her mother, infuriating her father with her unwillingness to accept either the Church of England or Anne's queenship. The turmoil took a physical and emotional toll on Mary. After more than a decade of family harmony, during which she enjoyed a close relationship with both parents, she spent her adolescence in direct conflict with her father, the king. Catherine feared for Mary's future. Before Catherine died in 1536, she wrote to Henry: "I commend unto you Mary, our daughter, beseeching you be a good father to her."[10] Despite Catherine's pleas, relations between Henry and Mary remained hostile. Even after Henry repudiated Anne and had her beheaded for treason in 1536, he still insisted that Mary accept her own illegitimacy. Henry's continued insistence on the illegitimacy of his eldest daughter demonstrated that Mary's position reflected, at least in part, her own father's will instead of Anne's influence. Mary signed a document stating that the marriage of her parents had been invalid, and she was publicly reconciled with Henry, though they would never again enjoy the close relationship of her childhood. Mary's relations with Henry's subsequent wives, Jane Seymour, Anne of Cleves, Catherine Howard, and Catherine Parr, were cordial, and she remained a prominent figure at her father's court.

Throughout his successive marriages, Henry attempted to present a public image of family stability through royal portraiture. As king, Henry commissioned the first realistic portraits of royal children, showing their distinct features and ages as well as their status. The earliest known portrait of Mary dates from her (later broken) betrothal to Charles V. The six-year-old princess appeared as a woman of marriageable age, and the artist's emphasis on her badge emblazoned with "The Emperour" made clear that the purpose of the portrait was to celebrate the alliance with the Holy Roman Emperor. In contrast, Henry's only legitimate son, the future Edward VI, born during the king's third marriage to Jane Seymour in 1536, appeared as a realistic infant in a portrait by Hans Holbein.

The portraits of Henry VIII's children were part of a wider European trend toward portraying the sons and daughters of monarchs as children rather than miniature adults in art. As a toddler, the future Charles V had posed for a triptych of paintings with his sisters Isabella and Mary. The three children were depicted with the solemn expressions and elaborate clothing suitable to their rank, but Charles's sister Mary held a doll in her hands, emphasizing her youth. Sixteenth-century royal family group portraits, however, remained stylized with little physical contact between the figures in the images. A 1545 portrait of Henry VIII and his family depicted the king with his arm around Edward but detached from the other figures in the painting. The queen shown at the king's side was not Catherine Parr, his wife at the time of the portrait, but Edward's deceased mother Jane Seymour. The king's daughters, Mary and Elizabeth, appeared on either side of the family group in the centre, with visible space between them and their father and brother, symbolizing their stated illegitimacy and distance from the throne.

Despite Henry VIII's efforts to ensure the existence of a continuing male line in the Tudor dynasty, his family circumstances required him once again to consider the possibility of female succession during the last years of his life. Edward was nine at the time of his father's death. At a time of high child mortality, a single male heir was not enough to secure the survival of a ruling house. In 1543, parliament passed the Third Act of Succession, acknowledging, "It is in the only pleasure and will of Almighty God how long His Highness or his said entirely beloved son, Prince Edward, shall live, and whether the said prince shall have heirs of his body lawfully begotten or not."[11] The act restored Mary and Elizabeth to the succession in order of age, but maintained their illegitimacy. Mary became England's first uncontested queen regnant in 1553.

After the king's three children, the senior claimant to the throne was Mary, Queen of Scots, the granddaughter of Henry's elder sister, Margaret. At the time of Mary's accession to the throne of Scotland at the age of just six days, Henry hoped that the Scottish queen would marry Edward, uniting England and Scotland. Mary's mother and regent, Marie de Guise, instead betrothed her daughter to the future King François II of France. Henry excluded Mary, Queen of Scots, from his will, placing the descendants of his younger sister Mary next in the line of succession. Despite Henry's efforts to exclude the Scottish succession, the accession of Henry's younger daughter Elizabeth I in 1558 was contested by Mary, Queen of Scots. Elizabeth never married or had children of her own, and her successor was Mary's son, King James VI of Scotland, who succeeded to the English throne as James I when Elizabeth died in 1603. James's two surviving children, Elizabeth, Queen of Bohemia, and King Charles I of England and Scotland, would raise their own respective children amid the political and religious upheaval of the Thirty Years' War and the English Civil Wars of the mid-seventeenth century.

NINE

Frederick V, Elector Palatine, (1596-1632) and Elizabeth of England and Scotland (1596-1662)

In 1620, King Frederick and Queen Elizabeth of Bohemia (an area overlapping the modern Czech Republic) had to flee Prague so quickly that they almost left one of their children in the city's castle. Frederick had just suffered a catastrophic defeat at the Battle of White Mountain that cost him the throne of Bohemia, which he had held for less than a year. The victorious Holy Roman Emperor Ferdinand II gave Frederick, Elizabeth, and their household mere hours to load their possessions into carriages and carts and leave the city. Elizabeth, who was seven months pregnant at the time, ordered her servants to gather up as much as they could carry. Ornate furniture, sumptuous court dresses, and the royal family's personal possessions were thrown haphazardly into overflowing conveyances. As the last carriages were preparing to leave the castle courtyard, a court chamberlain made a last inspection of the royal apartments. Following the sound of a baby's cries, he discovered Frederick and Elizabeth's eleven-month old son, Prince Rupert, who had been forgotten or abandoned by his nurse. The chamberlain tossed Rupert into the last carriage leaving the castle grounds, ensuring that he escaped with the rest of his family and household. The rescue of this royal child changed the course of Canadian history, as Prince Rupert grew up to become the first governor of the Hudson's Bay Company.

The infant Rupert's fortunes and those of his parents and siblings seemed to have changed overnight. When Frederick and Elizabeth married in 1612, they seemed destined to create a prosperous royal household that would allow their children to live in comfortable circumstances. Elizabeth was the only surviving daughter of King James VI of Scotland, who became King of England in 1603, and his queen, Anna of Denmark. The upbringing of Elizabeth and her siblings was the focus of a furious parenting debate between James and Anna. James had little experience of family life. His father, Henry Stuart, Lord Darnley, had been assassinated when James was just a toddler, and his mother, Mary, Queen of Scots, had lost her reputation and then her throne when she married a third husband who was widely believed to have arranged the murder of Darnley, her second husband.

When James was almost two years old, Mary fled to England, seeking assistance regaining her throne, but was instead imprisoned by Elizabeth I for nineteen years until her execution in 1587. James was crowned King of Scotland at the age of thirteen months and raised under the supervision of a series of Presbyterian governors, who prevented contact between the child king and his mother. In contrast, James's queen, Anna, had been raised by her maternal grandparents and then her mother, Sophie of Mecklenburg-Güstrow, who was praised as "a right virtuous and godly Princess who with motherly care and great wisdom ruleth her children."[1] When Anna and her siblings suffered from childhood illnesses, it was their mother who sat by their bedsides and comforted them.

Anna expected to have the same nurturing role in the upbringing of her own children, but she found that James had very different ideas. When their eldest son Henry was born in 1594, James entrusted his care to John Erskine, Earl of Mar, whose mother, Annabel Murray, had cared for James in his infancy. A furious Anna demanded that the Scottish council discuss these arrangements for the heir to the throne to occupy a separate household and began to cultivate allies in her effort to retain custody of her son. James refused to allow a debate about the circumstances of Henry's upbringing. Anna responded by attempting to kidnap her son from his guardians, prompting James to write to the Earl of Mar, "This present therefore shall be a warrant unto you not to deliver [Henry] out of your hands except I command you with my own mouth...."[2] To the amazement of English diplomats, who had been aware of Henry VIII's determination to father an heir, Anna threatened not to bear any further children unless she were permitted to raise her son. A single heir was not sufficient to guarantee the Scottish succession. The parenting dispute between the king and queen of Scotland also threatened James's hope of succeeding his cousin twice removed, Elizabeth I, to the English throne. Since James's contemporaries considered the family to be a microcosm of the state, a king unable to control his wife might be considered unsuitable to rule the state. Over the winter of 1591–92, James's cousin Arbella Stuart, who shared his Tudor ancestry, made a successful visit to Elizabeth I's court, and was rumoured to be a possible successor to the childless Queen of England. Under the circumstances, reconciliation between James and Anna was imperative. The royal couple reached a compromise: Henry would remain with the Earl of Mar, but Anna would be involved in the choice of guardian for her surviving younger children, Elizabeth (born 1596) and the future King Charles I (born 1600).

For James, fatherhood did not mean supervising the daily care of small children but directing their education, especially the training of the heir to the throne. James had already written extensively about political theory prior to the births of his children, and the arrival of an heir gave him the opportunity to shape the next generation of rulers. Following Henry's birth, he composed *Basilikon Doron* for the edification of his heir, explaining in the preface that he had written it "[s]ince I ... as your natural father, must be careful for your godly and virtuous education, as my eldest son, and the first fruits of God's blessing towards me in thy posterity; and as a king must timeously provide for your training up in all the points of a king's office since ye are my natural and lawful successor therein...."[3]

James paid less attention to the education of his daughter because of his suspicion of the impact of a classical education on women, declaring, "To make women learned and foxes tame has the same effect: to make them more cunning." He was also of the opinion "that even a man who was vain and foolish, was made more so by Learning, and as for Women, who he said were all naturally addicted to Vanity, where it did one good, it did harm to twenty."[4] The future Queen of Bohemia would not receive the humanist education enjoyed by Henry VIII's daughters. Elizabeth's mother, Anna, however, was a patron of art, architecture, and the theatre, and her daughter shared her cultural interests and passed them onto her own daughters.

Like Elizabeth's father, James, her husband Frederick's father Frederick IV, Count of the Palatinate (a region along the upper Rhine River in what is now Germany), was deeply concerned with the education of his heir, and drew up detailed instructions for his son's tutors. A 1604 educational treatise intended for the young Frederick made clear that the proper development of a prince's character affected entire kingdoms, stating that "someone who corrupts a child of middling social standing, the same only pours poison into a glass; however, someone who corrupts a young prince, the same throws poison into a well which flows through the common ground from which a whole fatherland drinks."[5] For Frederick IV, the most important lessons for his heir were a thorough grounding in the precepts of Calvinism, a strict form of Protestantism that had emerged from the teachings of John Calvin in Geneva in the sixteenth century. The young Frederick's tutor was encouraged to drill him in "our true Christian religion" and ensure that he heard regular sermons.[6]

Frederick's childhood came to an abrupt end at the age of fourteen when his father died and a religious dispute took place concerning his guardianship. Since 1356, the rulers of the Palatinate had held the title of elector, which meant that they were among the seven German archbishops and princes who chose the Holy Roman Emperor. The Protestant Reformation, however, had threatened the cohesion of the empire. Since 1440, the emperor had been a member of the Roman Catholic House of Habsburg, but three of the electors — the rulers of the Palatine, Saxony, and Brandenburg — now embraced Protestantism. According the Peace of Augsburg, concluded in 1555, each German ruler was permitted to choose whether to practise Catholicism or Lutheranism. All inhabitants of each German territory were expected to follow the same faith as their ruler or emigrate to the territory of another ruler who shared their religious beliefs.

At the time of his father's death, the young Frederick's closest male relative was Wolfgang Wilhelm, Count Palatine of Neuberg, a Roman Catholic grandnephew of Henry VIII's fourth wife, Anne of Cleves. Mindful of his late father's wishes concerning religion, Frederick prevented Wolfgang Wilhelm from entering his capital, Heidelberg, and instead invited a Protestant member of the same branch of the family, John II, Count Palatine of Zweibrucken, to assume the role of guardian. The Holy Roman Emperor settled the dispute by allowing Frederick to rule without a guardian before he reached the age of eighteen, under the guidance of his mother, Countess Louise Juliana of the Dutch ruling House of Orange-Nassau. The dispute over Frederick's guardianship demonstrated how tenuous the religious settlement in the Holy Roman Empire had become by the early seventeenth century.

Frederick and Elizabeth were married on Valentine's Day 1613 in London amid lavish celebrations that included a performance of William Shakespeare's latest play, *The Tempest*, and a wedding song written by the poet John Donne. The timing of the wedding was appropriate, as the seventeen-year-old bride and groom had developed a close relationship from their first meeting. John Chamberlain, an English guest at the wedding, wrote that since arriving in England, Frederick "has taken no delight at running at ring [jousting], nor tennis, nor riding with [Elizabeth's brother Henry] the Prince (as ... others of his company do), but only in her conversation."[7] Elizabeth's vivacious, lively temperament balanced Frederick's serious demeanour, and they shared a common Protestant faith, as Scottish Presbyterianism followed the theology of John Calvin. The early years of their marriage, spent at Heidelberg Castle overlooking the river Necker, were contented ones. Frederick commissioned renovations to the castle and English-style gardens for the comfort of Elizabeth and their growing family.

Frederick's and Elizabeth's tranquility, however, was disrupted by growing religious tensions in Europe. In 1618, the Protestants of Bohemia rejected the authority of the future Holy Roman Emperor Ferdinand II, who had been crowned King of Bohemia the previous year, and threw four of his officials out a window. This event that became known as the 2nd Defenestration of Prague and marked the beginning of the Thirty Years' War.

The discontented Bohemians then invited Frederick to become their king. Frederick ignored the warnings of his fellow electors and his father-in-law, James I, that it was unwise to challenge the powerful Holy Roman Empire, whose rulers were close allies and relatives of the King of Spain. Frederick's brief reign as King of Bohemia and subsequent exile shaped the upbringing of his children, their prospects as adults, and the way in which his family was perceived by observers across Europe.

For the rest of their lives, Frederick and Elizabeth would be known as the Winter King and Queen in reference to the single winter they spent in Prague before going into exile. Ferdinand II, who became Holy Roman Emperor in 1619, was determined to make an example of Frederick to discourage further rebellions, and he therefore pillaged the Palatinate. Frederick would never return to Heidelberg Castle. He eventually found refuge with his family in The Hague, living under the protection of the Protestant Princes of Orange with some financial support sent by James I. There was widespread sympathy for the royal couple and their growing family, which would eventually consist of thirteen children. The Venetian ambassador to England made clear that he believed James I could have done more for his daughter, son-in-law, and grandchildren, writing to the Doge, "the beggary of that prince and his children cannot fail to affect the interests of this crown and bring discredit upon it."[8] In the Protestant popular imagination, Frederick and Elizabeth were a suffering mother and father, forced to raise their children in exile because of the inhumanity of the Roman Catholic Holy Roman Emperor. A woodcut from the early 1620s depicted Frederick and a visibly pregnant Elizabeth on either side of their five eldest children, with their coats of arms and the Battle of White Mountain in the background. Not everyone viewed Frederick and Elizabeth and their children sympathetically, however; to observers who questioned Frederick's judgment in accepting the crown of Bohemia against overwhelming military odds, his circumstances as the father of a growing family were presented as a reason why he should have been content to remain in Heidelberg as Elector Palatine. Satirical cartoons depicted Elizabeth as a lioness with more cubs than she could feed, or with her children eating gruel out of an overturned crown.

The names Frederick and Elizabeth selected for their children reflected both their family connections and their changing political circumstances. Their eldest son Henry Frederick (1614–29) was named for both his father and Elizabeth's elder brother Henry, who died shortly before her wedding. A second son, Charles Louis (1617–80) bore the names of Elizabeth's younger brother, the future King Charles I, and Frederick's mother, Louise. The couple's eldest daughter, Elisabeth (1618–80), bore her mother's name. After Frederick accepted the crown of Bohemia, he named his fourth child Rupert (1619–82), after one of his most illustrious ancestors, King Rupert of Germany, reflecting the family's new status as a reigning house. In contrast, the fifth child, Maurice (1620–52), arrived during the flight from Prague and was named for Frederick's uncle, Maurice, Prince of Orange, who offered the family sanctuary in the Netherlands. Maurice's sister Louise Hollandine (1622–1709) similarly reflected the royal couple's gratitude for a refuge in the Netherlands. The younger children, Louis (1624), Edward (1625–63) Henriette Marie (1626–51), John Philip (1627–50), Charlotte (1628–31), Sophia (1630–1714), and Gustavus Adolphus (1632–41) bore the names of powerful European royalty with the potential to intercede on Frederick and Elizabeth's behalf in the Thirty Years' War, including Elizabeth's sister-in-law, Queen Henrietta Maria of England, and King Gustavus Adolphus of Sweden, who emerged as a key Protestant military leader over the course of the hostilities. By the time the couple's twelfth child, Sophia, the future Electress of Hanover, was born in 1630, Frederick and Elizabeth had trouble choosing a suitable name. Sophia recalled in her memoirs, "I can well believe that my birth caused them little satisfaction. They were even puzzled to find a name and godparents for me, as all the kings and princes of consideration had already performed this office for the children that came before me. The plan was adopted of writing various names on slips of paper and casting lots for the one which I should bear...."[9] The children shared an identity as royal exiles. In the palace in Leiden where they were raised apart from their parents, one of their favourite games was pretending that they were returning to Heidelberg, which even the younger children born in the Netherlands considered to be their home.

Frederick had lost his crown and his ancestral lands, but there was a key role that he maintained throughout these changes in fortune: the position of father to a large German Protestant family. The Reformation in Germany placed greater emphasis than elsewhere in Europe on the role of the father as a spiritual adviser and guide within his household, assuming that mothers would be too indulgent to provide the necessary discipline and instruction to transform impulsive children into restrained, pious adults. In Roman Catholic communities, a variety of adults influenced a child's moral and spiritual development, including neighbours, members of the extended family, and the parish priest. All of these figures might share the blame for a poorly behaved child or a young adult with a weak moral character. In contrast, parenting in the sixteenth- and seventeenth-century Protestant German states was ultimately the responsibility of the father. The increased significance of the father's role in childrearing after the Reformation informed a new genre of parenting literature known as *Hausväterliteratur,* or housefather books. This prescriptive literature emphasized universal parenting principles that were necessary for the upbringing of children of all social backgrounds. Elite parents who considered themselves above instructing their children personally were the target of particular censure in housefather books. Conrad Sam, a theologian writing in the German city of Ulm in the 1520s, sternly reminded his readers:

> Whether you are a king, prince, count, knight or servant, whether a townsman or a peasant, if you want to know joy in your children, take care that you teach them virtue. Do not do as is now done in the world, where children are taught to rule, but not to serve; to curse and insult but not to pray; to ride, but not to speak properly. Children today are badly raised; not only do parents permit them their every selfish wish, but they even show them the way to it. God will hold parents strictly accountable for their children, who [now] reward them [appropriately by their bad behavior].[10]

The housefather books allowed moderate corporal punishment to correct children's behaviour, but made clear that the most effective childrearing techniques were setting strict rules and acting as a strong moral example.

Fathers were responsible for warning their children about divine punishment in the event of their misbehaviour, and God's favour toward good character. The best environment for moulding this good character was one filled with work and study, leaving little time for idle pursuits.

Frederick took his responsibilities as a father seriously and spent time ensuring that his children were well-educated. Frederick's children developed a close relationship with their father, looking forward to his visits to Leiden. Frederick did not share his father-in-law James's prejudices regarding education for girls, and ensured that his daughters were tutored in the classics and philosophy alongside their brothers. Louise Hollandine became an accomplished portrait painter, and Elisabeth corresponded with the philosopher René Descartes. Frederick's sons also developed intellectual pursuits. Rupert became an accomplished artist and scientist, eventually bringing a kind of reinforced glass, now known as Prince Rupert's drops, to the attention of the Royal Society of London.

When Frederick was on military campaigns, attempting to regain the Palatinate, he wrote to Elizabeth about arrangements for the upbringing of their children, sharing his own opinions and those of his mother concerning nursery staff. In October 1621, he wrote, "Madam my Mother thinks it would be better if little Charles had a page who was a little older and who had the temperament to govern himself and look after the child…. As for Madam Michaloivitz I do not know what to say to you; she is a great misery. I do not know if she would be suitable to serve little Rupert…"[11] In addition to his concern for the management of the nurseries, Frederick frequently mentioned in his correspondence that his wife and children were always in his prayers during his military campaigns.

Elizabeth paid less attention to her children, seem to prefer her pets. Sophia recalled in her memoirs that after her birth, "No sooner was I strong enough to be moved than the Queen my mother sent me to Leyden [*sic*], which is but three days' journey from The Hague, and where her Majesty had her whole family brought up apart from herself, preferring the sight of her monkeys and dogs to that of her children."[12] Despite Elizabeth's distance from the daily care of her children, she was concerned about their health, ensuring that they were sent to the country during outbreaks of bubonic plague, and she grieved with Frederick over the children who predeceased them. The accidental drowning of their eldest son, fifteen-year-old Henry Frederick, in 1629, which Frederick witnessed but was unable to prevent, was especially devastating for both parents. For Elizabeth, concern for her children was inseparable from her strong relationship with Frederick. When she was widowed in 1632, she refused her brother Charles's invitation to reside in England, believing that it was her duty to remain in Europe and further her children's prospects there. She wrote that her own inclination was to return to the English court, but "I must prefer the welfare of my poor children to my own satisfaction. The last request that their father made me, before his departure, was to do all that I could for them; which I wish to do, as far as lies in my power, loving them better because they are *his* than because they are *my own*."[13] Elizabeth kept her daughters with her in The Hague and arranged for her sons to continue their education at the University of Leiden and at the English and French courts.

As the children grew older, Elizabeth became especially concerned for their futures. Without lands or reliable incomes, Elizabeth's sons seemed destined to become soldiers of fortune, and the marriage prospects of her daughters were uncertain. Elizabeth rejected the more outlandish plans proposed for her younger sons, such as establishing a colony in Madagascar, and instead encouraged them to seek their fortune at her brother Charles I's court. The outbreak of the English Civil Wars between Charles I and parliament in 1642 complicated relations among the brothers, as Charles Louis remained at Whitehall Palace in London and swore allegiance to parliament while Rupert and Maurice became prominent Cavalier commanders in the royalist army of their uncle. The upheaval raised the possibility that one of Elizabeth's sons would be offered the thrones of England and Scotland. Instead, England became a protectorate without a monarch from the execution of Charles I in 1649 until the restoration of Charles II in 1660.

The Treaty of Westphalia that ended the Thirty Years' War in 1648 restored part of the Palatinate to Charles Louis, but the younger children did not experience a marked improvement in their financial situations. Rupert and Maurice became privateers in the early 1650s, sailing to the Caribbean with the remnants of the royalist navy to seize Spanish galleons in support of the restoration of their cousin as Charles II. Maurice was lost in a hurricane, and a grief-stricken Rupert returned to Europe with little to show for their efforts. Another one of Elizabeth's sons, John Philip, killed an exiled French lieutenant colonel, Jacques de l'Epinay, in a duel in 1646 and then fled the Netherlands. There were rumours that the duel had been prompted by l'Epinay boasting that he had seduced both Elizabeth and her daughter Louise Hollandine. The loss of Maurice and disgrace of John Philip confirmed Elizabeth's worst fears about any of her sons becoming a "knight errant."[14] To Elizabeth's dismay, some of her other children found support and solace in Roman Catholicism. Edward converted to marry a wealthy noblewoman, Anna Gonzaga, ignoring Elizabeth's declaration that she would disown any child of hers who became a Catholic. Louise Hollandine fled her mother's home for France, where she became a Catholic in 1657 and a nun the Cistercian Maubisson Abbey in 1660.

Elizabeth spent her last years at the court of her nephew, King Charles II. Relations with many of her children remained strained, but her time in England brought her closer to her son Rupert, who became one of the most prominent figures in Restoration England. The diarist John Evelyn recorded on February 17, 1662, "This night was buried in Westminster-Abbey the Queen of Bohemia, after all her sorrows and afflictions being come to die in the arms of her nephew, the King."[15] At the time of her death, the most famous of her children was Rupert, who became first governor of the Company of Adventurers Trading into Hudson Bay in 1670 and lent his name to Rupert's Land in what is now Canada. In 1701, however, the Act of Settlement made her youngest daughter, Sophia, Electress of Hanover, heir to the throne, and Sophia's son became King George I in 1714. Throughout Elizabeth's lifetime, there was potential for her descendants to reign over England and Scotland, and that potential was realized with the eventual accession of the House of Hanover. In the 1660s, however, the immediate consequence of Elizabeth's death was that Charles II's mother, the Dowager Queen Henrietta Maria, became the sole representative of the older generation of the royal family at court. Charles presented a public display of family unity, but relations with his mother had long been strained because of their political and religious differences.

TEN

Charles I (1600-49) and Henrietta Maria of France (1609-69)

In 1632, the Flemish artist Anthony Van Dyck painted a family portrait of Charles I, his French queen, Henrietta Maria, and their two eldest children, the two-year-old future king Charles II and the infant Princess Mary. *The Greate Peece*, as the portrait became known, was an unprecedented artistic interpretation of the royal family's domestic life. For the first time, a queen of England was depicted in a portrait holding one of her children in her arms. Van Dyck painted Mary's tiny fingers intertwined with those of her mother, emphasizing the queen's attentive care for her daughter. The heir to the throne, in the floor-length gown and cap of a toddler, was shown holding onto the leg of his seated father, the king, a statement about the legitimacy of the royal succession as well as the bond between father and son. The intimacy of the scene was emphasized by the presence of the royal couple's two dogs.

Although the portrait depicts the royal regalia on a table next to the monarch, Charles I and Henrietta Maria are seated on chairs instead of thrones. The presence of two dogs at their feet as well the young children emphasized the domesticity of the scene. The marriage of the Protestant Charles and the Roman Catholic Henrietta Maria had been controversial when it took place in 1625, and the portrait emphasized the domestic harmony that seemed to have overcome the couple's religious differences. Van Dyck would paint numerous other portraits of the royal couple and their children, emphasizing their devotion to each other and their family. For Protestant observers in England and Scotland, however, these images appeared to demonstrate that Henrietta Maria exercised undue influence over her husband, especially from 1629 to 1640, when Charles ruled without parliament. The public also questioned the sincerity of the royal family's domestic harmony.

Charles's father, James I, predicted that a married couple with religious differences would have difficulty agreeing how to parent their children. When Charles's eldest brother Henry died in 1612, James passed along the *Basilikon Doron* to his younger son. In his advice for choosing a bride, James recommended that his heir marry another Protestant, because "[d]isagreement in religion bringeth ever with it disagreement in manners; and the dissention betwixt your preachours and hers will breede and foster a dissention among your subjectes, taking their example from your familie; besides the perell of the evill education of your children."[1]

England's political situation in the early seventeenth century, however, discouraged Charles from marrying a Protestant princess. Only the Catholic French and Spanish ruling houses could provide the necessary dowry to replenish the English royal treasury. A friendly Catholic power might also exert the diplomatic and military influence on the Holy Roman Empire necessary to restore Charles's sister Elizabeth and her husband Frederick to their lands in the Palatinate. Charles, therefore, set aside James's advice on the appropriate religion for his bride and instead pursued what his father considered to be the most important criteria for a royal wife and mother: beauty, wealth, and a favourable foreign alliance. In 1623, Charles travelled to Madrid to pay court to the Infanta Maria, one of the sisters of King Philip IV of Spain, passing through Paris on his journey, where he sighted another eligible princess, King Louis XIII of France's youngest sister Henrietta Maria. When negotiations for a Spanish match were unsuccessful, Charles claimed to have fallen in love with the French princess.

Henrietta Maria was only fifteen when she married Charles, but she had definite ideas concerning childrearing informed by her position as a Roman Catholic princess marrying a Protestant monarch. As she explained in a letter to Pope Urban VIII, "if it please God to bless this marriage, and if he grant me the favour to give my progeny, I will not choose any but Catholics to nurse or educate the children who shall be born, or do any other service for them, and will take care that the officers who choose them be only Catholics."[2]

The marriage contract granted Henrietta Maria an exclusively Catholic household and control over the upbringing and education of her children until they reached the age of thirteen. The contract was published in English printed pamphlets, allowing public discussion of its terms, particularly in urban areas where literacy rates were higher. Protestant observers were alarmed by the concessions granted Henrietta Maria because they seemed to inflame one of the key parenting debates of the period: whether "recusant" Catholic wives and mothers in otherwise Protestant families should be in a position to influence the religious education of their children. For English and Scottish Protestants, Henrietta Maria was not only a foreign, Catholic queen consort, but the most prominent recusant wife and mother in the British Isles.

Henrietta Maria's own experiences of family life were shaped by the political turbulence of early seventeenth-century France. Henrietta Maria did not have any memory of her father, King Henri IV, who was assassinated when she was an infant, but she had a close relationship with her mother, Marie de Medici, and her siblings. Marie was a distant parent to her younger children, even by seventeenth-century royal standards, as she was at first consumed by her duties as regent to the young Louis XIII, then was exiled from Paris when Henrietta Maria was only eight. Nevertheless, Henrietta Maria maintained a correspondence with her mother and accepted her advice on a variety of topics, including childbirth. By the mid-seventeenth century, male doctors attended royal confinements, and Charles expected his physician, Theodore Mayerne, to attend to his wife. Henrietta Maria, however, relied on the ministrations of her mother's midwife, Madame Peronne, and insisted that she travel to England to deliver the royal children. Peronne became a celebrity in England, as her arrival from France meant that a royal birth was imminent. Odes were composed for the French midwife who was even willing to cross the battle lines during the English Civil Wars to ensure that Henrietta Maria's youngest child was safely delivered.

Neither Louis nor Charles honoured the terms of Charles's and Henrietta Maria's marriage contract. The diplomatic accord between England and France broke down quickly. Louis made a secret treaty with his other brother-in-law, King Philip IV of Spain, and the Anglo-French war broke out in 1627, lasting until 1629. Charles's closest friend, George Villiers, Duke of Buckingham, led a disastrous naval expedition in an attempt to relieve the siege of French Protestants in the town of La Rochelle. In addition to the hostilities, Louis did not pay Henrietta Maria's full dowry. In these circumstances, Charles disregarded key clauses in the marriage contract, particularly those pertaining to the governance of the royal household. He dismissed the majority of the queen's French attendants and insisted that Henrietta Maria accept Protestant ladies-in-waiting, including Buckingham's female relatives. Henrietta Maria was distressed by the loss of her French household, which included numerous servants whom she had known since infancy, such as her former governess, Madame St. Georges. When Henrietta Maria gave birth to her eldest surviving son, Charles, in 1630, Charles I had the heir christened in the Church of England and appointed Protestant attendants for him over Henrietta Maria's protests. A Protestant governor, William Cavendish, 1st Duke of Newcastle, oversaw the prince's education. Like her mother-in-law, Anna of Denmark, Henrietta Maria had more influence over the attendants assigned to the care of her younger children, particularly her daughters. Charles I refused to allow Jean Kerr, Countess of Roxburge, a Scottish Roman Catholic, to care for the heir to the throne, but she was allowed to help raise the younger royal children.

Although Charles broke his marriage contract and insisted on making key decisions regarding the upbringing and education of his children, Henrietta Maria was still able to introduce influences from her own childhood into the royal nursery. In France, the eldest daughter of the sovereign was styled "Madame Royale" to denote her status and Henrietta Maria brought this practice to England. Her eldest daughter Mary was the first English princess to receive the title of Princess Royal, an honour that continues to be bestowed on the eldest daughter of the monarch at the discretion of the sovereign to the present day. (While Mary received the title as a child, subsequent royal women designated Princess Royal usually received the title as adults. In 1987, Queen Elizabeth II bestowed the title of Princess Royal on her only daughter, Princess Anne, in recognition of her philanthropic work with Save the Children.) Henrietta Maria also encouraged the strong bonds among siblings that existed during her own childhood. While Charles and his siblings, Henry and Elizabeth, spent much of their childhoods in separate households, Henrietta Maria kept her children together. Charles and Henrietta Maria's children maintained close relations with each other that transcended religion and politics. As king, Charles II would insist on the right of his brother to succeed him as James II despite James's Catholicism.

Charles and Henrietta Maria became the parents of six children who survived infancy. Prior to the Wars of the Roses, a large royal family attracted popular admiration, but the decades of conflict among the descendants of Edward III meant that the presence of too many male heirs appeared to be a source of political instability. When Charles and Henrietta Maria became parents of a fourth child and second daughter, the Venetian ambassador reported, "The generality are more pleased than if it had been a boy, because girls ensure posterity as much as boys, and the kingdom is relieved of the danger to which states sometimes succumb from there being too many princes of the blood royal."[3] The cost of raising and educating numerous children according to their status as members of the royal family also attracted criticism, and the expenses incurred by their attendants were closely scrutinized.

When Charles recalled parliament for financial reasons in 1640, the members of the House of Commons critiqued him as a father and head of household as well as a king. Although Charles and Henrietta Maria maintained a separate household for their children, visits were common. In contrast to previous kings and queens, Charles and Henrietta Maria rarely undertook royal progresses, and were therefore able to spend more time with their children. Protestant parliamentarians were critical of Charles's decision to allow the royal children to spend extended periods of time with their mother, who exposed them to Catholic rites. Parliament insisted that the ten-year-old heir to the throne leave his mother's household at once and return to the care of the Duke of Newcastle. Parliament also questioned Charles and Henrietta Maria's haste to conclude a marriage treaty between their nine-year-old daughter Mary and the fifteen-year-old William II, Prince of Orange, who were wed in 1641. Although the Dutch prince was suitably Protestant, Henrietta Maria's determination to escort Mary to her marital home in 1642 seemed to reflect an interest in concluding independent diplomatic and financial arrangements in Europe rather than Mary's readiness to live in her husband's household.

Relations between king and parliament broke down and the English Civil Wars began in 1642. Henrietta Maria was impeached in absentia by the House of Commons in 1643 on eight charges, including mismanagement of her household; the charges stated "that she hath put ill affected persons in great places and offices of credit, whereby to advance the Popish party."[4] Henrietta Maria took advantage of her time in the Netherlands with Mary to pawn crown jewels for the royalist cause, which became the basis of another one of the charges in her impeachment as queen.

The English Civil Wars changed the setting of royal childhood, as palaces where generations of royal children had been born and grew up were damaged or destroyed. The Palace of Placentia at Greenwich, which had been a favourite residence of Tudor monarchs and the birthplace of Henry VIII and his daughters, became a biscuit factory and then a prisoner-of-war camp during Oliver Cromwell's time as Lord Protector. The castle at Winchester commissioned by Henry III was destroyed during heavy fighting between supporters of the king and parliament, leaving only the Great Hall intact. Woodstock Palace outside Oxford, where Edward III's eldest son, the Black Prince, had been born in 1330, was reduced to ruins by the fighting, and the stones later became part of Blenheim Palace, residence of the Dukes of Marlborough. Those royal residences that survived the English Civil Wars were remodelled extensively after the monarchy was restored in 1660, and Charles I's children and grandchildren acquired new palaces. Charles II appointed his cousin Prince Rupert governor of Windsor Castle in 1668, and Rupert oversaw renovations until his death in 1682. Charles I's grandchildren William III (son of Mary, Princess of Orange) and Mary II (daughter of James II) added a new wing to Hampton Court Palace and acquired Kensington Palace, the current London residence of William, Kate, and their children.

For Charles I, fatherhood was part of the motivation to continue leading the royalist cause as the military situation turned against him after his defeat at the Battle of Naseby in 1645. Charles and Henrietta Maria saw each other for the last time in 1644, shortly before the birth of their youngest child Henrietta Anne and the queen's flight to France. The hostilities had brought the couple closer together, and Charles was reluctant to make key decisions concerning the royal children without consulting her. In October 1646, Charles wrote to her: "Prince Charles hath desired me to make Sir George Carterett his vice-chamberlain, which I think reasonable if thou dost; so give order for it; otherwise it shall pass in silence for me, because of thy desire that I should put none about the prince without thy advice."[5]

Charles I predicted that he might lose his life in the Civil Wars and beseeched Henrietta Maria to continue supporting the royalist cause after his death, writing, "I conjure thee, by thy love to me (if I knew a greater, I would name it), that thou wilt never retire thyself from my business, so long as I have a child alive, whatsoever becomes of me...."[6] Henrietta Maria remained devoted to the Stuart dynasty, but her political strategies for achieving the restoration of the monarchy often differed from the views of her adult sons.

After Charles was apprehended and imprisoned in 1648, he was allowed visits with those of his children who were in parliamentary custody, James (who soon escaped), Elizabeth, and Henry. Charles developed a close bond with thirteen-year-old Elizabeth and nine-year-old Henry in the last months of his life. Elizabeth recorded an account of their last meeting after Charles was convicted of treason against his people by the remaining members of the House of Commons and sentenced to death by beheading. She wrote, "He was glad I was come.... He wished me not to grieve and torment myself for him, for that would be a glorious death that he should die."[7]

While Charles was concerned with the emotional impact of his execution on Elizabeth, his words to Henry emphasized the political consequences of his death. Since Henry was in parliamentary custody and young enough to require a regent, Charles feared that he would be established as a puppet monarch to give legitimacy to parliament. Charles, therefore, spoke to Henry as a king as well as a father, warning him, "Mark child, what I say; they will cut off my head, and perhaps make thee a king. But mark what I say, you must not become king, you must not be a king so long as your brothers Charles and James do live; for they will cut off your brothers' heads (when they can catch them and cut off thy head too at last)."[8] Deeply affected by his father's words, the young Henry swore he would be torn to pieces before he would allow the crown to be placed on his head. Charles was beheaded on January 30, 1649, just two days after his last meeting with Elizabeth and Henry.

Henrietta Maria outlived Charles I by twenty years and continued to expect obedience from her children during their adulthood, even after the monarchy was restored in 1660. She had the greatest influence over Henrietta Anne. The child had been smuggled out of England by her governess at the age of two and reunited with her mother, who raised her as a Catholic and arranged her marriage to a French cousin, Philippe, Duc d'Orléans, brother of King Louis XIV. As an adult, Henrietta Anne shared her mother's interest in artistic patronage and a closer political relationship between England and France.

Henrietta Maria had less influence over her sons. After parliament released Henry from custody, he joined his mother and youngest sister in France. After an initial joyful reunion, Henry experienced pressure from Henrietta Maria to convert to Catholicism in 1654. Before his death, Charles I made clear to his children that they were to "obey [their mother] in everything, except religion,"[9] and Henry therefore refused to convert. Just as Elizabeth of Bohemia threatened to disown any child of hers who converted to Catholicism, Henrietta Maria threatened to turn Henry out of her household if he did not renounce his Protestant faith. At fourteen, Henry was caught between his elder brother Charles, who ordered him to remain steadfast in his faith, and his mother. Charles wrote to Henry, "The letter that came from Paris says that it is the Queen's purpose to do all that she can to change your religion, which if you hearken to her, or anybody else in that matter, you must never think to see England, or me again, and whatsoever mischief shall fall on me or my affairs at this time, I must lay all upon you as being the only cause of it...."[10] Henry obeyed his brother and was expelled from his mother's household.

Following her son Charles II's restoration in 1660, Henrietta Maria was in a position without clear expectations, as there had not been a Queen Mother figure at the English court since Henry VII's mother, Margaret Beaufort, and there would not be another until the reign of Queen Victoria. Due to his mother's Catholicism and controversial reputation, Charles II was encouraged to leave her in France when he became King of England. Even though Charles's relationship with his mother had been difficult throughout the 1650s, he was determined to ensure that the entire royal family returned to its former status. Henrietta Maria returned to England for extended periods during the Restoration and presided over a lavish court at Somerset House in London, overshadowing her daughter-in-law, Charles's Portuguese queen, Catherine of Braganza.

The controversial mother of the king became the subject of unfounded rumours that she had decided to start a secret second family with her steward, Henry Jermyn, Earl of St. Albans. The diarist Samuel Pepys wrote in 1662, "The Queen-Mother is said to keep too great a Court now; and her being married to my Lord St. Albans is commonly talked of; and that they had a daughter between them in France, how true, God knows."[11] Henrietta Maria's family grew smaller instead of expanding in her later years. Her daughter Elizabeth died of pneumonia in 1650 while still in parliamentary custody. Both Mary and Henry died of smallpox soon after the Restoration. Only Charles, James, and Henrietta Anne survived their mother, who died at the Château de Colombes in France in 1669.

During his exile, the future Charles II had received support and encouragement from a distant source. The news that Charles I had been tried and executed for crimes against his people spread quickly in 1649 and was particularly shocking to those monarchs who still enjoyed absolute power. In Russia, Czar Alexei I, the second ruler of the Romanov dynasty, established in 1613, was considered God's representative on earth. When Alexei learned of Charles I's execution, he sent the future Charles II financial aid and offered condolences to Henrietta Maria, "the disconsolate widow of that glorious martyr, King Charles I."[12] England and Russia had been trading partners since the establishment of the Muscovy Company, chartered in 1555 during the reigns of Queen Elizabeth I of England and Czar Ivan IV "the Terrible" of Russia, but an outraged Alexei expelled

English merchants from Russia's interior in the aftermath of the English Civil Wars. In contrast, royalists fleeing Cromwell's protectorate were welcome to settle in Moscow's Foreign Quarter, which was already inhabited by Dutch merchants and Germans escaping from the Thirty Years' War. Alexei intended for the Foreign Quarter to supply necessary technology and expertise for his military without influencing Russian society; nevertheless, social contacts between the czar's court and the Foreign Quarter developed. One of Alexei's closest friends and advisers, Artamon Matvayev, married a Scottish royalist refugee named Eudoxie Hamilton. Their ward, Natalya Naryshkina, became Alexei's second wife in 1671. Czar Peter I, called "the Great," son of Alexei and Natalya, would be inspired by the culture of the Foreign Quarter to remodel elite Russian society according to Western ideals. Peter's rapid introduction of social reforms inspired by English, German, and Dutch practices, however, would lead to a deadly conflict with his son and heir.

ELEVEN

Peter I "the Great" of Russia (1672-1725) and Catherine I (1684-1727)

In 1715, Czar Peter I "the Great" of Russia decided that he would give his twenty-five-year-old son and heir, Alexei Petrovich (son of Peter), one last chance to become a worthy successor to the throne. Peter was constantly finding fault with his only surviving son, who did not seem to resemble him in any way. Peter was an energetic ruler who spent much of his reign fighting the Great Northern War (1700–23) against Sweden to regain a Baltic coastline for Russia. He established the Russian navy, ordered the building of a new capital city (Saint Petersburg), challenged the Ottoman Empire (modern-day Turkey) for access to the Black Sea, toured Western Europe twice, passed new laws, reformed the tax code, and attempted to remodel his court and broader elite society along Western lines. As an absolute ruler, he did not tolerate opposition of any kind. Peter crushed a 1698 military revolt, ordering the execution of more than a thousand rebel soldiers. Hundreds more were branded with hot irons, flogged with a heavy rawhide cat o'nine tails spiked with metal barbs known as a knout, or sent to Siberia with their families. Peter's father and grandfather had been influenced by the Patriarch of the Russian Orthodox Church, but Peter replaced the old patriarchate with a Holy Synod subject to the state, and engaged in drunken revels at court that satirized Orthodox liturgy.

In contrast to the energetic, ruthless, and irreverent Peter, Alexei was a passive figure who often complained of illness and found comfort in religious literature and the traditional observances of the Russian Orthodox Church. While Peter appeared to be constantly in motion, involving himself in all aspects of ruling the Russian state, his heir was content to attend long church services or read books. The heir to the throne was seasick aboard his father's ships, and seemed incapable of assuming military command or even assuming an effective administrative role to ensure Russia's troops were well supplied. Alexei did not share his father's enthusiasm for Western technologies or culture, and was a natural figurehead for opponents of the czar's reforms. The only similarities between father and son appeared to be a taste for strong drink and an imposing height compared to the other men of the Russian court: Alexei was more than six feet tall, and Peter was six feet seven inches. Peter complained of what he perceived as his son's shortcomings, but there did not seem to be any clear alternative heir. The czar did not have any surviving brothers, nephews, or other male descendants.

The composition of Peter's family changed in October of 1715. Both Peter's second wife, the future Empress Catherine I (not to be confused with Catherine II, "the Great"), and Alexei's wife, the German princess Charlotte-Christine of Brunswick-Lüneburg, gave birth to boys within days of each other. Peter's new son and grandson were both named after him, and they represented new possibilities for the succession. In these new circumstances, Peter sent a long letter to his son that he had drafted some weeks before, offering him a final chance to be a worthy successor to the Russian throne, writing as a frustrated father:

> Remember your obstinacy and ill-nature, how often I have reproached you for it and for how many years I almost have not spoken to you. But all this has availed nothing, has effected nothing. It was but losing my time, it was striking the air. You do not make the least endeavors, and all your pleasure seems to consist in staying idle and lazy

at home.... If [you will not mend], I will have you know that I will deprive you of the succession, as one may cut off a useless member.[1]

If Peter hoped that his letter would shock Alexei into changing his conduct, he was soon disappointed. Alexei's wife, Charlotte-Christine, had died from complications following the birth of their son, and the letter arrived on the day of her funeral. With an infant son of his own to assume his place in the succession, Alexei decided to stop trying to meet his father's expectations. Just three days after Peter's letter arrived, Alexei wrote a short reply renouncing his place in the succession and his own parental rights to his toddler daughter and newborn son:

> I do not aspire after you (whom God preserve many years) to the succession to the Russian crown, even if I had no brother as I have one at present whom I pray God preserve.... I put my children into your hands, and as for myself, I desire nothing of you but a bare maintenance during my life....[2]

Peter refused to accept Alexei's renunciation of his place in the succession at face value. Although Peter's letter had accused his son of having "no inclination to learn war" because "you do not apply yourself," and concluded that Alexei was completely reliant on the judgment of others, "like a young bird that holds up his bill to be fed," he eventually became convinced that his son's submission was a pretext for a larger plot against his rule and reforms.[3] There had been numerous examples throughout Europe of royal fathers and sons who had clashed with each other and even led opposing armies on the battlefield. The conflict between Peter the Great and his son Alexei stands out because it turned fatal for the heir to the throne.

Father and son had been at odds since Alexei was a child. In 1698, eight-year-old Alexei had been forcibly separated from his mother, Yevdokia Lopukhina, a pious and conservative Russian noblewoman. Peter had just returned from his first European tour and was no longer interested in being married to a consort who viewed foreigners as dangerous heretics because they did not practise Russian Orthodox Christianity. Peter insisted that Yevdokia enter a convent where she would be isolated from the outside world, including her son. Yevdokia argued furiously for her right to remain at court as Peter's consort and the mother of the heir to the throne. After hours of heated discussion, Peter summoned an ordinary postal carriage bound for a remote convent in Suzdal, a small town on the Volga River. Once in Suzdal, Yevdokia was compelled to renounce her former life and take holy orders. Her head was shaved, and she was given the name Helena for her new life as a nun in an enclosed convent. Yevdokia was not the first Russian czarina to be repudiated by her husband in this manner. In the sixteenth century, Ivan the Terrible had sent two of his seven successive wives to convents. The discarded wives of Ivan the Terrible, however, were childless, and their perceived infertility provided the necessary pretext for the end of their marriages; for the mother of the heir to the throne to be stripped of her position and forced into a convent was unprecedented. Peter's treatment of Yevdokia was highly controversial at the time, and he would be the last Russian leader to divorce while in office until President Vladimir Putin in 2014.

At the time of the breakdown of Peter's first marriage, he was a virtual stranger to his son Alexei. During the seventeenth century, elite Russian boys remained in the care of their mothers and other female relatives before being entrusted to their fathers and male tutors around the age of seven. At the apex of Russian society during Alexei's childhood, the division between male and female spheres was stark, even inside the home. The nobility demonstrated their status by secluding the women of their families in special quarters within the home known as the *terem*. Elite social life was divided by gender, with noblemen and noblewomen socializing separately, only coming together for special occasions such as weddings. Princess Darya Golitsyn, a member of one of Russia's wealthiest and most influential families, lived through Peter the Great's social reforms and contrasted them with her childhood, explaining, "I was born a recluse, raised within four walls."[4] Until her marriage, the princess only set foot outside her home a few times per year for religious services and occasional visits to female relatives.

Women from the ruling Romanov dynasty and their young children were especially secluded from male company. From the reign of Ivan the Terrible's father, Vasili III, until Peter's marriage to Yevdokia, Russian rulers chose their consorts in bride shows at which hundreds of young women from landed gentry families were assembled in Moscow's Kremlin so that the czar could select his spouse. In contrast, Peter's seven sisters and three aunts remained unmarried. Women assumed the rank of their husbands, and marriage to Russian noblemen would therefore have reduced the status of the royal women. Foreign princes were equally unsuitable because they did not share the Russian Orthodox faith. The Romanov dynasty had come to power following a long interregnum known as the Time of Troubles, and sons-in-law were thought to create unnecessary complications for the succession.

Seventeenth-century Romanov women were expected to devote their time to prayer, embroidering altar cloths, and raising the children of their brothers. Alexei spent his early childhood in the *terem* and remained there longer than previous heirs because Peter was abroad when his son turned seven. The childrearing ideals of Alexei's early childhood were outlined in the *Domostroi* (household order), a sixteenth-century guide to managing a prosperous Russian household thought to have been written by Silvester, a priest at the Cathedral of Annunciation in Moscow's Kremlin. The author devoted several chapters to the importance of parents guiding their children and children being obedient to the wishes of their parents. Chapter 15, "How to Raise Your Children with all Learning and in Fear of God," begins,

> The parents must teach [their children] to fear God, must instruct them in wisdom and all forms of piety. According to the child's abilities and age, and to the time available, the mother should teach her daughters female crafts and the father should teach his sons whatever trade they can learn. God gives each person some capacity.[5]

Like the "housefather" books published in the German states following the Protestant Reformation, the *Domostroi* emphasized the importance of fathers in shaping the moral characters of their children. The author warned fathers that the whole family would "suffer eternal torment together" if the wife, children, or servants "because of your failure to instruct them, engage in evil deeds," such as carousing, theft or lechery.[6] The *Domostroi* urged fathers to set a good example for their children at all times to ensure that they would live godly lives.

Despite the importance the *Domostroi* gave to the father's role within the family, Yevdokia's forcible removal from Alexei's life did not result in Peter taking a greater personal interest in his son. Instead, Peter entrusted the upbringing of his son to his sister Natalya, with his closest friend, Alexander Menshikov, serving as governor to the heir to throne, in addition to foreign tutors appointed to give the heir a Western-style education. Natalya was a prolific playwright who turned one of her palaces into Russia's first public theatre. Alexei may have acquired his love of books from his aunt's influence, as she had a collection of more than one hundred printed and manuscript works on a variety of subjects, including the lives of saints and military history. Natalya may have also represented a connection to the mother Alexei had lost. Although Natalya favoured Peter's reforms and Yevdokia opposed them, the two women enjoyed a close friendship, and Natalya had attempted to intercede on behalf of her sister-in-law when Peter was determined to end the marriage.

For his part, Menshikov treated Alexei with casual brutality. An Austrian minister to the Russian court recounted that he had heard that Menshikov had dragged Alexei across the floor by his hair in Peter's presence and that the czar had done nothing to intervene. Alexei found this treatment particularly humiliating because Menshikov had come from a peasant background before Peter elevated him to high office. Alexei would later blame his governor for many of his failings, including his drinking. Peter spent most of Alexei's childhood at war with Sweden and supervising the building of his new capital, Saint Petersburg, occasionally reappearing in his son's life without warning to bring him to a battlefield or a ship christening. On the rare occasions when father and son met, Peter expressed disappointment in his son, and Alexei seemed terrified of his father.

While Peter took little interest in his own son, he had strong opinions about how the Russian nobility raised their children, including dress, education, social life, and parental involvement in arranging marriages.

Peter ended the practice of noblewomen being secluded in the *terem*, and mandated that marriageable daughters be brought out into society to meet young men at "assemblies" so that they would have the opportunity to get to know potential partners before marriage. A 1718 decree explained that an assembly was "a voluntary gathering or meeting in someone's home; it is held not merely for amusement but also for affairs, and there people may see one another and discuss whatever is necessary, hear about what is going on, and also amuse themselves."[7]

The fashions favoured by the German and English nobility whom Peter had met on his European tour were required for attendance at these new assemblies. Women were expected to give up their flowing caftans for the low-cut, corseted bodices and wide farthingale skirts worn by elite women elsewhere in Europe. The same Princess Golitsyn who recalled her childhood as a recluse complained that at the age of thirty-one, "I was reduced to showing my hair, arms, and uncovered bosom to all of Moscow."[8] Peter expected men to shave off their beards, unless they paid a beard tax toward the war with Sweden, and wear shorter coats and powdered wigs. The nobility of St. Petersburg and Moscow engaged foreign tutors to ensure that their children mastered the dress and deportment necessary to excel in the newly Westernized Russian court.

In place of the precepts of the *Domostroi*, Peter commissioned a new guide for elite childrearing entitled *The Honourable Mirror of Youth*, which explained proper table manners and conversation and encouraged women to display "maidenly honour and virtue" in their social life. Peter's plans for the upbringing of noble children went far beyond outward appearances. Perhaps inspired by his own failed marriage to Yevdokia, which had been arranged by his mother, Peter decreed that both men and women had the right to choose their own marriage partners and reject betrothals arranged by their parents. Peter also insisted that young noblemen complete their educations before marriage and advance through the newly created Table of Ranks for the military and civil service according to merit instead of lineage.

In contrast to his hostile relationship with Alexei, Peter enjoyed a warm relationship with the children of his second marriage. Like Menshikov, Peter's second wife was from a peasant background, and owed her rise to the top of Russian society to the czar's will alone. She was born Marta Stavronsky in the modern-day Baltic states and was a maid in the home of a Lutheran pastor, Johannes Gluck, who was responsible for the first translation of the Bible into Latvian before being captured by Russian troops during the Great Northern War. Peter and Marta began an affair around 1703 while she was working as a laundress in Menshikov's household. They married publicly in 1712, with their two young daughters, Anna and Yelizaveta, serving as bridesmaids. Marta converted to the Russian Orthodox Church in 1705, assuming the name Catherine.

Of the dozen children of Peter and Catherine, only Anna and Yelizaveta survived childhood, and they were cherished by their parents. Peter wrote them affectionate letters while he was away on his military campaigns, accompanied by Catherine. In 1721 he wrote, "Annushka and Lizenka, greetings! Your mother and I are well, thank God, and at this moment are on our way to Persia. God grant that we see you safe and happy."[9]

Catherine, who was universally praised for her good humour, made efforts to welcome Alexei into the family. She treated her stepson with a combination of warmth and deference and recognized his strengths, asking for his advice during her preparation for her conversion to Russian Orthodoxy. When Alexei's wife Charlotte-Christine witnessed violent quarrels between her husband and father-in-law, she asked Catherine to make peace between them.

Catherine was unsuccessful in her attempts to reconcile Peter and Alexei. During the summer of 1716, Alexei fled Russia for the court of his brother-in-law, Holy Roman Emperor Charles VI, in Vienna, expressing fear for his life. There was a chilling precedent in Russian history for a czar murdering his eldest son personally: in 1581, Ivan the Terrible had bludgeoned his eldest son to death with an iron-tipped sceptre following an argument that turned violent. Peter was outraged that Alexei had turned their hostile relationship into an international incident, and sent diplomats to persuade him to return to Russia. Alexei was promised forgiveness and reconciliation with Peter if he ended his self-imposed exile; instead, he faced charges of treason when he returned to Russia in 1718. Alexei's terrified mistress, Yefrosinya Fedorova, testified that he had intended to end his father's wars, return to old Russian customs, and move the capital back to Moscow from St. Petersburg when he became czar.

Alexei was convicted of conspiring against Peter in June 1718 and sentenced to death. He died in prison a few days later after being tortured on Peter's orders to name accomplices and beaten repeatedly with the knout. The long conflict between father and son ended with Alexei's death. Other monarchs had threatened rebellious heirs with violence, but Peter's willingness to carry out his longstanding threat to Alexei — "I will declare you a traitor and I assure you I will find the means to use you as such" — is almost unique in European royal history.

Peter forbade his court to go into mourning because his son had been found guilty of treason. Within months of the funeral, the czar had commissioned a new commemorative medal engraved with the words, "The horizon has cleared," which suggested that he felt little remorse regarding his son's fate.[10] Alexei's children were mentioned last in prayers for the imperial family. In 1722, Peter issued a new Law of Succession, enabling the ruler to choose anyone he or she wished as a successor. As far as Peter was concerned, primogeniture was a custom that an absolute monarch could easily set aside. Peter died suddenly in 1725 without exercising this right to choose an heir, and Menshikov engineered the succession of his political ally, Peter's widow, as Catherine I.

Peter's seeming indifference to his son's death contrasted with his reaction to the death of Britain's Queen Anne in 1714. Peter had met Anne in 1698 when he visited London at the invitation of her brother-in-law and predecessor, King William III. Peter ordered six weeks of court mourning in Russia to commemorate the passing of his fellow sovereign. In contrast to Peter, Anne mourned deeply the loss of her only son to survive infancy, becoming best known to her subjects as a disconsolate mother.

TWELVE

Anne (1665-1714) and George of Denmark (1653-1708)

On July 30, 1700, eleven-year-old William, Duke of Gloucester, the son of Princess Anne, heir to the English throne, died of "a malignant fever" that may have been smallpox or an acute bacterial infection associated with pneumonia.[1] Anne and her husband, Prince George of Denmark, were devastated. William had been their only child to survive past infancy. Anne disappeared from public view until November of that year, remaining secluded at Windsor Castle with George and her closest friend, Sarah Churchill, Duchess of Marlborough. The grief of the royal parents was shared by the monarch and the public. Anne's brother-in-law, King William III, had treated his namesake nephew as a surrogate son, and he put aside past personal conflicts with Anne to express his sadness, writing, "I do not believe it necessary to use so many words to tell you of the surprise and sorrow with which I learned of the death of the Duke of Gloucester. It is so great a loss for me and for all England that my heart is pierced with affliction. I assure you that on this occasion and on any other I shall be glad to give you any marks of friendship."[2] The public outpouring of grief confirmed the king's view that the death of Anne's son was a loss for all of England. Although the future queen's son had lived for only eleven years, the promise and symbolism of royal motherhood dominated Anne's entire adult life and, later, her reign.

Anne was the second daughter of King James II, whose marriage to her mother had been controversial. James was a promising candidate for dynastic marriage because the Restoration of the English monarchy in 1660 had made him heir to his brother Charles II. He had, however, entered into a relationship with Anne Hyde, a lady-in-waiting to his sister Mary, and the daughter of one of Charles's advisers. When the monarchy was restored in 1660, Anne was pregnant, and adamant that she was secretly betrothed to James.

Until the passing of An Act for the Better Preventing of Clandestine Marriage in 1753, a betrothal was considered almost as binding as a marriage in England. There were clear historical precedents for how secret betrothals could complicate the royal succession. Richard III, for example, had argued that his brother Edward IV's children were illegitimate because Edward had been pre-contracted to Eleanor Butler before he married Elizabeth Woodville. Charles II, therefore, insisted that James and Anne Hyde marry publicly so that there would be no question concerning their children's place in the succession. As a young child, the future Queen Anne had spent little time with her parents, instead living with her paternal grandmother, Henrietta Maria, and then her aunt Henrietta Anne in France, where she received medical treatment for an eye condition that would plague her throughout her life. By the time Anne was five years old, both her grandmother and aunt had died, and she returned to England.

As Duke and Duchess of York, Anne's parents continued to cause controversy when they both converted to Catholicism. Charles then took charge of the education of the couple's two surviving children, Mary and Anne, ensuring that they were raised in the Church of England by Protestant guardians. Anne's mother died when she was only six, and the difference in religion between James and his daughters complicated their relationship. Anne sought emotional solace beyond parent-child bonds, becoming extremely close to her sister and a circle of female friends whom she came to regard as her "family."[3]

In 1673, James married his second wife, Mary Beatrice of Modena. The new Duchess of York was only fourteen, and James introduced her to eleven-year-old Mary and eight-year-old Anne with the words, "I have brought you a new play-fellow."[4] While Mary treated her new stepmother as a friend, the younger Anne made clear that Mary Beatrice could not replace the grandmother, aunt, and mother that she had lost. As an adult, she complained to her sister that their stepmother "pretends to have a great deal of kindness for me but I doubt it is not real, for I never see proofs of it but rather the contrary."[5]

In contrast to most seventeenth-century princesses, including her sister Mary, who married the Dutch Prince William of Orange in 1677, Anne remained at home after marrying a foreign prince. Her consort, Prince George of Denmark, resided in England after their marriage in 1683. The hierarchy of their marriage was unusual for a seventeenth-century royal couple. Although Anne made the conventional displays of wifely devotion, she was the dominant partner in their relationship. George accepted his wife's leadership, acting as her representative in male political spheres such as the Privy Council, House of Lords, and the military, and describing himself as "Her Majesty's subject" once she succeeded to the throne.[6] Although George had acquired military experience in Denmark, he preferred a quiet life at home with Anne and their growing family. He wrote soon after his marriage, "We talk here of going to tea, of going to Winchester, and everything else except sitting still all summer, which is the height of my ambition."[7]

By 1687, George and Anne had two young daughters, Mary and Anne Sophia. That same year, a smallpox epidemic swept through London, including Whitehall Palace, where Anne was residing with her family. Anne had already contracted the disease around the time of her sister Mary's wedding, and was therefore immune, but George and the children fell ill. Anne nursed her family herself. George recovered, but both their daughters died of the disease. Rachel Wriothesley, Lady Russell, described the anguish of the bereaved parents, writing, "I never heard any relation more moving than that of seeing them together. Sometimes they wept, sometimes they mourned; in a word, then sat silent, hand in hand, he sick in bed, and she the carefullest nurse to him that can be imagined."[8] The loss of their children brought the couple closer together and they remained devoted to each other throughout their marriage.

In 1688, while Anne and George mourned their daughters, her father, who had succeeded to the throne as King James II in 1685, was hopeful that his queen, Mary Beatrice, would give birth to a healthy son. Like Anne, Mary Beatrice had suffered a series of miscarriages and the loss of daughters in infancy. James's confidence in the outcome of his queen's latest pregnancy, therefore, seemed suspiciously optimistic. The birth of a son to Mary Beatrice would displace Anne and her sister Mary and ensure a Roman Catholic succession. When Mary Beatrice gave birth to a healthy son on June 10, 1688, Anne lent credence to the rumours that the new heir was not a royal baby, but was instead the son of a commoner who had been smuggled into the birth chamber in a warming pan, a device for holding the warm coals needed to make beds more comfortable in the drafty residences of the period. Anne claimed that she had never been allowed to place her hand on her stepmother's abdomen to feel the baby kick, and wrote to her brother-in-law and sister, William and Mary, in Holland, of her doubts about the child. Although it would have been nearly impossible to smuggle a baby unnoticed into a palace crowded with courtiers awaiting news of the royal birth, the warming pan story suited Protestant popular opinion, and the political ambitions of William, Mary, and Anne.

The controversy surrounding the birth of James and Mary Beatrice's son precipitated the Glorious Revolution and the creation of the modern constitutional monarchy. William accepted an invitation from seven prominent Protestant English nobles to invade England, and Anne and George deserted James to support William's bid for the throne.

James fled England and was ultimately defeated by his son-in-law at the Battle of the Boyne in Ireland in 1689. Before their coronation as William III and Mary II, Anne's sister and brother-in-law accepted a Bill of Rights that decreed that they must accept the advice of parliament and rule according to English common law. Although this political settlement satisfied Protestant public opinion, there was widespread unease about a father being driven from his kingdom by his daughters. Performances of William Shakespeare's *King Lear* were censored during the reign of William and Mary as the new queen and her sister attempted to counter any insinuation that they were "unnatural" daughters. In these circumstances, the birth of a son to Anne in 1689 appeared to be evidence of God's approval of the overthrow of James II and the accession of William and Mary. The infant Prince William was not only welcomed by his parents and the Protestant public, but by his reigning aunt and uncle, who were childless.

The circumstances of the young William's childhood are better documented than that of any previous member of the English or Scottish royal families because his Welsh page, Jenkin Lewis, wrote a memoir about the prince's upbringing. In France, there were already examples of royal servants writing about the health and education of royal children. The youth of King Louis XIII was carefully documented in the diary of his doctor, Jean Heroard. The circumstances of the English Civil Wars, however, meant that English and Scottish court memoirs of the mid-seventeenth century focused on politics rather than parenting. In contrast to the political reminiscences of Charles I's reign, Lewis focused on the daily care of the young prince. He described the succession of wet nurses who were dismissed as unsuitable until the arrival of a Mrs. Pack, the wife of a Quaker, whom "Prince George of Denmark ... observ[ed] ... to be a strong healthy woman."[9] By the age of four, Lewis described William as already fascinated by the military, writing, "In 1693, he grew very inquisitive, by asking what everything meant that he saw and to throw off childish toys, saying he was then a man, calling himself a soldier. He liked to see the sentinels at two years old, saying Dub-a-Dub, and would have the boys of Kensington to Camden House ... leading them as their captain."[10] As William grew older, Lewis noted approvingly that he was well-behaved at public engagements and developed a close bond with his uncle, William III, even when there was a "misunderstanding between the Queen [Mary] and the Princess [Anne]."[11]

Like Heroard's diary, Lewis's memoir was not originally written for publication, but when the text was discovered and printed in the late eighteenth century, the publisher acknowledged the public's interest in the daily lives of royal children. The publisher's preface declared, "In all civilized nations of the world, the histories of distinguished characters have been read with eager attention by the most accomplished persons in every age. Nor have the early presages of future greatness, during the tender years of those whose high birth entitles them to the most exalted stations, been treated as trivial and uninteresting."[12] Since William had once been destined to be a monarch, anecdotes from his childhood, including the various medical treatments that he endured over the course of his short life, qualified as being of public interest, prefiguring future accounts of royal domestic life for a popular audience.

Lewis's account of the young William's health crises reflected the cultural climate of the scientific revolution that transformed Europe in the seventeenth century. When Richard III and Anne Neville lost their only son, chroniclers focused on God's will and the supposed signs that the king had incurred divine wrath, but seventeenth-century observers sought medical explanations for childhood illnesses and deaths. Royal doctors are a constant presence in Lewis's memoir, prescribing remedies for William's frequent illnesses. At the age of three, the young prince suffered from an ague, "which was cured by Doctor Radcliffe and Sir Charles Scarborough, who prescribed Jesuits's powder, which we now call bark, of which the Duke took large quantities also early in the spring of 1694, for the same complaint, most manfully."[13] When William suffered a subsequent childhood illness, his anxious mother "therefore sent for Mr. Sentiman, an apothecary, who had the receipt of a medicine approved of by King Charles II which had cured every kind of ague … it was a mixture of brandy, saffron etc. [William] took it twice; but it made him very sick the first day, and he vomited in my arms…."[14] Despite all their efforts, the medical professionals of William III's court were powerless to treat the young William's enlarged head, which impaired his co-ordination, or the final illness that cost him his life.

High infant mortality rates remained a sad fact of life for parents of all social backgrounds. The sixteenth-century French philosopher Michel de Montaigne attempted to remain emotionally detached from the children he lost in infancy, but he acknowledged that other parents were far more affected by the deaths of their sons and daughters, writing, "I have lost two or three children at nurse, if not without regret, at least without repining; yet there is scarcely any accident that touches men more to the quick."[15]

Anne hoped that her subsequent children might be more fortunate than their brothers and sisters and survive to adulthood. Sarah Churchill wondered at Anne's stamina, writing, "though she was not forty … she had had before seventeen dead ones."[16] Although there was sympathy for Anne's successive bereavements as a mother, her continued optimism about giving birth to living children eventually provoked criticism and satire. Churchill dismissed Anne's hopes for a child after her seventeen losses as "a very vain thought … which proceeded more from her pride," and a 1703 satirical poem imagined the queen knighting any doctor who would tell her that she was still capable of conceiving a child.[17]

The death of Anne's son provoked a succession crisis that contributed to the union of England and Scotland. William III had not remarried after the death of Mary II in 1694, and therefore seemed unlikely to have children of his own. The only surviving child of Anne's late aunt Henrietta Anne, Anne Marie d'Orléans, was known as "one of the most amiable and virtuous of women," but she was a French Catholic married to an Italian prince, Victor Amadeus II of Savoy.[18] After the circumstances of the Glorious Revolution, there was little Protestant popular support for a Roman Catholic succession. While Anne's contemporary, Peter the Great, had asserted his right to choose his own successor, the future succession of the English constitutional monarchy was determined by act of Parliament. The Act of Settlement, passed in 1701, decreed that in the event that William III and then his sister-in-law Anne died childless, the succession was to pass to Sophia, Electress of Hanover, and her Protestant descendants. The Act, which remains in force to the present day, excluded not only Henrietta Anne's descendants but also the children of Sophia's elder siblings. Roman Catholics remain excluded from the succession, and Protestant dynasts could not marry Catholics without losing their succession rights until 2015. The Act of Settlement had political as well as religious implications. The Act of Union between England and Scotland in 1707, which created a single British state, was informed by concerns that Scotland might not accept the Hanoverian succession.

Anne was not pleased with the terms of the Act; her second cousin, Sophia's eldest son, George of Hanover, had been one of her suitors during her youth, and he had made a poor impression during a visit to England. As late as 1703, thirty-eight-year-old Anne told Sarah that she still yearned for "the inexpressible blessing of another child, for though I do not flatter myself with thoughts of it, I would leave no reasonable thing undone that might be a means toward it."[19] The queen would never conceive again, but neither Sophia nor George was welcome in England during her lifetime.

As queen, Anne was without surviving children of her own, but she presented herself to the public as a mother to her subjects. There were past precedents for reigning queens affirming their legitimacy by describing themselves as mothers of their people, often during times of crisis. When Mary I's authority was threatened by the Wyatt Rebellion of 1554, she gave a speech at London's Guildhall that included the words, "I cannot tell how naturally the mother loveth the child, for I was never the mother of any; but certainly, if a Prince and Governor may as naturally and earnestly love her subjects as the mother doth love the child, then assure yourselves that I, being your lady and mistress, do as earnestly and tenderly love and favour you."[20] Mary I's half-sister, Elizabeth I, expressed similar sentiments when she was pressured by her councillors to marry and become the mother of legitimate heirs, telling the House of Commons not to "upbraid me with miserable lacke of children: for everyone of you and as many as are English-men, are children, and kinsmen to me; of whom if God deprive me not … I cannot without injury be accounted Barren."[21]

Neither Mary nor Elizabeth, however, ever became pregnant, and their subjects acted as substitutes for children. Anne's circumstances were different; she had known motherhood, and carried the memories of her deceased children. Her subjects were a consolation for the sons and daughters she had lost. For her coronation, Anne selected a passage from the Book of Isaiah to be the centrepiece of the Archbishop of York's sermon: "Kings shall be thy nursing fathers and queens thy nursing mothers,"[22] which inspired early-eighteenth-century writers, including Daniel Defoe, author of *Robinson Crusoe*, to compose odes to the queen as "the General Mother, the Guardian, the Refuge of all Her Subjects."[23] Anne's role as a mother long outlasted the lifetime of her only surviving son, and continued until the end of her reign.

Anne outlived her heir, Sophia, by a few weeks, and was therefore succeeded by George, Elector of Hanover, as King George I. There was no shortage of Hanover heirs. Fifty-four-year-old George had two children, the future George II, who became Prince of Wales the year of his father's accession, and Sophia Dorothea, the future Queen of Prussia. The Prince of Wales was married to Caroline of Ansbach, and four of their eight children had already been born at the time of George I's accession. These multiple generations of heirs, however, did not belong to a harmonious family. Throughout the eighteenth and early nineteenth centuries, the House of Hanover became synonymous with family conflict as generations of monarchs and their heirs quarrelled bitterly over a variety of personal and political grievances.

Anne viewed her "seventeen dead ones" as the will of God, and found solace in her strong Protestant faith, which had shaped the circumstances of her life and reign. In contrast, when the future George II and Queen Caroline lost one of their children in infancy, they would blame the baby's grandfather, George I. George II and Caroline's own son, Frederick, would make clear from the moment he became a father that he did not want his parents to be involved in any aspect of the upbringing of his children. The domestic turmoil of the House of Hanover occurred at the same time as a distinctive children's culture emerged in wider elite society, complete with storybooks and comfortable clothes specially designed for the very young. The contrast between emerging sentimental ideas of childhood and the discord in the Hanoverian royal household would give royal parenting a lasting negative image in the popular imagination.

THIRTEEN

George II (1683-1760) and Caroline of Ansbach (1683-1737)

On the evening of July 30, 1737, Augusta of Saxe-Gotha, Princess of Wales, went into labour with her first child at Hampton Court Palace, a royal residence since the reign of Henry VIII.

The arrival of a grandchild for King George II of Great Britain in the direct line of succession was an event of such public significance that it required official witnesses. George II and Queen Caroline expected to watch the birth alongside senior members of the government and clergy. Frederick, Prince of Wales, however, was rarely on speaking terms with his parents, and did not want them to be present for the birth of his child. Instead of summoning the king and queen and the other expected witnesses when Augusta's labour pains began, Frederick summoned a carriage to take him and his wife to St. James's Palace in London. When George and Caroline learned of their son and daughter-in-law's hasty departure, they were concerned for both the health of Augusta and her baby and the stability of the succession if a future king was born without multiple official witnesses to confirm the child's legitimacy.

Less than fifty years had passed since James II and his queen, Mary of Modena, had been accused of smuggling a baby into the royal bedchamber in a warming pan to replace a stillborn child and ensure a Roman Catholic succession. By 1737, the so-called warming pan baby, James Francis Edward Stuart, nicknamed "The Old Pretender," was a middle-aged man actively seeking the support of the French government for an invasion of England. His seventeen-year-old son, Charles Edward Stuart, better known as "Bonnie Prince Charlie" or "The Young Pretender," was in the process of gaining military experience in the War of the Polish Succession (1733–38). Charles would remain an active threat to George II's sovereignty until he was defeated at the Battle of Culloden in 1746. Since there was an alternate line of succession just across the English Channel with two generations of male heirs, George II was determined to ensure that his own grandchild's right to succeed to the British throne was unquestioned. George and Caroline set out for London in pursuit of their son and daughter-in-law.

Frederick and Augusta arrived at St. James's Palace in London just in time for the birth of their child. The palace staff had not expected the sudden arrival of the Prince and Princess of Wales. There were no clean sheets for the beds, so Augusta gave birth on tablecloths spread over a mattress. Frederick's parents did not arrive in time for the birth. For once, a reigning monarch and his consort were relieved that their first grandchild was a sickly looking baby girl who was unlikely to succeed to the throne. A girl would never be suspected of being a warming pan baby. Caroline described the baby, named Augusta after her mother, as "a poor, little, ugly, she-mouse."[1] Lord Hervey, who had been a close of friend of Frederick until they competed for the attention of the same mistress in 1723, was even more blunt in his description of the royal baby and the unusual circumstances of her birth. Hervey wrote, "At a quarter before eleven [the Princess of Wales] was delivered of a little rat of a girl, about the bigness of a good large toothpick case; none of the Lords of the Council being present but my Lord President [of the council] Wilmington, and my Lord Godolphin, Privy Seal."[2] Frederick may have disagreed with his parents on most issues, but he recognized the importance of witnesses to the royal birth, and had summoned Wilmington and Godolphin once he reached St. James's Palace.

The Prince and Princess of Wales's second child, the future King George III, was born the following year in more conventional circumstances. Instead of causing a succession crisis, Frederick's hasty departure from Hampton

Court with his labouring wife cemented his estrangement from his parents. Despite Augusta's attempts to reconcile her husband with her parents-in-law, they were ordered to leave St. James's Palace as soon as she had recovered from the birth. In medieval England, George and Frederick might have faced each other on the battlefield. In Peter the Great's Russia, the conflict between father and son might have cost Frederick his life. But in Britain's developing constitutional monarchy, the adversarial relationship between the king and his heir contributed to the development of the modern Westminster parliamentary system. The faction that surrounded Frederick and sympathized with his grievances with his parents would develop into the government's official opposition.

In the reigning House of Hanover, George and Frederick's estrangement was hardly unprecedented. George II's relationship with his own father, George I, had been even worse. When the future George I had married his cousin, Sophia Dorothea of Celle, it was to ensure that their respective landholdings, the German provinces of Hanover and Celle, would eventually be inherited by a single ruler. But the couple had little in common beyond their two children, and they each pursued extra-marital relationships. While George's decades-long affair with Melusine von der Schulenburg, later Duchess of Kendal, was acceptable behaviour for a prince, Sophia Dorothea's romance with a Swedish count, Philip von Königsmarck, threatened the succession. The royal couple divorced; George then imprisoned Sophia Dorothea in Ahlden Castle in Saxony for the rest of her life to prevent a remarriage from threatening the unification of Celle with Hanover.

The imprisoned Sophia Dorothea was not permitted to see her children, and her imprisonment permanently damaged the relationship between the future King George I and his son. Once George I became king in 1714, his estrangement from his heir became clear to observers in Britain. The Prussian envoy Frederick Bonet wrote: "They do not speak to one another; they have never gone to one another's apartments; they have never eaten together; they have never been together in the Royal or private houses, nor in the promenades, nor at the hunt, but only in Council, at Chapel, and in the evening in the circle of the princess [Caroline]."[3] Since her marriage to the future George II in 1705, Caroline of Ansbach had attempted to act as a peacemaker between father and son, but she had little success. When the king and Prince of Wales met at her social gatherings, they did not speak to each other.

George II's conflict with his father impeded his ability to make decisions concerning the upbringing of his own children. George I decided that his son and daughter-in-law were not suitable parents, and assumed custody of his young grandchildren. When Caroline gave birth to her second son in 1717, George I selected the infant's name, George William, and chose his godparents, including Thomas Pelham-Holles, Duke of Newcastle, whom the future George II despised. The furious royal father confronted Newcastle at the christening, shaking his fist and shouting, "You are a rascal, I shall find you out."[4] Since George had a heavy German accent, Newcastle heard, "I shall fight you" and assumed that he had been challenged to a duel. George I had to intervene to prevent a physical altercation between his son and his grandson's godfather.

Following the christening, George I expelled his son and daughter-in-law from St. James's Palace, while insisting that their three daughters and infant son remain there. The Prince and Princess of Wales moved to Leicester House, home of the Prince of Wales. Caroline was granted supervised visits, but the future George II was kept from his children for months at a time. When George William died of a heart condition at the age of four months, the grieving future George II blamed his father.

The differences between George I and George II, and then George II and Frederick, Prince of Wales, shaped the development of parliament in a constitutional monarchy. The office of prime minister emerged during the reign of George I as Sir Robert Walpole took charge of restoring confidence in Britain's economy following the South Sea Bubble crisis of 1720. Members of the royal household who became members of the House of Commons had to resign their positions at court, but the same restrictions did not apply to members of the Prince of Wales's household. Leicester House became the unofficial meeting place of members of the opposition. The future George II was determined to bring down his father's Whig government, and hosted members of the Tory party and discontented members of the Whig party. His political efforts, however, were inconsistent, and his supporters complained that he did not always use his personal influence in the House of Lords or order the members of his household to vote together in the House of Commons. Nevertheless, the heir to the throne maintained his separate household until his accession in 1727, and "the Leicester House faction" became an established part of the British parliamentary system over the course of the mid-eighteenth century.

The future George II recreated his acrimonious relations with his father in his dealings with his own eldest son, Frederick. When George I succeeded to the British throne in 1714, the future George II accompanied him to London, while fourteen-year-old Frederick remained in Hanover to represent the family there. Frederick became accustomed to being head of his own household and making decisions independently. When he rejoined his parents in England at the age of twenty, he made it clear that he had no intention of following their dictates. Frederick continued his father's tradition of hosting opposition politicians at Leicester House, achieving more political influence than his father had done as Prince of Wales. Frederick provided patronage for opposition politicians such as William Pitt the elder and George Lyttleton, and he controlled forty votes in the House of Commons by the late 1740s.

Frederick's decision to oppose his father in the political realm caused a permanent breach in his relationship with his mother. When the politicians under Frederick's patronage turned a dispute with his father over his allowance into the subject of a motion debated in the House of Commons in 1737, Caroline lamented to Hervey, "My dear firstborn is the greatest ass and the greatest liar and the greatest *canaille* and the greatest beast in the world, and I most heartily wish him out of it."[5] After the vote, which Frederick's faction narrowly lost, George and Caroline banned their son and daughter-in-law from their residences, even refusing them the use of trunks to transport their belongings. In contrast to his father, however, George II allowed his granddaughter Augusta to remain with her parents. Remembering the fate of his own son George William, George II's own resolution "was to leave the child with the princess, and not to take it (as the late king had taken the king's children upon the quarrel in the last reign) lest any accident might happen...."[6] George II never exercised his legal right to assume custody of his grandchildren, but relations with his heir remained hostile for the remainder of Frederick's life.

The conflict within the royal family contrasted with eighteenth-century British ideas of childrearing, which increasingly emphasized the importance of parents treating their children with patience and understanding. In 1693, philosopher and physician John Locke wrote *Some Thoughts Concerning Education*. Locke argued that infants were born with empty minds that were filled by experience. Good parenting and a stable atmosphere within the home were therefore crucial to the healthy development of children. Locke also encouraged regular feedings and plenty of sleep for infants, setting the tone for future childrearing manuals. In contrast to previous volumes of childrearing advice, which emphasized preparation for adulthood, Locke encouraged parents to allow their children to enjoy their youth, writing, "All their innocent folly, playing, and childish actions are to be left perfectly free and unrestrained as far as they can consist with the respect due to those that are present."[7] Locke encouraged parents to treat their children firmly but kindly and avoid imposing harsh punishments. At a time when treatises on family life and education were encouraging parents to treat their children with patience and pay close attention to their development, the discord within the royal family appeared particularly dysfunctional and undermined the popularity of the House of Hanover in Britain.

Frederick never became king, dying in 1751 at the age of forty-four. His eldest son, the future King George III, became Prince of Wales that same year and succeeded his grandfather George II in 1760. In their personal lives, a number of Frederick's children inherited his independence of thought and willingness to defy familial expectations. The practice of dynastic marriage had been the focus of increasing criticism since the reign of Henry VIII, but the emergence of romanticism later in the eighteenth century made arranged marriages between members of royal families seem particularly incongruous with the domestic lives of the rest of society. Frederick's son-in-law, Charles William, Duke of Brunswick, husband of Princess Augusta, complained, "Only private persons can live happily married because they can choose their mates. Royalty must make marriages of convenience, which seldom result in happiness. Love does not prompt these alliances, and these marriages not only embitter the lives of the parties to them, but all too frequently have a disastrous effect upon the children who are often unhealthy in mind or body."[8] Three of Charles William and Augusta's sons were declared unfit for military service. Their daughter Caroline was unhappily married to her cousin, the future King George IV. Another one of Frederick's daughters, Caroline Matilda, married King Christian VII of Denmark but had an affair with her husband's physician, Johann Struensee, events dramatized in the 2012 Danish film *A Royal Affair*. Two of Frederick's sons, Prince William Henry, Duke of Gloucester, and Prince Henry, Duke of Cumberland, married commoners in secret.

George III was shocked by the behaviour of his siblings, and put aside his own personal inclinations to make a suitable dynastic marriage to Princess Charlotte of Mecklenburg-Strelitz. To prevent future royal marriages from being contracted without the permission of the sovereign, George III proposed the Royal Marriages Act, which was passed by Parliament in 1772. The Act decreed that all descendants of George II, with the exception of the children of princesses married to foreign royalty, must receive permission to marry from the monarch in order for their marriages to be valid. By the reign of Elizabeth II, there were hundreds of eligible descendants of George II, and granting distant cousins permission to marry was therefore a frequent occurrence for the monarch. Twenty-first century succession reform limited the reach of the Royal Marriages Act to the first six people in the line of succession. The Queen granted the last official permission to marry under the original terms of the Royal Marriages Act in February 2015, just before the succession reforms came into force, allowing Juliet Victoria Katharine Nicolson, a descendent of Queen Victoria's granddaughter Princess Patricia of Connaught, to marry Simon Alexander Rood.

George III and Charlotte were determined to break with the Hanover tradition of acrimonious relations between monarchs and their heirs, and raised their thirteen surviving children in an atmosphere of warm domesticity. George was the first Hanoverian monarch born and raised in England, and he was nicknamed "Farmer George" by his subjects because he preferred a secluded domestic life at Kew Palace to a more public and ceremonial one. Visitors to Kew remarked on George and Charlotte's attention to their children, and the whole royal family came together for social occasions. This family cohesion did not continue into the next generation, however. George and Charlotte's seven sons rebelled against their parents' expectations and became notorious for their extravagant spending and unwillingness to contract suitably royal marriages unless absolutely necessary to the succession. As George's mental health grew more fragile later in his reign, he became increasingly unwilling to allow his six daughters to leave his household to marry foreign princes. George's difficulties with his adolescent sons and determination to keep his daughters close to home began around the same time that Britain lost the Thirteen Colonies during the American Revolution. A 1777 satirical poem by William Blake was entitled "Poor Old England Endeavouring to Reclaim His Wicked American Children."[9] As his reign progressed, the public observed George III lose control of his sons, colonies, and mental faculties. Having begun his reign as Farmer George, George III went down in history as Mad King George, overwhelmed by political, personal, and medical setbacks.

Like Henry III and Eleanor of Provence, George III and Charlotte popularized royal baby names, including their own, that remain in use to the present day. The name Edward had fallen out of fashion in the royal family after Henry VIII chose it for his only surviving son, and there had not been a senior member of the royal family who used William as a first name since Queen Anne's son. George and Charlotte chose the names William and Edward for their third and fourth sons respectively, reviving these classic royal baby names. The House of Hanover also introduced new baby names to the royal family and the wider British public. The names bestowed on Hanoverian princesses became especially popular. The British elites began giving their daughters names chosen by George and Charlotte, such as Amelia and Sophia, as well as the names of German princesses who married into the royal family, such as Caroline and Charlotte. These names continue to be popular in Britain. Not all Hanoverian names outlasted their own era, however; in addition to William and Edward, George and Charlotte also had sons with the now-obscure names Adolphus, Augustus, and Octavius. William and Kate named their own children George and Charlotte, reviving interest in Hanoverian royal baby names in the twenty-first century.

In addition to supervising the upbringing of her children, Queen Charlotte enjoyed a friendly correspondence with other royal women throughout Europe, including Marie Antoinette, an Austrian archduchess who married the future King Louis XVI of France in 1770. At first glance, the two queens had little in common. Charlotte was a decade older than Marie Antoinette and the consort of a constitutional monarch instead of an heir to an absolute monarchy. While Marie Antoinette was a leader of fashion who set trends emulated at other European courts, Charlotte dressed in an unremarkable manner, leaving the fashion statements to female members of the aristocracy such as another one of Marie Antoinette's correspondents, Georgiana Cavendish, Duchess of Devonshire. Marie Antoinette expected to wield political influence at the French court, while Charlotte restricted her activities to the domestic sphere. Nevertheless, when the French Revolution took place, Charlotte ordered apartments prepared in the event that Louis and Marie Antoinette fled to Britain, and expressed sympathy for the Queen of France, writing, "The poor unfortunate princess, what a bitter portion hers is. I pity both the King and her and wish anxiously that they meet with some well disposed people to extricate them hourly out of their great horrible distress."[10] Despite their differences, Marie Antoinette and Charlotte had common ground that created a bond between them: both queens were devoted mothers determined to assume an active role in the upbringing of their children. When Marie Antoinette was placed on trial by the French Revolutionary Tribunal in 1793, she would be judged as a mother as well as a former queen.

FOURTEEN

Louis XVI of France (1754-93) and Marie Antoinette of Austria (1755-93)

Marie Antoinette gave birth to her first child, Princess Marie-Thérèse, Madame Royale, in front of dozens of her husband's subjects in 1779. The Queen of France's bedchamber at the royal residence of Versailles was filled with courtiers and curious members of the public who climbed onto the furniture to get a better view of the queen in labour. One of the queen's ladies of the bedchamber, Jeanne Campan, recalled, "The etiquette of allowing all persons indiscriminately to enter at the moment of the delivery of a queen was observed with such exaggeration that when the *accoucheur* said aloud, '*La Reine va s'accoucher*,' the persons who poured into the chamber were so numerous that the rush nearly destroyed the Queen."[1]

Marie Antoinette fainted amid the crowd, and her husband, King Louis XVI, who was also present for the birth, had to push his way through the assembled masses to open a window. Campan noted with disapproval, "It was impossible to move about the chamber, which was filled with so motley a crowd that one might have fancied himself in some place of public amusement."[2]

The audience in Marie Antoinette's bedchamber was in keeping with the seventeenth- and eighteenth-century French conception of royal residences as public spaces. Any well-dressed member of the public was permitted to enter the palace at Versailles and observe the royal family eating their meals or walking in the garden. Enterprising merchants set up stalls outside the gates that offered the necessary attire for rent. The close proximity between the royal family and people of all social backgrounds allowed for critiques of the monarch's domestic life. Marie Antoinette's perceived failures as a mother undermined popular support for the monarchy during the decades preceding the French Revolution.

Marie Antoinette enjoyed far more privacy during her own childhood as the fifteenth of the sixteen children of Empress Maria Theresa of the Habsburg Empire (encompassing modern-day Austria, Hungary, Czech Republic, Slovakia, Slovenia, and parts of Italy and the Balkan states) and Francis, Duke of Lorraine. Since she was the youngest daughter, her parents assumed that she would marry a minor prince, and paid little attention to her education. A letter from Maria Theresa intended for either Marie Antoinette or the sister closest to her in age, Marie Caroline, emphasized the importance of being good-natured and obedient, stating, "My dear daughter, you merit well for your diligence in writing to me and the beauty of character and the dear Lord keep you and gently speak well of your talents that you will continue to employ and follow the good counsel of your faithful [governess] Brandeis and I promise that you will be happy and make your parents happy."[3] Habsburg monarchs and their families participated in formal court ceremonies and dined in public on special occasions, but their domestic life was shielded from the public gaze. As Queen of France, Marie Antoinette would look back on her childhood with nostalgia, remembering sleigh rides and skating with her brothers and sisters in the vast park surrounding the Schönbrunn Palace outside Vienna. This idyllic childhood came to an end after the deaths and disfigurements of a number of her elder sisters from smallpox, resulting in Marie Antoinette being chosen to marry the future King of France and cement a new alliance between France and Austria, two kingdoms that had been enemies since the Thirty Years' War.

Marie Antoinette was married to the future King Louis XVI in 1770 at the age of fourteen, and more than seven years passed before her first pregnancy. The long delay between marriage and motherhood gave her plenty of time to contemplate how she would raise her children. During the queen's lifetime, French Enlightenment philosophers debated the role of women within their families. Denis Diderot and Jean le Rond d'Alembert, the authors of the famous *Encyclopedia,* argued that women were subject to their husbands purely because of the laws that governed that state. In contrast, Jean-Jacques Rousseau, author of *Emile, or On Education,* argued that nature intended for women to be wives and mothers in the domestic sphere while men enjoyed a public life. Rousseau denounced what he considered to be unnatural childrearing practices, such as swaddling infants and hiring wet nurses to breastfeed newborns. These practices were not solely the preserve of wealthy people with vast households of servants; the wives of urban artisans often hired peasant women to breastfeed their children. Rousseau also disapproved of mothers who turned the upbringing of their children over to nannies, writing, "A child who passes through many hands in turn, can never be well brought up. At every change he makes a secret comparison, which continually tends to lessen his respect for those who control him, and with it their authority over him."[4]

Marie Antoinette became a mother in this climate of debate concerning the proper duties of mothers toward their children. The acquisitions by Marie Antoinette's librarian demonstrate that she preferred novels, plays, and biographies of female historical figures to Enlightenment philosophy, but she was exposed to new ideas through her family and social circle. Louis XVI, however, was an avid reader of Enlightenment philosophy, and Marie Antoinette's eldest brother, Emperor Joseph II of the Habsburg Empire, was an enthusiastic reformer according to Enlightenment precepts.

Marie Antoinette embraced the new trends in childrearing. When she was expecting her first child, she wrote to her mother, "In the manner they are brought up now, they are far less uncomfortable. They are not swaddled; they are always in a basket or in the arms and the moment they are able to be outside, they are accustomed to it little by little, and end up being there always. I believe this is the healthiest and best way to raise them."[5] By 1778, Rousseau's ideas of natural childrearing were not simply one set of ideas about parenting but "the manner they are brought up now" for the women of the queen's social circle.

Maria Theresa was less accepting of these new trends than her daughter, emphasizing in her letters the unique conditions facing royal parents whose marriages sealed diplomatic alliances. When Marie Antoinette proudly wrote about breastfeeding her newborn daughter, Maria Theresa encouraged her to entrust the infant to a wet nurse to ensure that a second pregnancy occurred as soon as possible. The fragile Franco-Austrian alliance would be strengthened by the birth of a male heir. The queen reluctantly followed her mother's advice. Louis and Marie Antoinette became the parents of three more children in the 1780s — Louis-Joseph (born 1781), Louis-Charles (born 1785), and Sophie-Beatrix (born 1786).

Louis XVI's subjects were uneasy about the prospect of the heir to the throne's character being shaped by a foreign queen surrounded by rumours of extravagance and immorality. Marie Antoinette appointed one of her closest friends, Yolande de Polastron, Duchess of Polignac, to the prestigious position of Governess of the Children of France, which allowed Polignac access to income and patronage usually reserved for more prestigious noble families. There was speculation that both Marie Antoinette and Polignac were neglecting the children, as Louis-Joseph's health declined through the 1780s. Even courtiers sympathetic to Marie Antoinette questioned her ability to parent the heir to the throne effectively. The Marquis de Bombelles wrote about Louis-Joseph's 1784 illness in his memoirs, "Again, the Queen did not know how much this child, so precious to the state and to her, has been in danger," concluding that Marie Antoinette "has a very good heart" but was too consumed by her social life to raise her children herself.[6] Louis-Joseph's death from tuberculosis in 1789 seemed to confirm rumours that the health of the royal children was being neglected, and Marie Antoinette's parenting received even greater scrutiny.

On the eve of the French Revolution, the popular press made it clear that Marie Antoinette was considered unfit to influence the future King of France. Subversive pamphlets, often smuggled into France from Britain or Belgium to evade censorship, critiqued Marie Antoinette. Despite the salacious content of many of these pamphlets, the often-anonymous authors assumed a serious tone, presenting Marie Antoinette's failings as information essential for patriotic French people. Since Louis-Joseph was the Dauphin, or heir to the throne, Marie Antoinette's critics believed that it was particularly important for him to be on guard against his mother's influence. In 1788, a political pamphlet written anonymously by the essayist and poet Sylvain Marechal entitled *Modern Apologues of the Dauphin, First Lessons of the Eldest Son of the King* was smuggled into France from Belgium.[7] The pamphlet was structured as a series of instructional allegories necessary to the future king's education. "Lesson 84: The Courtesan Reigns" was an implicit warning against Marie Antoinette, who had come to personify popular anxieties about the influence of both royal wives and mistresses over the state:

> I stayed to see the golden chariot pass. A woman was alone in the back. She was beautiful, this woman! Her bosom, to dazzle, did not need the river of diamonds of Golconda, which covered it. At her ears hung two pearls the price of two provinces. But her eyes eclipsed all that. Her mouth stuck out like that of an ingenious child, caressed by her mother. Sweetness characterized all her features. She was beautiful, this woman. I ask her name of an old man who had not had time to flee the procession: young man, it's the first of the courtesans of the kingdom…. Vice, under the mask of beauty, is very powerful.[8]

Marechal's description of this anonymous courtesan summarized numerous popular anxieties concerning Marie Antoinette's influence over her husband and children and therefore the government of France. Her presence alone in the golden chariot alluded to her trips to Paris opera performances, unaccompanied by Louis. The river of diamonds at her bosom was undoubtedly a reference to the Affair of the Diamond Necklace, which had occurred only three years before. A number of the jewels in the famous necklace had originally been mined in India, where the wealthy kingdom of Golconda had existed in medieval times, allowing the author to reference the rumours that the queen had secretly purchased the expensive necklace without stating her name in his pamphlet. The lavish earrings provided further evidence of her extravagance during a period of financial hardship for France. Marie Antoinette's foreignness and the perceived influence of her Austrian relatives were referenced through the mention of the courtesan's prominent mouth, a common physical feature among the

Habsburgs, and the caresses of her mother, an allusion to Maria Theresa. Through the pamphlet, the heir to the throne, and by extension the French people, were warned that Marie Antoinette's dazzling appearance and fashions disguised an immoral character.

Marie Antoinette had long been aware that she had critics at her husband's court and that their ideas were spreading to a wider audience. She attempted to counter the critiques in the pamphlets with official portraits that celebrated her close relationship with her children. A 1787 painting by Élisabeth Louise Vigée Le Brun showed Marie Antoinette sitting with Louis-Charles in her lap while Marie-Thérèse held her arm and Louis-Joseph pointed to an empty cradle, inviting the public to sympathize with the queen for the recent death of her younger daughter, Sophie-Beatrix. Instead of attracting sympathy, however, the portrait became an object of satire. Vigée Le Brun recalled that when the portrait was exhibited in public at the 1788 *salon*, "The frame, which had been taken there alone, was enough to evoke a thousand malicious remarks. 'That's how the money goes,' they said, and a number of other things which seemed to me the bitterest comments. At last I sent my picture, but I could not muster up the courage to follow it and find out what its fate was to be, so afraid was I that it would be badly received by the public."[9] Marie Antoinette found that the portrait evoked painful memories because it reminded her of Sophie-Beatrix's death, and it therefore went into storage after its poor reception at the *salon*. Vigée Le Brun believed that if the portrait had been on display during the French Revolution, it would have been destroyed by the Paris market women who marched on Versailles.

For Marie Antoinette, the French Revolution of 1789 was initially not only a source of political upheaval that transformed Louis XVI from an absolute monarch to a constitutional monarch, but a series of events that threatened the established routines of the royal nursery. In October 1789, the royal family was transferred from Versailles to the dilapidated Tuileries Palace in Paris, where they could be kept under closer surveillance by the new National Assembly. The Governess of the Children of France fled the country. While Polignac's departure was a relief to Marie Antoinette's admirers and detractors alike because of her reputation for corruption, the queen was dismayed by the loss of a cherished friend whom she could trust to implement her views on childrearing. Marie Antoinette wrote detailed instructions for the new governess, Louise-Élisabeth de Croÿ, Marquise de Tourzel:

> One had always accustomed my children to have great confidence in me, and when they were in the wrong, they had to tell me themselves. When they were scolded, I looked more pained and afflicted with what they had done than angry. I have accustomed them to it that yes or no delivered by me is irrevocable but I always give them a reason within the scope of their age, for they cannot believe it is my temper. My son [Louis-Charles] cannot read and learns very badly but is too giddy to apply himself. He has no idea of his station in his head and I strongly desire that this continue; our children learn soon enough what they are.[10]

Marie Antoinette's instructions to Tourzel demonstrate both her close relationship with her children and the influence of Rousseau's philosophy of close childrearing on her approach to parenting. The queen cultivated a close bond with her children and observed their personalities, tailoring her parenting to their characters. Rousseau distrusted formal education for young children because he viewed them as mirrors who would reflect back the words and ideas of their elders without understanding them. Marie Antoinette was patient with her son, assuming that he would apply himself to his education as he grew older. The queen also tried to delay a distinctly royal upbringing for her children for as long as possible, attempting to shield them from the unique demands of their position. Tourzel accepted Marie Antoinette's parenting philosophy and became a trusted member of the queen's household, accompanying the royal family when they attempted to flee France in 1791.

Louis XVI was forced to abdicate in 1792 after the royal family was recognized and recaptured in the town of Varennes. The former king was placed on trial for crimes against the sovereignty of the French people later that year and executed by guillotine in 1793. Others members of the royal family were also tried and executed during what came to be known as the

Terror. The formal charges Marie Antoinette faced at her trial before the Revolutionary Tribunal in 1793 pertained to her contacts with Austria during the French Revolutionary Wars with the Habsburg Empire and other European powers, but the legal proceedings are remembered today for the accusations that she faced as a mother. Louis-Charles was taken from her care after Louis XVI's execution, and his new guardian Simon Hebert claimed to have discovered evidence that the queen had sexually abused her son. The accusations were intended to discredit Marie Antoinette as a wife and mother as well as a former queen. Instead, Marie Antoinette's reaction to the fabricated charges attracted widespread sympathy for her plight. According to the *Moniteur Universel* newspaper, Marie Antoinette declared: "'[I]f I have not responded, it is because nature refuses to respond to such a charge made against a mother.' (Here the accused appeared deeply moved) 'I appeal to all mothers who may be found here.'"[11] The tribunal recognized that this line of questioning might encourage the public to sympathize with the queen as a mother, and quickly returned the proceedings to her dealings with the Habsburg dynasty. Marie Antoinette was convicted of the charges of conspiring with foreign powers and guillotined on October 16, 1793.

The execution of Marie Antoinette orphaned her children. Louis-Charles died in prison in 1795. Marie-Thérèse was permitted to depart France for Austria in 1796. She married her cousin, Louis Antoine, Duke of Angoulême, and returned to France in 1814 when the monarchy was restored after the overthrow of Napoleon Bonaparte. Marie-Thérèse went into exile once more when her uncle and father-in-law, Charles X, was forced to abdicate in 1830, and died in 1851.

Marie Antoinette's possessions and those of her husband and children were sold by successive French governments in the aftermath of the revolution. Despite hostilities between Great Britain and France that continued until the end of the Napoleonic Wars, British collectors were particularly interested in eighteenth-century French art. During the reign of Queen Victoria, Marie Antoinette's personal possessions became especially popular collector's items. In 1839, two years after Victoria became queen, her aunt, Queen Louise of the Belgians, helped her acquire a series of French decorative pieces, including an ivory brisé fan with mother-of-pearl handles and a watercolour pastoral scene. Victoria was delighted with the items, and showed them to her prime minister, Lord Melbourne, during one of their regular meetings. Louise wrote to her niece, "I am very glad to hear that you approved of my modest offering [a dress] and that you were pleased with the fans. That of Marie Antoinette is really curious and I am glad that you purchased it. It would have been a pity if it had fallen into bad hands."[12]

Over the course of the nineteenth century, Marie Antoinette became part of popular culture in the English-speaking world, sentimentalized in historical novels and popular biographies. The fan became one of the most famous pieces in the Royal Collection.

Victoria's interest in Marie Antoinette, however, did not extend to emulating her approach to parenting. While Marie Antoinette expected the Governess of the Children of France to respect the individual personalities of her charges, Victoria required all nine of her children to absorb the values and demanding educational requirements imposed by her consort, Prince Albert of Saxe-Coburg-Gotha. The result was a continuation of the Hanover family tradition of the monarch disapproving of the conduct of the heir to the throne.

FIFTEEN

Victoria (1819-1901) and Albert of Saxe-Coburg-Gotha (1819-61)

In 1918, long after the deaths of her parents Queen Victoria and Prince Albert, Princess Louise, Duchess of Argyll, explained how parenting practices had evolved since her own childhood in the 1850s. Louise explained, "Luckily the habit of moulding all children to the same pattern has gone out of fashion. It was deplorable. I know, because I suffered from it. Nowadays individuality and one's own capabilities are recognised."[1] As the sixth of nine children, Louise received less attention from her parents than her elder siblings, and struggled to be recognized as a distinct personality in the crowded royal nursery. As she grew up, she attempted to distinguish herself by both defying her parents and attempting to outshine them in their own interests. The young Louise was nicknamed "Little Miss Why" for her willingness to question authority. After the death of her father Albert in 1861, Louise observed that public opinion was against Victoria's long seclusion as a widow, and encouraged her to be more visible to her subjects, a stance that brought her into conflict with her mother. At the same time, Louise inherited Victoria and Albert's love of art, and became the most accomplished amateur artist within her family, specializing in painting and sculpture. During her husband Lord Lorne's tenure as the fourth Governor General of Canada following Confederation (1878–83), Louise played a key role in the establishment of the Royal Canadian Academy of Arts and the National Gallery of Canada. Despite their frequent conflicts during her daughter's youth, Victoria acknowledged that the adult Louise was "(and who would some years ago have thought it?) a clever dear girl with a fine strong character, and a very marked character — unselfish and affectionate, a good daughter with a wonderful talent for art."[2]

Victoria's conflicts with the young Louise and then her ability to recognize the good qualities possessed by her adult daughter were characteristic of her relationships with all nine of her children. Victoria had little patience with childrearing and left the management of the nurseries to her consort, Albert. When her children became adults, Victoria was able to recognize their positive qualities, though she became critical again when she observed the upbringings of her grandchildren. Victoria's relationship with her eldest son and heir, the future King Edward VII, however, remained difficult over the course of her reign.

Both Victoria and Albert had experienced unhappy childhoods supervised by a lone parent, and therefore sought parental figures outside their immediate families. Victoria's father was George III's fourth son, Prince Edward, Duke of Kent. As a younger son with a dozen surviving siblings, Edward never envisioned a role for himself as father of the heir to the throne. Instead of contracting a dynastic marriage to a suitable princess, he enjoyed a decades-long relationship with a French mistress, Julie St. Laurent. Julie was treated as Edward's official companion during his extended residence in what is now Canada in the 1790s, which culminated in his appointment as Commander-in-Chief of the British North American forces. The death of Edward's niece, Princess Charlotte, daughter of the future George IV, and only legitimate grandchild of George III, in 1817, made a dynastic marriage imperative for the middle-aged prince. He proposed to Victoire of Saxe-Coburg-Saalfeld, a thirty-year-old widow with two children. Edward was proud of their only child, Victoria, and brought the infant out of the nursery to appear with him at public events, including military reviews. Edward's death from pneumonia when Victoria was only nine months old changed the course of the infant princess's upbringing. The upbringing of a fatherless royal child with the potential to succeed to the throne usually occurred under the supervision of the monarch. Instead of granting custody to George IV, however, Edward gave Victoire guardianship of Victoria in his will. There had not been a document granting such authority over childrearing to a British royal mother since the marriage contract between Charles I and Henrietta Maria in 1625. Victoire did not get along with her brothers-in-law, and kept the young Victoria from court as much as possible, raising her in comparative isolation at Kensington Palace. Fearing plots against her daughter's life, Victoire insisted that they share a bedroom and that a servant accompany the princess up and down staircases. The only respite from this routine was a series of public engagements initiated by Victoire to show Victoria to her future subjects. The young princess recorded these excursions in her journal, which was read by her mother. As she grew older, Victoria became increasingly discontented with her mother's strictures and idealized the memory of her father, admiring a series of paternal figures over the course of her youth, including her uncle, Leopold I, King of the Belgians, and her first prime minister, Lord Melbourne.

While Victoria grew up without a father, Albert grew up without a mother. The marriage of his parents, Ernst I, Duke of Saxe-Coburg and Gotha, and Louise of Saxe-Gotha-Altenburg, was unhappy, and they were unfaithful to each other. Ernst and Louise separated when Albert was five and divorced when he was seven. Ernst retained custody of his sons, and Albert never saw his mother again. The family scandal shaped Albert's approach to fatherhood as an adult, and he was determined to ensure that his children grew up in a stable family environment. He had little tolerance for what he perceived to be the moral lapses of others.

While Victoria was more forgiving of courtiers who engaged in extramarital affairs, she had absorbed her mother's disapproval of the conduct of her uncles and predecessors, George IV and William IV. Victoria and Albert therefore shared a commitment to making the monarchy respectable again after the excesses of the Hanoverian monarchs. In contrast to George and William, who were best known for their gambling, mistresses, and extravagant spending, Victoria's family would present an image of domestic virtue in tune with the values of the growing urban middle class of nineteenth-century Britain.

Victoria and Albert were married in 1840, three years after Victoria succeeded to the throne, and ultimately became the parents of nine children — Victoria ("Vicky") (1840–1901), Albert Edward ("Bertie") (1841–1910), Alice (1843 –78), Alfred (1844–1900), Helena (1846–1923), Louise (1848–1939), Arthur (1850–1942), Leopold (1853–84), and Beatrice (1857–1944).

In just a few generations, the childrearing practices of Britain's elite had been transformed by the development of a distinct nursery culture. While eighteenth-century parents incorporated their children into their social lives, Victoria and Albert's children lived in a parallel world to that of their mother and father, with their daily routines shaped by nursemaids and tutors. The self-functioning nursery followed the parenting dictates of the mid-nineteenth century.

In 1861, the published volume of *Mrs. Beeton's Book of Household Management*, edited by Isabella Beeton, a middle-class wife and mother in her twenties, stated with authority, "The nursery is of great importance in every family, and in families of distinction, where there are several young children, it is an establishment kept apart from the rest of the family, under the charge of an upper nurse, assisted by under nursery-maids proportioned to the work to be done."[3] Beeton emphasized the importance of separate spheres for parents and children throughout her text. She accepted the practice of women hiring wet nurses and stated that even women who nursed their own infants should allow a nursemaid to take charge of them when it was time for weaning. Children were not supposed to accompany their mothers on social calls unless there was a very close friendship between the caller and woman receiving the visit, and the children were exceptionally well-behaved. The nursery had its own routines separate from the rest of the household, and the children were fed bland meals designed to aid their developing digestive systems.

The separation of the nursery from the rest of the household was part of a wider trend toward separate spheres within the family following the Industrial Revolution. Prior to industrialization, the entire family had participated in the household economy, but increased urbanization and new modes of work meant that middle-class men increasingly left the home to work while the domestic sphere became a female domain. Within that distinct domestic sphere, the nursery had its own place apart from the rest of the household.

A nursery wing separate from the usual functioning of the household suited Queen Victoria, who was deeply ambivalent about motherhood. She had a strong aversion to childbirth, which she described as "the only thing I dread."[4] Her views may have been informed by accounts of the death of her cousin Charlotte in childbirth. The rituals surrounding the births of royal children also offended the queen's sense of modesty. The wives and daughters-in-law of the Hanoverian monarchs usually gave birth in the presence of government officials, but Victoria insisted that the prime minister, the Archbishop of Canterbury, and other witnesses remain in the adjoining room. The actual birthing chamber was restricted to the queen herself, her female attendants, doctors, and Albert, who was the first British royal father to be present for the births of his children since James II in 1688. After Vicky was born in 1840, Victoria wrote in her journal, "Dearest Albert hardly left me at all, & was the greatest support & comfort."[5]

Albert would continue to be a support to Victoria in the nursery, as the queen had little interest in young children, complaining when Vicky was expecting her own firstborn that "an ugly baby is a very nasty object — and the prettiest is frightful when undressed — till about four months; in short, as long as they have their big body and little limbs and that terrible frog-like action."[6] In contrast, Albert visited the nurseries frequently during the infancy of his elder children, insisting on the removal of Victoria's former governess Baroness Louise Lezhen from the royal household after Vicky developed an illness that he attributed to poor care from her nursemaids.

Victoria was the first reigning queen in the British Isles to balance monarchy with motherhood since James I's mother, the ill-fated Mary, Queen of Scots, in the sixteenth century. Victoria made clear that she did not consider the family circumstances of past reigning queens to have any influence on her own position. When Albert was granted an annual stipend of £30,000, which was £20,000 less than the annuity that had been awarded to Queen Anne's consort, George, Victoria protested that her husband should not be treated as less important than Anne's "stupid and insignificant husband."[7] Instead, Victoria sought support and advice in her unusual position from her female royal contemporaries in Europe. One of her closest friends and correspondents was Queen Maria II of Portugal, who also raised a large family while reigning as queen. Victoria wrote to Maria's consort and co-ruler, Ferdinand of Saxe-Coburg-Saalfeld, in 1847: "Our positions, yours and Albert's, and Maria's and mine, are so similar that we understand each other thoroughly."[8] Victoria admired Maria's deference to Ferdinand within the family circle and allowed Albert a similar leadership role in the upbringing of their children.

Albert's involvement in the royal nursery differentiated Victoria's family from that of her subjects. Nineteenth-century British childrearing advice emphasized the mother's responsibility for the moral character of her children. Even elite women who spent little time in the nursery were expected to select nursemaids who would ensure that their children absorbed proper values. According to *Cassell's Household Guide*, first published in 1869, "A mother, as the being nearest and dearest to the almost unconscious infant, should act not only as the appointed guardian of its bodily welfare, but should also extend her care and effect to the proper development and culture of its mind."[9] If a child developed a weak moral character, the mother was solely responsible. In contrast, Victoria left the education and moral development of her children to Albert. Victoria and Albert's family was therefore structured in a manner closer to that of the German housefather books that shaped Frederick of Bohemia's approach to fatherhood in the seventeenth century than to nineteenth-century British conceptions of a mother's responsibility to her children.

Albert planned the education of his children, especially the two eldest, Vicky and Bertie, with great care. In consultation with his mentor, Baron Christian von Stockmar, Albert approved a demanding educational program with lessons from 9:00 a.m. to 7:00 p.m., Monday to Saturday, including English, French, German, history, geography, math, music, drawing, and handwriting. Stockmar explained the importance of a thorough education for the royal children, stating, "The first truth by which the Queen and the Prince ought to be thoroughly penetrated is, that their position is a more difficult one than that of any parents in the kingdom: because the Royal children ought not only to be brought up to be moral characters, but also fitted to discharge successfully the arduous duties which may eventually devolve upon them as future sovereigns."[10]

In Stockmar's view, the failings of George IV and William IV were the result of poor parenting by their father, George III, who did not pay sufficient attention to their education. While Vicky thrived on Stockmar's rigorous curriculum, Bertie was not academically inclined and often cried during his lessons. Albert reacted to Bertie's outbursts by administering corporal punishment personally. Victoria and Albert both favoured strict discipline for their children. When Vicky lied about whether she was permitted to wear a new bonnet, her hands were tied behind her back.

Victoria and Albert also expected their children to acquire practical skills, a practice that continued among their descendants. When their granddaughters married into Europe's royal houses, their ability to make beds and cook simple meals distinguished them from other women at court, and these domestic abilities were seen as distinctively British characteristics for royal women.

For the British public, Albert's position as royal consort was inseparable from his role as a father to a large family. Satirical cartoons depicted Albert surrounded by numerous children, the youngest riding on his back. Although Victoria and Albert were admired for their domestic virtues, these portrayals of the Prince Consort as a doting family man were not always positive. When Victoria and Albert married, the press lampooned him as a poor German prince, travelling to England to make his fortune by marrying the queen. As the royal children grew older, the cost of providing dowries and annuities for such a large royal family became a matter of public and parliamentary debate. The maintenance of nine royal children appeared to be a drain on public expenses rather than a benefit to the nation, despite the extensive philanthropy undertaken by all of the royal children as they grew older. Albert's lofty educational goals were greeted with skepticism among Britain's elite. Lord Melbourne, cautioned the queen, "Be not over solicitous about education. It may be able to do much, but it does not do so much as is expected from it. It may mould and direct the character, but it rarely alters it."[11] Victoria herself appears to have questioned the suitability of Stockmar's educational program for Bertie on occasion, but she did not interfere with Albert's authority over the upbringing of their children.

Victoria may have been ambivalent about motherhood, but as queen of an expanding British Empire in the age of railways, steamships, telegrams, and photography, she had a greater global impact on parenting practices than any previous monarch. In Canada, Lucy Maud

Montgomery, author of *Anne of Green Gables*, reminisced more than two decades after the queen's death, "When I was a child and young girl the Victoria myth was in full flower. We were brought up to believe that 'the Queen' from babyhood to old age was a model for all girls, brides and queens to follow. In those days, every home boasted a framed picture of 'the Queen'."[12]

Victoria demonstrated her ability to influence cultural trends from the moment that she married Albert. In contrast to previous royal brides, such as her cousin Charlotte, who chose an elaborate cloth-of-silver gown that was difficult for ordinary women to copy, Victoria was married in a comparatively simple white dress with orange blossoms. Engravings of the queen in her wedding dress were printed in newspapers around the world, starting a trend for white wedding dresses that continues to the present day.

When the royal children were born, the public were curious to learn about life in the royal nursery. The new medium of photography brought images of the royal family to a wide audience. Victoria was the first British monarch to be photographed, and early images emphasized her role as a mother. The earliest known photograph of Victoria, dating from 1845, portrays her in a comparatively simple lace-trimmed dress without any royal regalia, with a protective arm around her five-year-old daughter Vicky.

Postcards depicting photographs of the royal children on holiday with their parents at Osbourne House on the Isle of Wight and at Balmoral Castle in Scotland were purchased by middle-class consumers. Victoria and Albert were the first royal couple to take family holidays with all of their children. The growth of railways and statutory holidays in Britain over the course of the nineteenth century made family vacations accessible to a broader range of the queen's subjects than ever before, allowing people from a variety of social backgrounds to take their children for a day at the seaside.

The public also emulated royal Christmas celebrations. In the eighteenth century, Christmas was a comparatively modest holiday spent with friends and neighbours. When the *London Illustrated News* published a cover image of Victoria, Albert, their children, and Victoria's mother, Victoire, gathered around a Christmas tree in 1848, accompanied by a detailed article about Christmas celebrations at Windsor Castle, the holiday was transformed into a family occasion centred around children. The German-style Christmas tree had been part of royal celebrations since the reign of George III, but increased press coverage of royal occasions during Victoria's reign resulted in the custom being associated with Albert in the British popular imagination.

Perhaps the greatest impact of Victoria's motherhood on the experiences of mothers from a diverse range of social backgrounds was her use of anesthesia to mitigate the pain of childbirth. Chloroform was first administered during childbirth in 1847. This intervention was controversial because the Bible stated that women were destined to suffer in labour as punishment for Eve's disobedience in the Garden of Eden. Professor Charles Meigs objected strongly to providing anesthesia for childbirth in an article for the 1849 edition of *The British and Foreign Medico-chirurgical Review* in which he compared mothers who used chloroform to drunkards and implored physicians not "to contravene the operation of those natural and physiological forces that the Divinity has ordained us to enjoy or suffer."[13] Victoria disregarded these critiques of childbirth anesthesia and breathed chloroform from a handkerchief for the births of her two youngest children, Leopold and Beatrice. The queen made it clear that she was pleased with the results of this new medical innovation, describing chloroform as "soothing, quieting and delightful beyond measure."[14] Once chloroform had the royal seal of approval, it became known as *anaestheasia à la Reine* and became fashionable for women in labour.

Victoria also set precedents that would have a lasting impact on the upbringing of future generations of royal children. Buckingham Palace — known in the eighteenth century as Buckingham House — was a favourite home of Queen Charlotte, and had been renovated according to designs drawn up by her eldest son, George IV. St. James's Palace, however, remained the official residence of the royal family in London. Victoria's uncle and immediate predecessor, William IV, twice attempted to give Buckingham Palace away, once to the navy and once to the government (after the Houses of Parliament burned down in 1832). Only during Victoria's reign did Buckingham Palace assume the significance it enjoys today as both an official royal residence and a family home for royalty. Victoria commissioned an additional wing to provide nursery rooms for her growing family, and Buckingham Palace assumed its current shape and status as both a family home and a setting for official entertaining. In Scotland, Balmoral Castle remains the private property of the monarch, and is the place where Queen Elizabeth II and members of her family spend part of the summer and autumn.

When it was time for her children to be christened, Victoria introduced new customs, popular in the royal family to the present day, to separate her own family from Hanoverian court ceremonies and scandals. The existing baptismal font had been used for both royal children and the ten children of the future King William IV and his mistress Dorothea Jordan. A new silver gilt font, known as the lily font, designed by Albert, was introduced for Vicky's christening in 1841 and has been used for most British royal christenings to the present day. Victoria also commissioned a Honiton lace christening gown for Vicky that would be worn by generations of royal children. By 2004, the original gown was too delicate to be worn, and Elizabeth II's dressmaker created an exact replica for subsequent royal babies. In 2015, William and Kate's daughter Charlotte became the seventh royal baby to be christened in the replica of the gown first designed for Victoria's children.

When they married and became parents themselves, Victoria and Albert's children experienced the tension between the tradition of dynastic marriage and the expectation of both their parents and the public that they would find a degree of personal happiness with their spouses. In 1855, Vicky became privately engaged to Crown Prince Frederick of Prussia when she was only fourteen and "Fritz" was twenty-four. Victoria wrote that her daughter was "nervous but did not hesitate or falter in giving her very decided answer" and "behaved as a girl of 18 would, so naturally, so quietly & modestly & yet showing how strong her feelings are."[15] The newly engaged couple had met only once before. Vicky's strong feelings, therefore, may have included the desire to please her parents, who had long been in favour of the match, and the knowledge that there was a limited range of suitable spouses for the eldest daughter of the British monarch.

Bertie's choice of bride was even more circumscribed. A careful study of the *Almanach de Gotha*, a guide to Europe's royal houses, revealed that there were only seven Protestant European princesses of the right age to marry the heir to the throne. In 1863, he married Alexandra of Denmark. She was a politically sensitive choice because of territorial disputes between the German and Danish monarchs, but Queen Victoria admired her comparatively modest upbringing and Bertie considered her to be the most beautiful of the princesses under consideration.

For Victoria and Albert's younger daughters, the range of available spouses was slightly broader. Louise married a Scottish aristocrat, John Campbell, Lord Lorne, the future Duke of Argyll, becoming the first British princess to marry a non-royal spouse since Henry VIII's sister Mary secretly married Charles Brandon, Duke of Suffolk, in 1515.

With the exception of Louise, all nine of Victoria and Albert's children had children of their own, providing the queen with more than forty grandchildren. Victoria expressed little excitement about her growing family. When Bertie's daughter Victoria was born in 1868, the queen remarked that the arrival of her fourteenth grandchild and seventh granddaughter was "a very uninteresting thing — for it seems to me to go on like the rabbits in Windsor Park."[16]

While parents all over the English-speaking world made efforts to follow aspects of the queen's example in their family life, her own sons and daughters made decisions about the upbringing of their own children that broke with the practices established by Victoria and Albert. The conflicts over parenting between Victoria and her grown children began when it was time to choose names for the royal grandchildren. In the names she chose for her own children, Victoria distanced herself from her Hanover ancestry. Her two eldest children were named Victoria after herself and Albert Edward after her husband and father respectively. The younger children were named for figures who were important to Victoria and Albert rather than past royalty. Arthur honoured the elderly Duke of Wellington, who had defeated Napoleon at the battle of Waterloo and served as the infant prince's godfather. Louise was named for Prince Albert's mother and Leopold for their uncle, King Leopold of the Belgians. For her second daughter, Victoria chose the name Alice in consultation with Lord Melbourne after a long discussion about the girls' names that they found most attractive. Victoria expected to be consulted in the choice of names for her grandchildren and made clear that Victoria and Albert should continue to appear as royal baby names to mark the line. In some instances, the queen's wishes prevailed. At her insistence, Bertie named his eldest son Albert Victor. Alice named her eldest daughter Victoria Alberta. There were so many Victorias among the queen's granddaughters that they were differentiated by nicknames such as Toria (Bertie's second daughter, Princess Victoria of Wales), Moretta (Vicky's second daughter, Princess Viktoria of Prussia), and Ducky (Alfred's second daughter, Princess Victoria Melita of Saxe-Coburg-Gotha).

To Queen Victoria's dismay, however, her children also revived royal names popular with the Hanoverian monarchs. Bertie chose the names George Frederick for his second son, who eventually reigned as King George V, prompting Victoria to write, "I fear I cannot admire the names you propose to give the Baby. I had hoped for some fine old name. Frederick is, however, the best of the two and I hope you will call him so; George only came over with the Hanoverian family…. Of course you will add Albert at the end, like your brothers …"[17]

When Vicky chose to name her eldest daughter Victoria Elizabeth Augusta Charlotte and call her Charlotte, Victoria scolded her in a letter, "I do hope one of your daughters, if you have any more will be called Victoria, so that there may be the 4 generations of Victorias." Victoria continued to make her views known about the names of her great-grandchildren. When George and his wife, Mary of Teck, chose the name Edward for their eldest son, the future Edward VIII, in honour of George's deceased brother, Albert Victor, who was nicknamed Eddy, Victoria wrote, "Of course if you wish Edward to be the first name I shall not object, only I think you write as if Edward was the real name of dear Eddy, while it was Albert Victor."[18] Queen Victoria's correspondence with her children and grandchildren demonstrates that names that are now considered timeless for royal babies such as George, Charlotte, and Edward were reintroduced into the royal family over the objections of the queen, and paired with Victoria or Albert to acknowledge her wishes.

The disagreements between Victoria and her grown children over the upbringing of her grandchildren did not end with choices of names. While Victoria complained of the physical hardships endured by women who experienced pregnancy and childbirth, her three elder daughters idealized the process of creating and nurturing a new life and embraced the physical bond with their children. Vicky breastfed her children herself over the objections of both her mother and her mother-in-law. When Victoria complained in a letter to her half-sister Feodora that Vicky was breastfeeding, Feodora replied, "I am sorry to find that Vicky's determination to nurse makes you so angry.... the Queen of Prussia feels the same as you. I have no opinion ... as I have always felt it a duty for a mother to nurse a child if she can and if the doctors approve."[19] Alice followed her sister's example, prompting Victoria to give the name Princess Alice to a cow in the royal dairy. Alice's interest in motherhood extended beyond her own family, and as Grand Duchess of Hesse-Darmstadt, she founded hospitals to care for expectant mothers, reducing maternal mortality.

Queen Victoria's third daughter, Helena, Princess Christian of Schleswig-Holstein, kept her own daughters close to her from a young age, involving them in her philanthropic activities. Helena's daughter, Princess Marie Louise, recalled in her memoirs, "I can still remember, at the age of six, trying to roll a bandage destined to be sent out to the sick and wounded in the Russo-Turkish war of 1878."[20]

Only Beatrice maintained a degree of distance from the physical demands of motherhood as her responsibilities as her mother's unofficial secretary and devotion to her husband, Prince Henry of Battenberg, precluded spending large amounts of time of the nursery. The very fact that Beatrice was married with children of her own, however, was an act of defiance against Victoria's conception of the duties of a youngest daughter to her mother. Victoria intended to keep an unmarried Beatrice at home as her companion and only allowed the twenty-eight-year-old princess to marry in 1885 on the condition that she and her husband would continue to make their home with the queen. Victoria's expectations of Beatrice were in keeping with broader parenting trends among Britain's elite, where it was assumed that one of the daughters in a large family would remain at home.

While Victoria's daughters embraced the physical demands of parenting, her sons left childrearing to their wives, rejecting Albert's example of close involvement in his children's upbringing and education. For Victoria's male-line grandchildren, fathers were distant or absent figures idealized by their children. Bertie ceded childrearing almost entirely to his wife Alexandra, and showed little interest in their schooling. His sons Albert Victor and George received undemanding lessons from a mediocre tutor before being sent to sea, and his daughters Louise, Toria, and Maud "could just read and write, period,"[21] according to their nephew, Edward VIII.

A demanding schedule of naval duties and tours of the British Empire separated Prince Alfred, Duke of Edinburgh, from his family for months at a time, and he allowed all major decisions concerning his son and four daughters to be made by his wife, Grand Duchess Maria Alexandrovna of Russia, including those regarding their marriages. When Maria selected the future King Ferdinand of Romania as a husband for her eldest daughter, Marie, Alfred did not interfere even though Victoria observed "it was the dream of [Alfred's] life" for Marie to marry her English cousin, the future King George V.[22]

Prince Arthur, Duke of Connaught, allowed his wife, Louise Margaret of Prussia, to impose her frugality on their three children. Their younger daughter, Princess Patricia, wore her elder sister's hand-me-down clothes and developed lifelong foot pain from the ill-fitting shoes that her mother insisted that she wear as a child. Patricia became closer to her father as an adult when she acted as his hostess while he served as Governor General of Canada from 1911 to 1916.

Prince Leopold, Duke of Albany, died of complications from hemophilia before his son was born and when his daughter was still an infant, and therefore could not be a presence in the lives of his two children.

Victoria's granddaughters often became mothers far from their childhood homes. In addition to Queen Marie of Romania, four of the queen's granddaughters became queens or empresses consort. Bertie and Alexandra's daughter Maud married her cousin Prince Charles of Denmark and they became King and Queen of Norway in 1905. Vicky's daughter Sophie married King Constantine I of Greece. Beatrice's daughter Victoria Eugenia married King Alfonso XIII of Spain. Both Sophie and Victoria Eugenia raised their families amid political upheaval and ended their lives in exile from their marital homes.

Of all the illustrious marriages contracted by her granddaughters, however, Victoria worried the most about Alice's youngest daughter Alix, who married Emperor Nicholas II of Russia in 1894 and took the name Alexandra upon her conversion to the Russian Orthodox faith. Victoria wrote to Alexandra's eldest sister, Victoria of Battenberg, at the time of the engagement, "Oh! darling Victoria, the more I think of sweet Alicky's marriage the more unhappy I am! *Not* as to the personality, for I like him *very much* but on acct. of the Country the policy & differences with us & the awful insecurity to wh. that sweet Child will be exposed."[23] Victoria's concerns for her granddaughter were prescient. Nicholas, Alexandra, and all five of their children would become victims of the Russian Revolution.

SIXTEEN

Nicholas II of Russia (1868-1918) and Alexandra of Hesse-Darmstadt (1872-1918)

In 1896, the newly crowned Emperor Nicholas II of Russia embarked on a coronation tour of Europe with his wife, Empress Alexandra, and their ten-month-old baby daughter, Grand Duchess Olga. Royal babies rarely accompanied their parents on foreign tours in the nineteenth century.

When Queen Victoria had visited the court of Napoleon III in 1855, she was accompanied by Albert and her two eldest children, but her six younger children remained in England. Nicholas and Alexandra's itinerary also included a state visit to France, to cement the Franco-Russian alliance concluded during the previous reign. The other countries on the tour, however, were monarchies with close ties to Nicholas, a grandson of King Christian IX and Queen Louise of Denmark through his mother, and Alexandra, a granddaughter of Victoria.

Then, as now, including a baby in a royal tour was a complicated endeavour, as Olga's public appearances had to be carefully balanced with her daily routines. Nicholas was not enthusiastic about a multi-month royal tour so soon after his coronation, and he complained in a letter to his brother Grand Duke Georgy about the expected rigours of travelling with a baby: "We shall have to drag our poor little daughter with us, as all the relatives want to see her. I can imagine what the French will get up to in Paris — maybe they really will rename [her] Napoleondra or something like it!"[1]

Nicholas was correct to surmise that a royal baby on tour would quickly become a celebrity, particularly in countries such as France that were no longer monarchies and rarely saw royal children in person. Olga attracted press attention everywhere she went. In Paris, French crowds cheered "*Vive la bebé*" every time she appeared in public and Olga became a popular girls name in France in 1896. Even Olga's nanny became a celebrity during her time in France, prompting cheers of "*Vive la Nounou*" when she appeared in public with the imperial baby.[2] The lavish gifts bestowed on the infant as she toured Europe received widespread press coverage and even impressed royal relatives. Grand Duchess Marie Pavlovna, a cousin of Nicholas II who was just five years older than Olga, recalled in her memoirs, "[My brother] Dmitri and I spent hours examining our young cousins' toys; one could never tire of them, they were so fine. Especially enchanting to me was the French President's gift to Olga.... In a trunk covered with soft leather was a doll with a complete trousseau: dresses, lingerie, hats, slippers, the entire equipment of a dressing table, all reproduced with remarkable art and fidelity."[3] Alexandra's cousin, Kaiser Wilhelm II of Germany, also presented Olga and later her younger sisters with life-sized dolls.

In England, a photograph of Nicholas, Alexandra, and their baby daughter made the front cover of the *London Illustrated News.* The imperial family's visit to Queen Victoria at Balmoral was the first royal tour to be captured by newsreel cameras. Olga made a good impression on her great-grandmother. Despite Victoria's long history of criticizing daughters and granddaughters who engaged in what she considered "baby worship," the queen wrote to Alexandra's sister, Victoria, "Is not Baby Olga too delicious? She is one of the most charming babies I ever saw."[4] Olga returned to Russia with the approval of both her royal relatives and the public across Europe.

Olga and her younger sisters, Tatiana (born 1897), Maria (born 1899), and Anastasia (born 1901), as well as her brother Alexei (born 1904), all accompanied their parents on subsequent royal visits across Europe, continuing the popular fascination with the imperial children. Both Nicholas and Alexandra were fascinated by photography and film and passed these interests to their children, encouraging them to take and develop photographs and create scrapbooks of family holidays. Anastasia may have been the first teenager to take a selfie, holding her camera in front of the mirror to take a photograph of her reflection. Nicholas and Alexandra were also enthusiastic diarists and letter writers and encouraged their children to also keep careful records of their lives. The result is one of the best-documented reigning families in history, living at a technological crossroads when photography had become a popular elite pastime but extensive written correspondence had not yet been superseded by the telephone.

The careful records that Nicholas, Alexandra, and their children kept of their family life were not only for private consumption. The Russian imperial family were among the first reigning houses to craft a public image through the use of modern media. Alexandra gave her children's Irish nanny Margaret Eagar permission to write a memoir of her years working in the Romanov nursery. Eagar explained to the British magazine the *Leisure Hour*, "Shortly after the birth of the Czarowitch [Alexei], I said to the Empress that I often had thought of writing my memoirs. She encouraged me to do so, saying so many untruths had been published, that it would be a relief to have an account of the Russian court that was absolutely true."[5] When the Romanov dynasty celebrated its tercentennial in 1913, Nicholas commissioned an authorized biography of himself for Russian readers, emphasizing the virtues of his family's comparatively modest domestic life. Like Victoria and Albert, Nicholas and Alexandra attempted to differentiate themselves from the decadent image of the aristocracy, issuing postcards depicting their children in comparatively casual dress on family holidays in addition to formal portraits in court dress. Nicholas and Alexandra's efforts to engage with the public made their children international celebrities who received fan mail from as far away as the United States, but did not succeed in improving the imperial family's reputation in Russia. Nicholas may have embraced modern technologies, but he remained Europe's last absolute monarch.

Behind the official image of the imperial family was another narrative that was carefully censored by Nicholas and Alexandra. Like her cousin, Victoria Eugenia, Queen of Spain, and her sister Irene, Alexandra was a carrier of hemophilia, a disease inhibiting the clotting of the blood, passed by female carriers to their sons. Of Victoria Eugenia's four sons, two suffered from hemophilia. Nicholas and Alexandra had only one son, Alexei, who was diagnosed with the disease soon after birth when a midwife swaddled him too tightly. The imperial couple lived in fear that a bruise or nosebleed would be fatal. There were no effective medical treatments for hemophilia in the twentieth century, making the condition seem more like a curse than a disease. Alexandra explained to a lady-in-waiting, "If only you knew how fervently I have prayed for God to protect my son from our inherited curse."[6] In desperation, Alexandra turned to peasant faith healers, most famously Grigori Rasputin, who seemed to be able to alleviate Alexei's symptoms through his prayers. The public was unaware of both the precise nature of Alexei's illness and the purpose of Rasputin's visits with the imperial family. This uncertainty fueled salacious rumours about the Siberian peasant's personal and political influence over the empress. Concern for Alexei shattered Alexandra's own health. Her daughters took turns caring for her in private and, as they grew older, representing her in public. The fundamental laws promulgated by Catherine the Great's son Paul I in 1797 forbade women from succeeding to the Russian throne while there were living male members of the House of Romanov, but Alexei's health meant that Nicholas considered amending the line of succession to place his daughters immediately after his son.

Nicholas was closely involved in the upbringing of his children and integrated them into the spheres in which he was most comfortable, including outdoor pursuits and the military. Nicholas's own parents had emphasized the importance of family cohesion and a close domestic sphere secluded from court ceremonies. His mother, Princess Dagmar of Denmark (Empress Marie Feodorovna), was close to her parents and extended family, and Nicholas had therefore attended numerous family gatherings in Denmark as a child, developing lasting friendships with his cousins, including the future King George V. Nicholas's father, Alexander III, enjoyed spending time in nature with his children, taking them hiking and mushroom picking in the islands in the Gulf of Finland. Nicholas inherited his father's love of the outdoors and scheduled daily exercise in the company of his children. Olga, Tatiana, Maria, and Anastasia joined their father for long walks, rowing, and tennis matches. Alexei was not permitted to play tennis because of the risk of injury, but he enjoyed boating and swimming.

The happiest period of Nicholas II's life before becoming czar was his military service, and he also passed this interest to his children. At the age of fourteen, each of his four daughters became an honorary Colonel-in-Chief of her own regiment, attending military reviews in dress uniform, creating a further bond with their father. Olga and Tatiana's second cousin Prince Gabriel Constantinovich described them reviewing their regiments at a 1913 military parade, writing, "They mounted their horses in a horsewoman way sitting sidesaddle. They wore their regiment uniforms in the rank of colonels…. Olga Nicholaevna greeted the regiment and made her rounds…. The heir with his younger sisters watched the parade from their tent…. I believe the Emperor was very proud as he watched his daughters for the first — and alas! — for the last time in a military line-up."[7]

During the First World War, Olga and Tatiana trained as nurses alongside their mother and chaired philanthropic committees, while Maria and Anastasia volunteered in a hospital. They were among the few women permitted to enter Russian military headquarters in Mogliev during the First World War, visiting Nicholas and Alexei with their mother. After Nicholas appointed himself Commander-in-Chief of the Russian Army in 1915, Alexei resided with him in Mogliev for months at a time. When Alexei's health made it necessary for him to receive care at home, Nicholas wrote to Alexandra of how quiet and lonely military headquarters seemed without the presence of his son.

While Nicholas incorporated his children into his public role and recreational pursuits, enjoying their companionship as they grew older, Alexandra treated parenthood as a sacred duty. In a series of private notes about marriage and parenting, she outlined her philosophy, writing, "The greatest treasure that parents can leave their children is a happy childhood, with tender memories of father and mother. It will lighten the forthcoming days, it will preserve them from temptation, and it will help them face the harsh realities of life after they leave the parental roof." According to Alexandra, a happy childhood was not an indulgent one. Instead, "Children should learn self-denial. They cannot have everything they want. They should learn to reject their own desires for the sake of other people." Alexandra's parenting philosophy did not reflect the values of the Russian elite; English governesses employed by Russian noble families often commented on the relaxed attitude toward young children's behaviour, who took their meals with their parents and adult guests instead of being sequestered in the nursery.[8] Alexandra's parenting philosophy made her seem more British than Russian.

Alexandra's own upbringing had been strongly influenced by her grandmother Queen Victoria, and she brought British customs to Russia. While the adolescent daughters of Russian noble families in Moscow and St. Petersburg had busy social schedules and often slept until noon, Alexandra insisted that her daughters rise early and occupy themselves with useful pursuits, including lessons, reading, and handicrafts such as knitting and embroidery. The empress's efforts to encourage Russian noblewomen to knit a certain number of garments each year for the poor were unsuccessful, but her own daughters were involved in numerous philanthropic endeavours from childhood, including selling flowers to fund tuberculosis sanitariums in the Crimea. Alexandra expected her daughters to set an example to others both at home and in public, and her notes to them encouraged good behaviour at all times.

Not all of Alexandra's parenting was prescriptive. At Christmas time, Alexandra hosted festive celebrations reminiscent of her own childhood in England and Germany. Her friend Anna Vyrubova wrote, "The first fir-tree to be lit was that in the nursery and it was the time when the children got presents. Sometimes their presents were very expensive but the Tsar's children never thought of how much they might cost. They were equally happy when they got a small crafted thing or a cheap toy."[9] Alexandra also ensured that there were presents for the servants as well as the soldiers and officers who guarded the imperial palaces. The children joined their parents in distributing these gifts, with the grand duchesses presenting silver coins to the military personnel.

Although Nicholas and Alexandra employed a British nursery staff while their daughters were young, following a tradition that had existed at the Russian court since the early nineteenth century, they did not allow nannies and governesses to interfere with their individual parenting philosophies. Nursery staff who questioned the imperial couple's parenting were quickly dismissed. Nicholas wrote to Georgy of his disagreements with the nursery staff, complaining in December 1895 about the arrival of one of Olga's first nursemaids from England, "In general she's going to be a lot of trouble and I am ready to bet that things are not going to go smoothly. For instance, she has already decided that our daughter does not have enough rooms, and that, in her opinion, [Alexandra] pops into the nursery too often. How do you like that? It's all very boring, especially when the first apple turns out to be rotten."[10] The troublesome nanny was quickly dismissed. Subsequent English nannies proved equally unsatisfactory. A nursemaid was dismissed after developing a drinking problem and being caught in bed with a soldier. Margaret Eagar became so engrossed in a discussion with a fellow nanny about the Dreyfus case in France that she forgot the toddler Maria in the bathtub, an incident that may have contributed to her eventual dismissal.

After the birth of their only son Alexei in 1904, Nicholas and Alexandra began to appoint more Russian nursery staff. Marie Pavlovna recalled, "two of their Russian nurses were peasants and wore magnificent native peasant costumes."[11]

The introduction of Russian nursery staff did not end the turmoil in the imperial nurseries. While foreign tutors assigned to teach the imperial children English or French wrote of Rasputin as a colourful character whom they rarely saw in person, certain Russian members of the household were shocked by his visits and voiced their disapproval. Alexandra Bogdanovich, the wife of one of Nicholas's generals, recorded in her diary in 1910 that Empress Alexandra "is incensed with those who have been saying that [Rasputin] is a scoundrel and so on. [The grand duchesses' governess] Tiutcheva and the senior nanny Vishniakova have therefore been placed on leave for two months."[12] Nicholas considered Sophia Tiutcheva's disapproval of Rasputin's visits to the nursery to be a critique of his actions as a father. The imperial children managed to maintain warm relations with their former servants, even those who had been in conflict with their parents. When they visited Moscow in 1913, the grand duchesses visited Tiutcheva and maintained a correspondence with her. In all their dealings with their household, Nicholas and Alexandra's daughters insisted on being addressed by their names, instead of their titles, and expressed embarrassment on being introduced as "Imperial Highness" at philanthropic committee meetings.

When Nicholas and Alexandra's children grew to adulthood, their parents' concerns shifted from finding suitable nannies to finding suitable sons-in-law. The fundamental laws governing the succession required all grand dukes and grand duchesses to make equal marriages to members of other royal houses. Nicholas II's two sisters had married members of the extended Romanov family and remained in Russia, but at the beginning of the First World War, foreign princes were under consideration for his daughters. In 1914, the Russian and Romanian royal families met to discuss a possible match between Olga and the future King Carol II of Romania, the eldest son of Alexandra's cousin Marie. Alexandra explained to the Russian foreign minister Sergei Sazonov, who favoured the match, "I could desire nothing more than they should remain in Russia after marriage. But I have four daughters, and it is, of course, impossible. You know how marriages are in reigning families…. The Emperor will have to decide whether he considers this or that marriage suitable for his daughters, but parental authority must not extend beyond that."[13]

In addition to Carol, whom Olga rejected as a possible husband, other potential foreign royal bridegrooms included Prince Christopher of Greece, Crown Prince Alexander of Serbia, Crown Prince Boris of Bulgaria, and the future British kings Edward VIII and George VI. The First World War introduced new possibilities. All four of the grand duchesses developed close emotional attachments to Russian officers whom they met through their work in military hospitals, and Alexandra wondered in a letter to Nicholas why the foreign princes could not be as nice. Nicholas granted his youngest sister, also named Olga, permission to contract a morganatic second marriage to a Russian officer in 1916. If the Romanovs had still been a reigning house at the end of the First World War, the question of whether marriages to commoners were suitable for daughters of the czar would undoubtedly have arisen again.

All discussion of royal marriages for Nicholas and Alexandra's daughters came to an end in March 1917, when Nicholas II abdicated on behalf of himself and his son Alexei following bread riots in Saint Petersburg (called Petrograd during the First World War) and military defeats. Nicholas and Alexandra were placed under house arrest in the Alexander Palace outside Saint Petersburg, and their children and dozens of members of their household chose to remain with them. During the imperial family's captivity, their daughters, now in their late teens and early twenties, assumed leadership roles within the household, particularly after the Bolshevik Revolution of

November 1917 when the conditions of the family's captivity became more restrictive. When Nicholas and Alexandra were transferred from Tobolsk, the Siberian town where the family spent the winter of 1917–18, to the Ural mining town of Ekaterinburg in the spring of 1918, Alexandra wrote in her diary, "Marie comes with us, Olga will look after Baby [Alexei], Tatiana the household & Anastasia will cheer all up."[14] Alexei's health precluded the entire family being transferred at the same time and the separation resulted in Olga, Tatiana, Anastasia, and Alexei spending several uncertain weeks separated from their parents and sister. They passed the time by hiding their family's remaining jewels, code named "medicines" and "candy" in their diaries and correspondence, sewing the gems into corsets and pillow linings before departing for Ekaterinburg.

Once the family was reunited in Ekaterinburg, the grand duchesses continued to advocate for their parents, and even contemplated a possible escape attempt. In June 1918, Olga, aged twenty-two, replied to a series of letters from an anonymous officer who proposed to help the family escape from captivity. Unaware that these letters were most likely composed by the local Bolshevik authorities as a pretext for the former imperial family's execution, Olga wrote on behalf of her family, "All of the windows are glued shut and painted white. The little one [Alexei] is sick in bed and cannot walk at all — every jolt causes him pain.... No risk whatsoever must be taken without being absolutely certain of the result. We are almost always under observation."[15] In consultation with her family, Olga ultimately rejected the proposed escape plan. Like Louis XVI and Marie Antoinette more than a century before, Nicholas and Alexandra wanted any escape attempt to liberate the entire family and household at the same time, and they were therefore reluctant to leave their few remaining servants behind to answer for their actions in the event of an escape.

Meanwhile, twenty-one-year-old Tatiana made use of her training as a nurse to alleviate health problems within the household. She also acted as a spokesperson for her family's interests, approaching the commandant with requests for necessary household supplies. Nineteen-year-old Maria became especially friendly with the guards assigned by the provisional government, then their Bolshevik replacements, which included members of the Red Army. She attempted to gather news about the outside world and the

Bolshevik government's plans for her family. Her sociability was interpreted as flirtatious by Bolshevik observers, but more likely reflected her years of experience engaging with soldiers as a volunteer in a military hospital and honorary Colonel-in-Chief of a regiment. Seventeen-year-old Anastasia raised morale over the winter of 1917–18, performing in amateur comic theatricals for her family and household. By the spring of 1918, however, her own spirits had begun to decline. An engineer in Ekaterinburg who witnessed the arrival of Olga, Tatiana, Anastasia, and Alexei from Tobolsk wrote, "I was overwhelmed by pity for them — me, a confirmed revolutionary.... Anastasia seemed like a frightened, terrified child, who could, in different circumstances, be charming, light-hearted and affectionate."[16]

The imperial family never left their final place of imprisonment, a prosperous merchant's home, which became known as the House of Special Purpose. All five of the imperial children were murdered alongside their parents in the cellar of the House of Special Purpose in July 1918. The tragedy had a profound impact on popular perceptions of the Romanovs. While they were alive, press coverage of the imperial family discussed their adult roles, including the philanthropic committees chaired by the grand duchesses, future dynastic marriages, and Alexei's position as the future Emperor of Russia. After the murder of the family, the four grand duchesses and Alexei were instead immortalized as martyred children better known for their deaths than their lives. The memoirs of the members of the extended Russian imperial family, nobility, and household who survived the Russian Revolution and fled abroad emphasized Nicholas and Alexandra's seclusion in a vanished world rather than how modern their family had seemed to the public in the early twentieth century. Popular-culture portrayals of the grand duchesses after their deaths focused on the rumours that one of them had survived the massacre rather than their actual experiences before and during the revolutions. The remains of Nicholas, Alexandra, all five of their children, and the four members of their household who died with them have been excavated and DNA-tested against samples from numerous royal relatives, but the legend of Anastasia's survival continues to be a part of popular culture. A musical theatre production based on the 1956 film *Anastasia* (which starred Ingrid Bergman) and on a 1997 animated film of the same name was part of the 2016–17 Broadway season.

When George V learned of the murder of the Russian imperial family, he attended a memorial service in a Russian Orthodox church and expressed his grief in his journals and correspondence. George wrote to Victoria of Battenberg, "[Mary] and I feel most deeply for you in the tragic end of your dear sister and her innocent children. But perhaps for her, who knows, it is better so; as even after Nicky's death she could not have wished to live. And the beautiful girls may have been saved from worse than death at the hands of those horrible fiends."[17] George had withdrawn an offer of asylum for the family in 1917, fearing that the presence of an unpopular former ruling family would undermine his own position as king in Britain. That same year, George was so concerned about the royal family's public image that he introduced a new name for his dynasty, previously known as the House of Saxe-Cobourg and Gotha: the House of Windsor. The changes introduced to the royal family's name and titles in 1917 affected more than his direct descendants: Victoria of Battenberg's surname became Mountbatten, and she received a new title, Marchioness of Milford Haven. The fate of the Romanovs, however, had a lasting impact on George's willingness to intervene when members of his extended family were in danger. In 1922, a British warship rescued Victoria's daughter, Princess Alice, her husband Prince Andrew, and their children from turmoil in Greece. Among the evacuees was the infant Prince Philip, who would grow up to marry George V's granddaughter, Queen Elizabeth II. The Second World War precipitated a further displacement of Europe's reigning houses, including the Dutch royal family, who found refuge in Canada.

SEVENTEEN

Juliana of the Netherlands (1909-2004) and Bernhard of Lippe-Biesterfeld (1911-2004)

On January 19, 1943, a royal baby was born in Ottawa, Canada. Princess Juliana, only child of Queen Wilhelmina and heiress to the Dutch throne, had settled in Canada following the Nazi occupation of the Netherlands in 1940. Like the younger children of King Frederick and Queen Elizabeth of Bohemia in the seventeenth century, Juliana's third child was born far from home to a royal family displaced by a larger war in Europe. Every aspect of the baby's birth and christening was shaped by her status as the newest member of the Dutch royal family in exile and a symbol of the continued survival of the House of Orange.

At the time of her arrival in Canada, Juliana was the mother of two daughters: Beatrix (born 1938) and Irene (born 1939). In the event that her third child was a boy, he would be second in line to the Dutch throne after his mother. Canada's governor general, Alexander Cambridge, Earl of Athlone, therefore issued a proclamation stating that part of the Ottawa Civic Hospital was to be declared temporarily extraterritorial so that the newborn would have Dutch citizenship alone. Four rooms were set aside for the birth: a maternity ward for Juliana, a nursery for her baby, and a room each for the nurse and security detail. Juliana recalled, "At first we thought the baby should be with the other babies.... I wanted us to be treated like any other mother and child. But later that didn't seem wise. So many people had to visit her officially, and they might have carried infection to the other babies. It wouldn't have been fair to them."[1]

The baby was a third daughter for Juliana and her husband Bernhard, who was present in Ottawa for the birth. She was named Margriet, in honour of the daisies worn by members of the Dutch resistance. The Dutch flag flew from Ottawa's Peace Tower to celebrate Margriet's arrival, and the bells played the Dutch national anthem.

News of Juliana's pregnancy and the birth of a new princess received a joyful reception in the occupied Netherlands. Bernhard announced the news of the forthcoming birth on the radio in the fall of 1942. In hiding with her family in Amsterdam, Anne Frank wrote in her diary on September 21, "I sometimes listen to the Dutch broadcasts from London. Prince Bernhard recently announced that Princess Juliana is expecting a baby in January, which I think is wonderful."[2]

German authorities in the Netherlands attempted to censor all news and discussion of the royal baby. Radios were confiscated and private letters opened. Concerned for the safety of the Dutch people, Bernhard warned in one of his broadcasts against celebrating the royal birth too openly. He spoke about his family's joy about the new arrival in a Radio Orange address that combined parental pride with concern for the Dutch people in the occupied Netherlands: "You could have imagined our happiness if you had seen our sweet little girl. Even before my wife had seen her, she said to me: 'I'm really glad it's a girl. If it had been a son, perhaps there would have been too much excitement in Holland and even victims, now I can breathe easier.'"[3] Underground newspapers published by the Dutch resistance hailed Margriet as a princess of peace and a symbol of better times to come for the Netherlands.

In her memoirs, Wilhelmina expressed concern that her daughter Juliana's public image as a mother raising her children in exile had superseded all her other efforts on behalf of the Dutch war effort during the Second World War. Wilhelmina made it clear that her daughter had acted not only as a wife and mother but also as a future sovereign, writing, "Some readers may think that Juliana devoted the years of her exile almost exclusively to her children. This idea is the most understandable as little news from faraway Canada ever reached the occupied fatherland, but it's decidedly incorrect. Of course, she gave much attention to her children, but at the same time she devoted much of her time and energy to the 'good cause.'"[4] Juliana represented the exiled Dutch royal family in diplomatic negotiations with Canada and the United States, volunteered for the Red Cross, and undertook a goodwill tour of the Dutch Caribbean, affirming the independence of the islands from the Nazi occupation in Europe. In the European popular imagination, however, Juliana was best known as an exiled mother, raising her children far from home because of the political upheaval created by the war.

Succession crises in the House of Orange that long predated the Second World War made the safety of Juliana and her children imperative to the continued survival of the dynasty, which had come to power following the Eighty Years' War (1568–1648) of independence against Spain. In common with Queen Victoria, whose reign overlapped her own, Wilhelmina was born in the aftermath of a series of untimely deaths in her family and a desperate need for new royal heirs. Her father, King William III of the Netherlands, first married his cousin, Princess Sophie of Würtemberg, but his wife and all three of their sons predeceased him. In the event of William's death without children, the Dutch throne would pass to a German relative of the king, an outcome that dismayed his subjects. The king was therefore encouraged to remarry a princess of childbearing age. The aging king, who was known for his erratic temperament and autocratic tendencies, had difficulty finding a young princess willing to marry him. William approached the four surviving daughters of George Victor, Prince of Waldeck and Pyrmont, the titular ruler of a tiny German principality with a long history of providing regiments for the Dutch military. Sixty-one-year-old William ultimately married twenty-year-old Emma of Waldeck and Pyrmont in 1879, after having been rejected by her elder sister, Pauline. The marriage seemed undistinguished for a reigning monarch at the time, but it ultimately provided the Dutch royal family with connections that proved valuable during the Second World War. In 1882, Emma's youngest sister, Helena, married Queen Victoria's youngest son Prince Leopold, Duke of Albany. Leopold and Helena's daughter, Princess Alice, Countess of Athlone, ultimately became viceregal consort of Canada from 1940 to 1946.

William had treated his late sons harshly, but Wilhelmina, born in 1880, remembered her father fondly in her memoirs. She recalled, "I had my daily hour of play with Father; I seem to remember that it began at five o'clock. I was dressed in a beautiful sleeveless open-necked frock, with a wide sash of the same colour as the bows on my shoulders.... Once dressed, I was taken to my father's study by way of the main staircase and the big drawing-room; and then the fun started."[5]

The parent with the greatest influence over Wilhelmina's upbringing, however, was her mother, Emma, who instilled in her only child an unwavering sense of duty that would serve her well as queen during the Second World War. Emma acted as regent when Wilhelmina succeeded to the throne at the age of ten in 1890, and reminded her that she belonged to her people. The young queen's education was accelerated to ensure that she could reign in her own right by the time she was eighteen, in 1898, and she socialized with few other children her own age. Marriage to Prince Henry, Duke of Mecklenburg-Schwerin, in 1901 expanded the queen's social circle, and she was devoted to her husband during the early years of her marriage.

Wilhelmina's only child, Juliana, was born in 1909. As in the reign of Wilhelmina's father, there was concern about the succession, as the queen had suffered a series of miscarriages prior to Juliana's birth. The arrival of a Dutch heir was greeted with widespread celebrations. Wilhelmina reduced her schedule of public engagements to spend more time with her daughter, recalling later in life, "In summer and autumn I considered myself exempt from many duties which had no bearing on my official task. As soon as I had a moment free, I lived only for my child."[6] Remembering the isolation of her own childhood, Wilhelmina ensured that Juliana was educated alongside other children in the palace. After completing her secondary education, Juliana attended the University of Leiden, earning a bachelor's degree in international law in 1930. Juliana met Bernhard of Lippe-Biesterfeld at the 1936 Summer Olympics in Berlin, and they married the next year.

In Canada, Juliana was determined to ensure that her children had friends their own age and blended into society. In a CBC radio address broadcast upon her arrival in 1940, Juliana explained, "You will see [the children] in your midst. You will see them quite often because we don't like locking ourselves up — that is not in our nature."[7] The princesses' playmates included the grandchildren of the Earl and Countess of Athlone. The Countess recalled, "In those days of sadness and anxiety our three grandchildren and the … Dutch children made merriment in the house and helped take our minds off the seriousness of those tragic times."[8] After spending a few weeks at Rideau Hall with the Earl and Countess, Juliana and her children settled in small house near Rockcliffe Park. They then moved to Stornoway, which is currently the residence of the leader of Canada's Official Opposition, after Margriet's birth. Queen Wilhelmina and Juliana's husband, Prince Bernhard, remained in the United Kingdom for much of the war to assist Dutch resistance efforts, but they visited Juliana and the children and praised their "charming house" in Ottawa.[9]

The First Canadian Army liberated the Netherlands between September 1944 and April 1945, allowing the Dutch royal family to return home. Juliana sent 100,000 tulip bulbs from the Netherlands to thank Canadians for providing a refuge for her family during the Second World War. An annual gift of 10,000 tulip bulbs continues to be delivered to the present day, and Ottawa has celebrated a tulip festival every year since 1953.

By the end of the Second World War, Canada was the only home Juliana's children could remember, and they had difficult readjusting to life in the Netherlands. Juliana and Bernhard were determined to maintain a lifestyle that was sensitive to the continuing privations experienced by the Dutch people, and the young princess Beatrix noticed that a number of her favourite foods were no longer served to her. At their first family dinner at the Soestjik Palace in the Netherlands after the war, Bernhard observed with dismay that "two-year-old Margriet beat a spoon on her plate, Irene sat with a leg curled underneath her and Beatrix, seven, talked incessantly with her mouth full and said she would prefer the steak and ice cream her mother had given her in Canada to the Dutch food on their plate."[10] The restoration of the House of Orange meant that Juliana's children received a conventional royal upbringing for the rest of their childhood, the older ones remembering Canada as a place where they enjoyed an unusual amount of freedom and anonymity.

Juliana became Queen of the Netherlands when her mother abdicated in 1948. The new queen was popular with her people because she was an approachable figure who did not stand on ceremony, but her reign was characterized by both personal and political turmoil. Wilhelmina had been a symbol of unity during the Second World War, but one of Juliana's first acts as queen was to preside over the breakdown of the Dutch empire as Indonesia achieved independence.

Juliana also faced challenges as a mother during the early years of her reign. In 1947, the year before she became queen, Juliana gave birth to her youngest daughter, Princess Marijke Christina. The baby was born nearly blind due to complications from the German measles Juliana suffered during her pregnancy. Like Empress Alexandra of Russia in the first decades of the twentieth century, Juliana blamed herself for her child's condition and sought advice from a faith healer. Juliana's confidante Greet Hoffmans became known as the Dutch Rasputin, interfering in politics and damaging the queen's reputation.

In common with past generations of royal parents, Juliana faced challenges when it came time for her daughters to marry. Both Wilhelmina and Juliana had married German princes, but popular opinion favoured Dutch spouses for the next generation of princesses. Of Juliana's four daughters, only Margriet chose an uncontroversial husband, Pieter van Vollenhoven, whom she met while studying at the University of Leiden. Her sisters Irene and Christina married Roman Catholics, waiving their succession rights in the staunchly Protestant House of Orange. Irene's marriage was particularly politically sensitive because her husband, Carlos Hugo, Duke of Parma and Piacenza, was a claimant to the Spanish throne. A Spanish prince, particularly one with close links to Francisco Franco's dictatorship, was not an acceptable husband for a Dutch princess. The Dutch government refused to consent to the marriage, and Juliana attempted to persuade her daughter to cancel the wedding. When Irene and Carlos Hugo were married in 1964, Juliana and Bernhard watched the ceremony on television instead of attending in person. Beatrix's marriage to a member of the German nobility, Klaus von Amsberg, brought demonstrators out onto the streets, chanting, "Claus, raus! [Claus, out!]." The Dutch press questioned whether a former member of Hitler Youth was a suitable consort for a future Queen of the Netherlands.

Parenthood restored the popularity of Beatrix and Claus, who obtained Dutch citizenship and began spelling his name in the Dutch fashion in 1965. In 1967, Beatrix gave birth to her eldest son, Willem-Alexander, the first male heir born to the House of Orange since 1851, and the Dutch watched the young prince and his two younger brothers grow up. Beatrix became queen when Juliana abdicated in 1980, becoming a respected elder stateswoman over the course of her reign.

In 2013, Queen Beatrix of the Netherlands followed the example of her mother and grandmother by abdicating the Dutch throne. The ceremony was an opportunity for the Dutch people to look back on the queen's reign and welcome the first reigning king since 1890 to the throne. In Canada, the CBC interviewed people who recalled her time in Ottawa during the Second World War and "remember[ed] that she was known as Trixie Orange."[11]

Beatrix's abdication allowed her eldest son, Willem-Alexander, to begin his reign while still in his mid-forties. Willem-Alexander is part of a new generation of European monarchs who succeeded to their respective thrones following the abdications of their predecessors. King Albert II of the Belgians abdicated for health reasons in 2013, leaving the throne to his fifty-three-year-old son Philippe. The following year, King Juan Carlos of Spain abdicated following a decline in his popularity due to his perceived extravagance and the involvement of his daughter and son-in-law in a financial scandal, and was succeeded by his forty-five-year-old son, who became King Felipe VI.

For the former monarchs of the Netherlands, Belgium, and Spain, royal parenting includes stepping aside to allow their children to begin their reigns at a comparatively young age. As former sovereigns, abdicated monarchs have the potential to act as valuable resources for their reigning children, guiding them through the challenges of the early years of their reigns. The wave of European royal abdications in 2013 and 2014 led to speculation about whether Queen Elizabeth II would abdicate the thrones of the United Kingdom and Commonwealth realms to allow the accession of her eldest son, Charles, the Prince of Wales, who is currently the oldest heir to the throne in British history. Elizabeth, however, pledged in a radio broadcast on her twenty-first birthday in 1947 that her "whole life, whether it be long or short, shall be devoted to your service and the service of our great imperial family to which we all belong."[12] The Queen's commitment to serve her people predated marriage and motherhood and endures over the course of a reign that surpasses the record set by her great-great-grandmother Queen Victoria. From her accession in 1952 until the present day, the Queen has reigned over a period of unprecedented political and social change, including a transformation of popular attitudes toward parenting.

EIGHTEEN

Elizabeth II (1926–) and Philip of Greece and Denmark (1921–)

In honour of Queen Elizabeth II's ninetieth birthday in 2016, Prince William reflected in a documentary about his grandmother's life and reign, "I've been able to explore, understand, slightly carve my own path. So I greatly appreciate and value that protection…. She's never dictated what we should do. It's a quiet guidance. It's sometimes never seen, but it's always there, and I think that has allowed me personally to explore and understand more about who I am and what I have to do."[1]

The Queen's position as the longest-reigning monarch in British history and head of state of sixteen Commonwealth realms has shaped her public image as a model of tradition and constancy. In 1973, the Queen visited Bath Abbey to commemorate the one thousandth anniversary of the coronation of Edgar the Peaceable and Elfrida of Northampton, demonstrating a millennium of continuity for the monarchy. William's description of the Queen as a grandmother, however, demonstrates that she has developed her own approach to influencing the younger generations of her family. Previous reigning monarchs who were also grandparents, including George I and Victoria, attempted to control the upbringings of their grandchildren — the choice of names, godparents, and education.

The conflicts between monarchs and their heirs that were endemic to the House of Hanover often stemmed from this determination to overrule the wishes of adult children and take control of grandchildren. The current Queen avoided this approach, allowing her adult children and grandchildren autonomy not known since Edward III and Philippa of Hainault granted their sons independent incomes and their daughters the freedom to refuse dynastic marriages.

The Queen's willingness to allow her children and grandchildren independence unknown to past generations of royal children reflected evolving parenting trends in the late twentieth century that emphasized the distinct personalities of individual children. Just as the Queen has incorporated new technologies, from television to social media, into the public image of the monarchy, her approach to engaging with her children, grandchildren, and great-grandchildren has evolved over the course of her reign. Nevertheless, the Queen's approach to parenting received public scrutiny when the marriages of three of her four children broke down during the 1990s, raising the question of whether she should have managed her adult children more closely and provided their spouses with a greater degree of guidance in their adjustment to life within the royal family.

Increased media coverage of the private life of the Queen and her family informed popular opinion concerning her choices as a mother. Throughout the Queen's reign, the public has assumed that royal parenting would be distinct from the childrearing trends that shaped the decisions of other parents. When parenting advice of the 1950s and 1960s recommended that mothers spend as much time as possible with their children, the public accepted that the Queen had responsibilities to the United Kingdom and Commonwealth that would keep her away from home for long periods of time. While other parents of the 1980s and 1990s were advised to allow their adult children to make their own decisions regarding their marriages and childrearing, the public wondered why the Queen had not managed her children and their families more closely. Today, the Queen is in the public eye as a grandmother and great-grandmother, and there is great interest in her involvement in the upbringing of the youngest generations of the royal family. As William's recollections demonstrate, the Queen has developed her own conception of her role as a mother, grandmother, and great-grandmother, breaking with royal tradition to allow her descendants to pursue their own interests and forge their own paths.

The future Queen Elizabeth II married Prince Philip of Greece and Denmark (Lieutenant Philip Mountbatten) in 1947. Prince Philip received the title of Duke of Edinburgh. Elizabeth and Philip had contrasting childhoods. Elizabeth had a close relationship with her parents, King George VI and Queen Elizabeth, and younger sister, Princess Margaret, and they referred to themselves as "We 4." The princesses were educated at home by a governess, Marion Crawford, with Elizabeth receiving additional instruction in history from the provost of Eton. Details of the princesses's childhood became well known to the public because Crawford published her memoirs of working in the royal household, *The Little Princesses*, after she retired in 1948. In contrast to Nicholas and Alexandra's children's nanny, Margaret Eager, Crawford did not have permission to share her experiences with the public, and her relationship with the royal family ended when the book was released in 1950.

In contrast to Elizabeth, Philip, born on the island of Corfu, saw little of his parents during his adolescence. The family's flight from Greece precipitated the disintegration of his immediate family. His mother, the former Princess Alice of Battenberg, was committed to a mental hospital when he was ten years old, and his father, Prince Andrew of Greece and Denmark, moved to Monte Carlo with his mistress. All four of Philip's elder sisters married German princes and left home in 1930 and 1931. Philip's grandmother Victoria, Marchioness of Milford Haven, and maternal uncles George and Louis Mountbatten took charge of his upbringing. He attended a series of boarding schools, including Cheam in Hampshire and then Gordonstoun in Scotland, before beginning a career in the Royal Navy, in which he served with distinction during the Second World War. While the circumstances of Elizabeth's childhood were well known to the public, Philip remarked to one of his biographers, "I suppose they know I was born a Prince of Greece, but one impression that I think needs to be corrected is that the whole of my life has been spent here and that I was brought up by Lord Mountbatten.... I don't think anybody thinks I had a father. Most people think that [Louis Mountbatten is] my father anyway."[2] Compared to Elizabeth, who made headlines in the years immediately preceding her marriage by training as a mechanic for the auxiliary territorial service and touring South Africa with her family, Philip was a comparatively obscure figure to the British public.

The arrival of Philip and Elizabeth's eldest child, Prince Charles, in 1948 prompted changes to long-established traditions concerning royal births. Since the Glorious Revolution of 1688, the presence of at least one government minister had been vital to ensuring that a royal baby was accepted as a legitimate heir to the throne. The Home Secretary was present for the births of Elizabeth, her sister Margaret, and their cousin Prince Edward, the future Duke of Kent, but in the late 1930s and 1940s this official presence was deemed unnecessary for the arrivals of other cousins who were further down the line of succession. For the arrival of his first grandchild, George VI decreed that the presence of the Home Secretary was no longer necessary for any royal births, a change in policy that remains in effect. In keeping with the choices of numerous other fathers of his generation, Philip was absent for Charles's birth, and received the news of his son's arrival while playing squash with his secretary, Michael Parker.

Charles had long been out of favour as a royal baby name because of the execution of Charles I in 1649, but Elizabeth chose the name out of personal preference, and selected another name popular with the Stuart monarchs, Anne, for her second child, who was born in 1950. The younger children received traditional family names: Andrew (born 1960), for Philip's father, and Edward (born 1964), a name that had been given to English princes for more than a thousand years.

George VI issued letters patent in recognition of his grandchildren's place in the succession. There had not been a son born to an adult heiress presumptive[3] since the future Queen Anne gave birth to Prince William, Duke of Gloucester, in 1689. During the First World War, George V affirmed that titles passed through the male line, with the exception of children of a female sovereign. Without George VI's 1948 Letters Patent, Elizabeth's children would have been styled the Honourable Charles Mountbatten, Earl of Merioneth, and Lady Anne Mountbatten until their mother's accession to the throne. As Queen, Elizabeth would issue similar letters patent in 2012, allowing all of the children of William and Kate, male and female, to hold the title of Prince or Princess, instead of the eldest son alone, as George V intended for great-grandchildren of the sovereign.

Elizabeth entered the 1950s as heiress presumptive to the throne, wife of a naval officer, and mother of two young children. These roles were difficult to reconcile with the domestic ideology of the time. Parenting manuals of the time assumed the mother's constant presence within the home. According to Dr. Benjamin Spock's influential parenting guide *The Common Sense Book of Baby and Child Care*, first published in the United States in 1946, parenting was nearly synonymous with mothering, and mothers were encouraged to trust their own instincts rather than relying on neighbours or other authorities within the community. Spock stated in a 1969 interview with *Redbook* magazine, "Biologically and temperamentally, I believe, women were made to be concerned first and foremost with child care, husband care and home care."[4] Spock softened his views on this subject over the course of his career and introduced gender-neutral language in later editions of his books, but during the early decades of the Queen's married life, the opinion of childcare experts was that mothers should make their children the primary focus of their lives. Spock explained: "I agree that we all have a serious obligation to the community…. But the most important way for a mother to carry this out is to bring up children who will be fine citizens."[5] Spock's sentiments were remarkably similar to popular interpretations of Jean-Jacques Rousseau's ideas of the family during the French Revolution, demonstrating continuity in philosophical debates concerning the role of women in their families that shaped the cultural climate of successive reigns.

When Elizabeth became Queen in 1952, the demands on her time outside the domestic sphere increased. At the same time, the emphasis on the bond between mother and child increased in parenting literature of the period. John Bowlby's study of institutionalized children, *Child Care and the Growth of Love*, further emphasized the importance of a strong mother-child bond, arguing that separations between mothers and children increased the likelihood of mental health disorders for young people. Joan Bakewell, a television journalist born in 1933 who became a Labour Party peer, explained the impact of Bowlby's writing on her generation, stating, "We applied his ideas to ourselves, seeing it as our duty to stay close to our babies' development.... It became central to our lives and brooked no argument about careers and part-time work."[6]

Being Queen of the United Kingdom and Commonwealth realms, however, was a full-time career. Elizabeth and Philip spent much of the 1950s undertaking overseas tours. They sailed around the world on the Royal Yacht *Britannia*, visiting Australia and New Zealand in addition to Pacific and Caribbean island realms for six months during 1953–54, and spent six weeks on a whistle-stop tour of Canada in 1959. As a result, Charles and Anne spent extended periods apart from their parents, and Charles in particular developed a close relationship with his grandmother Queen Elizabeth, the Queen Mother. In her letters to her daughter and son-in-law, the Queen Mother shared anecdotes about the children, writing in January 1954, "Charles has started his lessons with Miss Peebles [governess], & seems to be happy with her."[7] The Queen Mother and her grandchildren followed the royal tours through newsreel coverage and newspaper articles. Film footage of the Queen shaking Charles's hand after a long separation later became famous as supposed evidence of the unhealthy degree of formality between royal parents and children, but at the time, the public accepted that the Queen's family operated differently from other families in terms of relations between parents and children.

The Queen's marriage also differed from the prevailing gender roles of the 1950s and 1960s. Early in her reign, the Queen followed the example of her grandfather, George V, by confirming the name of her reigning house. Since the Norman Conquest of 1066, a king or queen descended from a previous ruler through the female line had started a new dynasty with his or her father's family name. When James I succeeded Elizabeth I in 1603, the reign of the House of Stuart began in England, even though James derived his claim to the English throne through his descent from Henry VIII's sister, Margaret Tudor. This practice of changing the name of the royal house continued even after female monarchs were succeeded by children of their own. Queen Victoria, the last British monarch from the House of Hanover, was succeeded by her son, Edward VII, who became the first monarch from the House of Saxe-Coburg and Gotha, Prince Albert's royal line. The Queen and Prince Philip, however, were in a unique situation, as neither of them bore the names of long-established royal houses;

George V had created both Windsor and Mountbatten as royal surnames in 1917. After the Queen ascended to the throne, Philip's uncle, Louis (Earl Mountbatten of Burma), told Prince Ernst August of Hanover that "The House of Mountbatten now reigned"[8] and later referenced "Elizabeth Mountbatten" becoming Queen in his privately published family genealogy.[9] The unique circumstances of the House of Windsor's family name, however, made it unclear whether the Queen's accession necessarily led to a change in dynasty. The Queen's grandmother, Queen Mary, made it clear that she considered the establishment of the House of Windsor to be permanent, irrespective of the marriages of future sovereigns. Elizabeth followed the advice of her grandmother and her first prime minister, Winston Churchill, and confirmed that the reigning dynasty would remain the House of Windsor, with the younger members of the royal family assuming the surname of Mountbatten-Windsor.

While Elizabeth was the dominant figure in the royal family's public life, Philip assumed a leadership role in the domestic sphere. Like Queen Victoria, Elizabeth allowed her consort to assume control of the household, including the educational program of the royal children. Philip had not experienced a conventional royal upbringing, and he wanted his children to experience life outside the palace walls. He explained during a 1956 tour of the United States, "The Queen and I want Charles to go to school with other boys of his generation and learn to live with other children, and to absorb from childhood the discipline imposed by education with others."[10] Past generations of heirs to the throne had been educated privately, whether in the households of members of the nobility or via tutors or governesses. A princess did not attend a public educational institution until Victoria's daughter Princess Louise enrolled in the National Art Training School in London in 1863, attending only intermittently because of her royal duties. Her elder brother, the future Edward VII, completed terms at Oxford and Cambridge, but he was not allowed to attend lectures or socialize with fellow students.

After completing his early education at home, Charles was sent to Cheam and Gordonstoun, following in the footsteps of his father. Charles was unhappy at school. When Philip was asked how Charles was enjoying Gordonstoun, Philip replied, "Well, at least he hasn't run away yet."[11] The younger children, Anne, Andrew, and Edward, had a more positive experience of boarding school. Andrew completed an exchange term from Gordonstoun at Lakefield College outside Peterborough in Canada. The Queen's role as Head of the Commonwealth shaped the choices of secondary school overseas programs for her children: Charles spent time in Australia and Papua New Guinea, while Andrew went to Canada, strengthening the royal family's personal relationships with the Commonwealth realms and continuing the long tradition of royalty residing for extended periods in the Dominions. After graduating from Gordonstoun, Charles became the first British heir to the throne to earn a post-secondary degree, receiving a Bachelor of Arts in Anthropology, Archaeology and History from Cambridge University in 1970, with an exchange term at the University of Aberystwyth to learn Welsh in preparation for his formal investiture as Prince of Wales in 1969.

Philip reflected on fatherhood in a speech to London's Guildhall at the time of his golden wedding anniversary in 1997, stating, "Like all families we went through the full range of the pleasures and tribulations of bringing up children. I am naturally somewhat biased but I think our children have done rather well under very difficult and demanding circumstances, and I hope we can be forgiven for feeling proud of them. I am also encouraged to see what a good start the next generation is making."[12]

While Philip and Elizabeth have been widely praised for their philanthropy, engagement with the Commonwealth, and devotion to their royal duties, their parenting became the focus of criticism in the 1990s as the marriages of three of their four children came to very public ends. The author Maureen Waller, who has written about all six of England's reigning queens, stated that Elizabeth's children had "an old-fashioned upbringing surrounded by servants, with Mummy holding them emotionally at arm's length. They needed more than she was able to give."[13] Numerous journalists questioned the Queen's approach to childrearing and suggested that she should have played a more active role in her children's upbringing. Criticism of the Queen's comparatively laissez-faire approach to childrearing occurred at the same time as parenting experts were critiquing the rise of "helicopter parenting" in the rest of society. Benjamin Spock's widow, Mary Morgan, declared in 2007 that "Parents Take Parenting Too Seriously" and explained that her husband had been concerned by the rise of overprotective parenting in the 1980s. Morgan said that Spock "blamed all the experts that told parents they're doing it wrong."[14] In common with the beginning of the Queen's reign, popular opinion on how royalty should parent differed from the accepted advice for mothers and fathers in the rest of society.

On the occasion of her ninetieth birthday in 2016, the Queen commissioned official photographs by Annie Leibowitz that celebrated her roles as a mother, grandmother, and great-grandmother. A photograph with Anne illustrated her bond with her only daughter, who shares her commitment to public service. Another image depicted the Queen surrounded by the children in her family: her two youngest grandchildren, Lady Louise and James, Viscount Severn (children of Prince Edward), and her great-grandchildren, Savannah and Isla Phillips, and Mia Tindall (grandchildren of Princess Anne), Prince George, and Princess Charlotte. Just before the official celebrations began in the United Kingdom, a final photograph showed the Queen with the Duke of Edinburgh after almost seventy years of marriage. The images demonstrate her commitment to her family as well as her people over the course of her reign, quietly challenging popular criticism of her domestic life. When her former daughter-in-law, Diana, Princess of Wales, died in 1997, the Queen prioritized her role as a grandmother, remaining with her family at Balmoral Castle to give her grandsons William and Harry the space to mourn in private amid the beauty of the Scottish countryside. The Queen's cousin Margaret Rhodes explained, "To take them away to have nothing to do in Buckingham Palace would have been horrible."[15]

When the royal family returned to London for Diana's funeral, the Queen addressed her people "as a grandmother." The Queen and Prince Philip had provided stability for William and Harry during the breakdown of their parents' marriage and their grief following Diana's death. The upbringing of the two young princes combined royal tradition with innovations introduced by Charles and Diana.

NINETEEN

Prince Charles (1948-) and Diana Spencer (1961-97)

A few weeks before his ninth birthday in 1991, Prince William was hospitalized after one of his classmates accidentally hit him in the forehead with a golf club. As William explained to a ten-year-old cancer patient interviewing him for the Children's BBC in 2009, "We were on a putting green and the next thing you know there was a seven-iron and it came out of nowhere and it hit me in the head. So, yeah, I was in hospital for that, but that was very minor compared to how many times you've been into hospital."[1]

For William's parents, Charles and Diana, Prince and Princess of Wales, however, the accident did not seem "very minor," and they rushed to the Royal Berkshire hospital in Reading to be with their son. The royal couple arrived in separate cars. Charles was at Highgrove House in Gloucestershire when he received the news of William's accident; Diana, in contrast, was living in the couple's London apartments in Kensington Palace. Their ten-year marriage had broken down, and they spent little time together outside of official engagements; British Prime Minister John Major would announce their official separation the following year. William's accident, however, briefly brought them together in shared concern for their son's condition. As William was wheeled into a hospital room for a CAT scan, both Charles and Diana "were walking behind his stretcher, reassuring him."[2] William was diagnosed with a depressed fracture of the skull and underwent a seventy-minute operation to correct the dent and check for bone splinters. The operation was a success, leaving William with no lasting effects beyond a mark on his forehead that he would later describe as his "Harry Potter scar."[3]

William's accident, however, had a lasting impact on popular perceptions of Charles and Diana as parents. While Diana remained at the hospital during William's operation, Charles proceeded to a previously scheduled engagement, attending a performance of *Tosca* at the Royal Opera House with two government ministers. Charles assured his guests that William's condition was "not too bad" and travelled to an environmental conference after the opera, remaining in contact with the hospital by phone. The public was already closely following the growing distance between Charles and Diana and speculating about their marital problems. There was widespread popular sympathy for the princess, an international celebrity who had developed a rapport with the public. Charles had already received criticism as a husband, but his decision to continue his planned schedule of engagements while William was in surgery resulted in accusations in the press that he was a distant father to his two sons. The British tabloid newspaper the *Sun* sensationalized William's accident with headlines such as "Wills in the Brain Scan Scare" and "Blood Soaked Out of His Bandages" and their front page asked of Charles, "What Kind of a Dad Are You?"[4]

In the United States, *People* magazine interviewed childrearing experts about the effects of being raised by an absentee father. British psychologist Dr. David Lewis argued that simply being born into the royal family precluded William and his younger brother Harry from experiencing an ordinary family life, stating, "These are not going to be normal children … because this family is in a completely different ball game,"[5] and royal experts opined that Charles's distance from his children was in keeping with the culture of the British aristocracy. The press coverage of William's accident demonstrated how popular opinion could misinterpret events unfolding behind palace doors, creating a received wisdom about royal parenting that was not necessarily accurate. The relationship between Charles and his sons was far closer than the public could tell from media coverage of the royal family. The breakdown of Charles and Diana's marriage encouraged the public to focus on their differences, but the fact is, they shared a common rapport with children and an interest in ensuring that their sons would experience happier childhoods than their own.

Charles's two younger brothers, Prince Andrew and Prince Edward, were born in 1960 and 1964, when Charles was twelve and sixteen respectively, and he took a strong interest in them from babyhood. Charles's biographer, Anthony Holden, wrote that when Andrew was born, "Cheam [school] staff were accustomed to boys being somewhat dashed by the news of the arrival of a younger sibling. They were struck by Charles's delight at having a baby brother and the almost excessive enthusiasm with which he relayed the latest news from home."[6] As Charles grew older, he took his responsibilities as a godparent seriously, purchasing birthday and christening gifts and providing counsel as they grew older.

Diana, the third daughter of John Spencer, eighth Earl Spencer, and Frances Shand Kydd, also took a strong interest in children and their welfare from a young age. Kay King, who ran the Young England kindergarten where Diana worked as an educational assistant, recalled that "[the children] responded so well to her, and she was completely at ease with them."[7] In contrast to Charles, Diana's rapport with children became a key element of her image from the beginning of her time as a recognizable public figure. Her first photo session in front of assembled journalists took place on September 18, 1980, at the kindergarten. The iconic photograph depicted Diana holding two of her pupils, with the sun outlining her legs through a summer skirt. Her public appearances as Princess of Wales emphasized her ability to communicate with children, crouching down to their level on royal walkabouts to engage with them.

Charles and Diana became parents less than a year after their 1981 wedding. William was born on June 21, 1982. At twenty-one, Diana was three years younger than the average British first-time mother that year, and the royal couple's decision to start a family so quickly seemed to reflect royal tradition rather than the changing social norms of 1980s Britain. The circumstances of William's birth, however, reflected the royal couple's willingness to break with the past. Charles was present for all sixteen hours of

Diana's labour, the first heir to the throne to be present in the delivery room since the future Edward VII witnessed the premature birth of his eldest son, Albert Victor. William was also the first future monarch to be born in a hospital, St. Mary's, in West London. The medical personnel present at a royal birth had changed over the centuries, from female midwives in the sixteenth century to a male doctor and female midwife working in tandem in the mid-seventeenth century to male doctors in the nineteenth century, but the setting had always been a private residence. The birth of royal children in hospital created new traditions, including journalists and members of the public gathering outside the maternity wing and the new parents posing for photographs with their baby on the hospital steps.

Charles and Diana also broke with tradition by bringing nine-month-old William along on an official tour of Australia and New Zealand. Since the nineteenth century, royal tours of the British Empire, then Commonwealth, separated royal children from their parents for months at a time. When the future Queen Elizabeth II was an infant, her parents were sent on a Commonwealth tour that kept them away from home for six months. The Queen Mother, then Duchess of York, wrote, "Feel very miserable at leaving the baby. Went up & played with her & she was so sweet. Luckily she doesn't realize anything…. I drank some champagne and tried not to weep."[8] The 1983 royal tour allowed Charles and Diana to visit their son between days of royal engagements. Like the infant Grand Duchess Olga in 1896, the sight of a royal baby on tour captured the public's imagination. Charles wrote to William's godmother, Lady Susan Hussey, "I must tell you that your godson couldn't be in better form. He looks horribly well and is expanding visibly and with frightening rapidity. Today he actually crawled for the first time. We laughed and laughed with sheer hysterical pleasure and now we can't stop him crawling everywhere."[9]

Charles was pleased by the public's interest in his son, writing to another friend, "You may have seen some photographs of him recently when he performed like a true professional in front of the cameras and did everything that could be expected of him. It really is encouraging to provide people with some nice jolly news for a change!"[10] The interest in the royal baby on tour prompted one adviser to British prime minister Margaret Thatcher to suggest releasing new footage of William in Australia over Easter weekend in

1983 to divert attention from Campaign for Nuclear Disarmament protests against the deployment of American cruise missiles in Britain.[11]

As Charles and Diana spent increasingly long periods of time apart in the late 1980s, the public scrutinized both their marriage and their individual relationships with their children. Like their father and other children of Britain's elite, William and Harry attended boarding school from a young age and therefore spent school terms apart from their parents. Charles did not send his sons to Cheam and Gordonstoun, where he had been unhappy, but instead chose Ludgrove School in Wokingham and then Eton College, which were both close proximity to Windsor Castle.

When William and Harry were with their parents, they were exposed to very different experiences. Charles shared his love of the natural world with his sons at Highgrove House. Diana took her children to Disneyland and McDonalds, insisting that they stand in line with the other customers. The media judged Diana to be the more demonstrative parent. When Charles and Diana visited Canada with William and Harry in 1991, a photograph of Diana embracing her sons aboard *Britannia* in Toronto harbour was published in newspapers and magazines around the world. Photojournalist Jayne Fincher recalled, "A few seconds behind her Prince Charles did the same thing. He came down; he was hugging and kissing the boys too. But the sad thing was that all the pictures that were used were her with her arms out, and nobody ever used a picture of him."[12] Public opinion turned against Charles as both a husband and father as he and Diana spoke to the press separately about the breakdown of their marriage. Diana stated in a 1995 BBC panorama interview that "there were three of us in this marriage, so it was a bit crowded,"[13] referring to Charles's affair with Camilla Parker Bowles. She also questioned Charles's suitability to be king.

Diana died in a car accident in 1997, the year after her divorce from Charles was finalized. Both William and Harry have spoken about Diana's enduring influence on their development. When Harry appeared on *Good Morning Britain* to promote the Invictus Games, he discussed his mother, stating, "It's a great shame she's not here, but every day I wonder what it would be like if she [were] here, what she would say and how she'd be making everyone laugh…. There's all sorts of emotions as I'm here trying my best to make her proud."[14]

Harry's choices of charitable patronages reflect his mother's interests in children's welfare and HIV/AIDS patients. In 2006, Harry founded Sentebale with Prince Seeiso of Lesotho, a charity devoted to improving the lives of AIDS orphans in Lesotho. In July 2016, Harry took an HIV test live on camera to encourage others to be tested for the virus. While much of William's philanthropy is closer to his father's interests, including wildlife conservation, he has also been involved in anti-bullying initiatives, reflecting Diana's view that "the biggest disease this world suffers from in this day and age is the disease of people being unloved," words that have made their way into contemporary parenting advice manuals.[15]

In the years following Diana's death, Charles attracted popular sympathy as a single parent. Past breakdowns of royal marriages resulted in the children siding with one parent, usually their mother. The future Queen Mary I supported her mother, Catherine of Aragon, over her father Henry VIII when Henry sought an annulment of the marriage, and George I's decision to repudiate his wife, Sophia Dorothea, permanently damaged his relationship with his son, the future George II. In contrast, William and Harry maintained a close relationship with both their mother and father during the separation and divorce. William spoke warmly of his father in an interview for a documentary celebrating the 40th anniversary of the Prince's Trust, describing him as "incredibly hard-working" and praising his sense of humour as "a family trait."[16] William also recalled anecdotes about Charles attending his school plays, prompting one journalist to conclude from the interview, "It is evidence that beneath the awkward exterior the heir to the throne is a pretty decent father."[17]

William and Harry's acceptance of Charles's second marriage to Camilla in 2005 helped the public accept the new Duchess of Cornwall as a member of the royal family. Charles has expressed pride in his sons and his grandchildren, George and Charlotte. After years of being viewed as an absent father, Charles's warm relationship with his sons and grandchildren is now part of his public image.

Popular perceptions of Charles as a father have been transformed in the decades since William's accident with the golf club at Eton. Charles's rehabilitation as a father in the popular imagination has informed more recent press coverage of his generation of royal parents. In April 2012, Lady

Louise Windsor, daughter of Charles's younger brother Edward, Earl of Wessex, and Sophie, Countess of Wessex, suffered a riding accident at the age of eight. In contrast to her grandmother the Queen, who does not wear a helmet while riding so that her hair will not have to be restyled for subsequent royal engagements, Louise was wearing full safety gear, including a helmet and back brace, and it was therefore clear that she would make a full recovery. The official statement from Buckingham Palace informed the public, "The Countess of Wessex was supposed to go to Manchester today with the Earl but understandably stayed with her daughter." Just as Diana had remained at the hospital with William following the golf accident while Charles attended to his royal engagements, Sophie remained with her daughter while Edward continued to a planned joint engagement at the Christie Cancer Hospital.

The press coverage of Charles and Diana in 1991 versus Edward and Sophie in 2012, however, was very different. Edward did not receive criticism as a father for leaving his injured child's bedside to undertake a planned public engagement. *Hello!* reported without critical comment, "Edward went ahead with the engagement, visiting the Christie in Withington, after learning his daughter hadn't been seriously injured."[18] The nature of Edward's public engagement may have influenced the coverage, as a visit to a cancer hospital appears to be more important than a night at the opera, but knowledge of Charles's bond with his sons may have also demonstrated that the press had been too quick in the past to describe similar actions as a manifestation of absentee fatherhood.

The year before her riding accident, Louise was a bridesmaid at the wedding of her cousin Prince William to Catherine "Kate" Middleton. When William was a child, parenting experts who assumed that Charles was an absentee father argued that the young prince would not be capable of bonding with a family of his own. Dr. Ronald Levant, author of *Between Father and Child* and the former director of Boston University's Fatherhood Project, explained to *People* that "when [the sons of such fathers] grow up, they have trouble forming intimate relationships with their wives and children, and will repeat the experience with their own children, whether they like it or not."[19] At the time of William and Kate's wedding, the public perception of William as a potential father was far more optimistic. Not only did William clearly have a warm relationship with Charles, but he was also marrying into a close family. *Newsweek* explained that the Middletons personified "the ordinary domestic happiness William would like to achieve in his own life. It's definitely something he aspires to — settled, contented domesticity."[20] Kate was the first woman from a middle-class background to marry a direct heir to the throne since the future James II married Anne Hyde in 1660. Like the foreign princes and princesses who married into the British royal family in previous centuries, she brought new ideas about parenting to her marriage, based on her own experiences. By the time Buckingham Palace announced that William and Kate would become parents for the first time in 2013, it was clear that the new generation of royal children would have an upbringing that blended royal traditions with twenty-first-century parenting trends.

TWENTY

Prince William (1982-) and Catherine Middleton (1982-)

In January 2016, Prince George of Cambridge started attending a Montessori preschool near Anmer Hall, the country estate in Norfolk where his parents William and Kate, the Duke and Duchess of Cambridge, have spent most of their time since his birth in 2013. George was only the second generation in his family to attend preschool, and at two-and-a-half, he was younger than Prince William was when he started attending Jane Mynors' nursery school near Kensington Palace at the age of three years and three months.

George's first day of school attracted intense media scrutiny because it was one of the rare occasions when authorized photographs of the young prince were issued to the media. The photographs were taken by Kate, who also took official photos of her daughter, Princess Charlotte, at the age of six months. Although royalty have taken family photographs themselves since Queen Victoria's reign, Kate has often assumed the role traditionally given to official photographers of creating and curating the images of her family seen by the public. By taking and sharing pictures of her children personally, Kate is mirroring the activities of other parents of her generation. George is the first direct heir to the British and

Commonwealth thrones to be born into the age of social media, when parents from all walks of life proudly post pictures of their children on Facebook and Instagram.

In contrast to most other children, there is a global audience for photographs of George and Charlotte. During the weeks prior to George's birth on July 23, 2013, journalists from around the world gathered around the Lindo maternity wing of St. Mary's Hospital in London, eagerly awaiting a chance to take the first picture of the newborn. The announcement of the prince's birth was broadcast on Twitter as well as the traditional easel behind the Buckingham Palace gates. Photographs of Prince George making his first appearance outside the hospital were broadcast worldwide as part of the twenty-four-hour news cycle. The public expected that there would be frequent film footage and photographs of George as he grew from a baby into a toddler, but William and Kate proved to be extremely protective of their family's privacy.

George and Charlotte have made the occasional appearance at official events, most notably appearing on the Buckingham Palace balcony together for the first time during Queen Elizabeth II's ninetieth birthday celebrations, but they are rarely in the public eye compared to other European royal children close to their own age, such as Princess Estelle of Sweden. As a result, the press eagerly reports anecdotes about George and Charlotte that William and Kate mention during informal conversations in royal walkabouts. During one of Kate's final royal engagements before Charlotte's birth, travel adviser Claudia Gordon "asked her if Prince George was excited about the new Prince or Princess that was coming, and she said yes and that he is a toddler and is talking and walking."[1] These glimpses into family life behind palace doors provide few details that demonstrate a distinctly royal upbringing for George and Charlotte, encouraging the public to identify with William and Kate as young parents.

Even though he is a future monarch, George is being educated to forge his own path in the world. The philosophy of renowned educator Maria Montessori (1870–1952) matches William and Kate's desire for their children to develop according to their individual personalities, even though they have been born into more than a thousand years of royal tradition.

Montessori encouraged children to learn at their own pace, arguing that their minds naturally absorbed new experiences and ideas. In her 1949 book, *The Absorbent Mind*, Montessori explains:

> Our work is not to teach, but to help the absorbent mind in its work of development. How marvelous it would be if by our help, if by an intelligent treatment of the child, if by understanding the needs of his physical life and by feeding his intellect, we could prolong the period of functioning of the absorbent mind! What a service we should render if we could help the human individual to absorb knowledge without fatigue, if man could find himself full of knowledge without knowing how he had acquired it, almost by magic.[2]

The Montessori approach is completely different from the rigid educational program designed by Baron Stockmar for Victoria and Albert's children in the nineteenth century, and assumes that George and Charlotte possess an innate capacity for knowledge and self-discovery. Montessori's philosophy also theorizes that all young children learn in a similar fashion. While past educational programs for royalty referenced their status as an issue to be emphasized or minimized in early childhood according to their circumstances and the wishes of their parents, the Montessori program takes succession out of the equation and treats royal children exactly the same as their peers.

Kate has brought her own parenting philosophy to the royal family. Although William and Kate were both raised in privileged circumstances in the United Kingdom, Kate's upbringing bore little resemblance to the royal splendour that surrounded William from the time of his birth. Kate's mother, Carole Goldsmith, came from a working-class background, and met her future husband, Michael Middleton, while working as a flight attendant for British Airways. The couple started Party Pieces, a mail-order children's party supply business, and became self-made millionaires. Income from Party Pieces and from the trust established for the fortune of Michael's grandmother, wool manufacturing heiress Olive

Lupton, allowed Kate and her siblings to be educated at elite boarding schools, although weekends and holidays were spent with family. Denise Allford, who taught Kate and her sister Philippa "Pippa" at St. Andrew's Prep School in Pangbourne, Berkshire, recalled that the Middleton family often spent their holidays together in the Lake District, stating, "The girls would talk about these wonderful holidays they had at the cottage with no water and no electricity…. They never came back with suntans; they holidayed in the UK most of the time. It was typical of their very grounded life."[3]

Kate's close relationship with her family endured through her years at Scotland's University of St. Andrews, where she began a relationship with William. Kate continued to take frequent holidays with her family, and worked as a photographer for Party Pieces after graduation. William admired the close bonds within the Middleton family, and developed a strong bond with his future parents-in-law. As parents, William and Kate are attempting to recreate the tranquil home environment created by the Middletons, spending plenty of time with George and Charlotte.

The difference between William and Kate's social backgrounds and the closeness of the Middleton family has fueled press speculation in the United Kingdom about the degree of influence Kate's parents will have over the upbringing of George and Charlotte. While Diana's relationship with her mother and sisters was often strained, Kate has remained close to her family through marriage and motherhood. William also enjoys a warm relationship with the Middletons. William and Kate have changed their participation in royal holiday traditions to ensure that George and Charlotte have time with both their royal and Middleton relatives. Kate, George, and Charlotte spent Easter with the Middletons in 2016 instead of attending church services with the Queen, and William and Kate have created their own Christmas traditions, which include time with the Middletons and celebrations at Anmer Hall. Like the families of other "commoners" who have married into the royal family over the centuries, such as Elizabeth Woodville and Anne Boleyn, there has been enormous speculation about the Middleton family's ambitions. Carole Middleton in particular has been singled out for her influence. *Town and Country* magazine argued that Kate is part of a rising British upper-middle or "upper Middleton" class that is increasingly intermarrying with royalty and the aristocracy, stating, "This sub-class has a strategist in its midst who is almost always 'mum.' The Upper Middleton mother is the social class equivalent of the Tiger Mother.... Think of the UM mother as Churchill standing beside a big social map and slowly but methodically shunting her children into the right places at the right time."[4] The press has also speculated about how much time George and Charlotte were spending with their paternal grandfather Charles, compared to Carole Middleton's frequent visits to Anmer Hall.

In the wider Commonwealth, the Middleton family has received far less scrutiny concerning their influence over a future monarch and wider trends regarding social mobility. Outside the United Kingdom, the term "middle class" is not applied to self-made millionaires like the Middletons, and Kate's close family is viewed as a welcome counterpoint to the more distant parenting practices that prevailed in the royal family during much of the nineteenth and twentieth centuries. When William and Kate visited Canada in 2016 with their children, they were praised for keeping to a schedule that enabled them to spend most evenings with George and Charlotte at Government House in Victoria.

William and Kate's charitable patronages demonstrate their concern for issues facing twenty-first-century children, including bullying and effective treatment for children's mental health problems. While previous generations of royalty have become patrons of a broad range of philanthropic organizations, the Royal Foundation of the Duke and Duchess of Cambridge and Prince Harry focuses on three core causes: conservation, the armed forces, and young people. William has been particularly concerned with bullying in schools. In September 2015, he attended a #Back2School anti-bullying ambassador training session hosted by the Diana Award, named in memory of his late mother. During the event, he affirmed that he would confront the abuser if he witnessed a homophobic bullying episode and revealed his own strong family relationships, writing that the five most important people in his own support network are his wife Kate, brother Harry, father Charles, and grandparents, the Queen and Prince Philip.

In June 2016, just days after a mass murder in an Orlando gay nightclub, William became the first member of the royal family to appear on the cover of a magazine for gay readers, stating, "No-one should be bullied for their sexuality or any other reason."[5] Kate has given speeches in support of effective care for mentally ill children. During Children's Mental Health week in February 2016, she released a video message in which she affirmed that "every child deserves to grow up feeling confident that they won't fall at the first hurdle — that they [can] cope with life's setbacks. This resilience, our ability to deal with stressful situations, is something we begin to learn in childhood, as we respond to each challenge and problem life presents."[6]

William and Kate's concern for bullied and mentally ill children suggests that they will be particularly focused on ensuring George and Charlotte experience a secure and supportive upbringing that respects their individual personalities. As William explained in an essay for the British mental health charity *Heads Together* on Father's Day 2016, "it is a day ... to reflect on just how much I've learned about fatherhood and the issues facing fathers in all walks of life. In particular, it is a time to reflect on my responsibility to look after not just the physical health of my two children, but to treat their mental needs as just as important a priority."[7] George and Charlotte will be treated by their parents as distinct personalities with individual needs, an approach that is unusual in the history of royal parenting.

Despite William and Kate's determination to ensure that George and Charlotte experience as normal an upbringing as possible, their place in the direct line of succession has resulted in them being at the centre of political controversies, including gender-neutral succession reform and Scottish independence, began before they were born. The place of women in the royal succession and the relationship between the English and Scottish crowns has been debated since the Middle Ages, and continues to be part of the lives of the youngest generation of the royal family. Over the course of William's and Kate's lifetimes to date, a profound change in attitudes toward royal succession has swept Europe's royal houses, that will have lasting consequences for the upbringing of future generations of royal children, starting with George and Charlotte. The institution of monarchy had grown out of a need for strong military leadership, and for centuries, it was taken for granted that a male sovereign was preferable to a female one. In England, Common law regarding inheritance of property supported the development of male-preference primogeniture in the succession. There was no need for the 1701 Act of Settlement to state that younger brothers would take precedence over their elder sisters in the succession because male-preference primogeniture was almost universally accepted as the natural method of determining the succession within a hereditary monarchy. As late as the reign of George VI, the future Elizabeth II was heiress presumptive rather than heir apparent. She was never created Princess of Wales, a title associated with the consort of a Prince of Wales rather than the daughter of a monarch.

The other European royal houses either followed similar succession patterns or placed even more stringent restrictions on women becoming reigning monarchs. In the 1980s and 1990s, however, a number of Europe's royal houses changed their succession laws to introduce absolute primogeniture, ensuring that the eldest child of a monarch, male or female, would succeed to the throne and therefore require an upbringing for an heir, regardless of gender. The first country to introduce this succession reform was Sweden where "King" Christina had once struggled to reconcile expectations of her roles as a ruler and woman in the seventeenth century. In 1980, the Swedish parliament reformed the 1810 Act of Succession, which restricted the succession to Napoleon Bonaparte's general Jean Baptiste Bernadotte and his male descendants, to allow the throne to pass to the monarch's eldest child, male or female. King Carl XVI Gustaf of Sweden had two young children at the time, Victoria (born 1977) and Carl Philip (born 1979). In Sweden, succession reform changed the existing line of succession, as Victoria became Crown Princess, superseding her younger brother. Carl Gustaf was reportedly displeased by the change because it stripped his son of his existing place in the succession. The King stated on Swedish television, twenty-three years after the change, "a constitution that works in retroactive force is strange."[8] The Swedish reforms have influenced the order of succession for multiple generations, as Victoria's daughter, Estelle, also has a younger brother.

In the United Kingdom and Commonwealth realms, succession reform was more complicated because the Queen reigns not only in the United Kingdom but in fifteen other Commonwealth Nations. As absolute primogeniture was introduced in the Netherlands (1983), Norway (1990), Belgium (1991), Denmark (2009), and Luxembourg (2011), discussion concerning how succession reform would be introduced in sixteen nations sharing a single monarch intensified. Future Prime Minister David Cameron, then-leader of the Conservative Party, explained in 2009, "The Queen is not just our Queen. She is the Queen of all the Commonwealth countries that have her as their head of state so this is not an easy change to make."[9] The Commonwealth Heads of Government expressed little interest in starting the reform process. Canadian Prime Minister Stephen Harper stated during his 2011 election campaign, "The successor to the throne is a man [Charles]. The next successor to the throne is a man [William]. I don't think Canadians want to open a debate on the monarchy or constitutional matters at this time."[10] The prospect of one of William and Kate's children reigning over Canada seemed remote at the beginning of the twenty-first century.

The debate concerning succession reform assumed a new urgency after William and Kate married that same year. In an effort to avoid the retroactive constitutional change that took place in Sweden, changing the existing line of succession, the process of reform began before William and Kate became parents. In October 2011, the leaders of the Commonwealth realms agreed in principle to introduce absolute primogeniture at the Commonwealth Heads of Government Meeting in Perth, Australia. In contrast to the King of Sweden, Queen Elizabeth II appeared to favour the reforms, attending the summit and mentioning the importance of gender equality in her speech, stating, "The theme of this year is 'Women as Agents of Change.' It reminds us of the potential in our societies that is yet to be fully unlocked, and it encourages us to find ways to show girls and women how to play their full part."[11] The press reported optimistically that succession reform was now settled and that William and Kate's eldest child, male or female, would eventually succeed to the throne.

The succession reforms agreed upon at the 2011 Commonwealth Heads of Government Conference would not come into force until March of 2015, just one month before Charlotte's birth. While there was broad agreement on the importance of absolute primogeniture for a twenty-first century monarchy, the process of reform raised other concerns with the United Kingdom and the Commonwealth. In the United Kingdom, succession reform prompted broader questions about the inheritance of lands passed down through the royal family since the fourteenth century, and the broader implications for the peerage. Since the reign of Edward III, the eldest son of the monarch has automatically held the title of Duke of Cornwall and enjoyed financial independence through the extensive landholdings belonging to the Duchy. In early 2014, William completed a ten-week course in Agricultural Management at Cambridge University in preparation for succeeding to the Duchy upon Charles's accession to the throne. The Succession to the Throne Act 2013 introduced by then Deputy Prime Minister Nick Clegg received criticism because it did not take into account succession to royal lands intended for the sovereign or heir to the throne, raising the possibility that a future royal daughter might become heir to the throne while her brother inherited the Duchy of Cornwall, intended for the heir's income. Clegg argued that these details could be addressed in the future, once succession reform was in place.

Discussion of the future of the Duchy of Cornwall raised the question of how gender informs succession to English peerages, which often become extinct in the absence of a male heir. One of the most vocal advocates of peerage reform is Julian Fellowes, the creator of the television series *Downton Abbey*, who observed, "My wife [Lady Emma Kitchener-Fellowes] was born female. The fact remains that had she been born male she would now be the fourth Earl Kitchener of Khartoum."[12] In the aftermath of the British debate over royal succession reform, a campaign group emerged to lobby for absolute primogeniture to determine succession to the peerage. While this campaign did not prompt legislation for absolute primogeniture in the peerage, a private member's bill before the House of Lords calls for the inheritance of all peerages to be determined by male-preference primogeniture, which would prevent peerages from becoming extinct in the absence of male heirs. Although the Succession to Peerages Bill does not provide the same inheritance rights for women as the recent royal succession reforms, the passing of the legislation would have a profound impact on future generations of royal children. Prince Andrew's title, Duke of York, is currently expected to revert to the Crown upon his death. Under the terms of the bill, the title would be inherited by his elder daughter Princess Beatrice and pass through her line, making it unlikely that it would ever again be bestowed on the second son of the sovereign.

In the Commonwealth realms, succession reform raised questions about the future of a united Commonwealth and the monarch's role within federal systems of government. The Commonwealth nations where the Queen reigns as Head of State adopted a variety of approaches to implementing succession reform. Canada passed an act to assent to alterations in the law touching the Succession to the Throne in 2013. The legislation proved controversial because Canada's constitution requires amendments to "the office of the Queen, the Governor General and the Lieutenant Governor of a province" to be authorized by the legislative assembly of each province instead of the federal government alone. There were also concerns raised about whether Canada could "assent" to British legislation in the twenty-first century because the 1931 Statute of Westminster created an independent Canadian Crown. The legislation faced a court challenge in Quebec on the grounds that the provinces had not been consulted regarding the change to the office of the Queen. In February 2016, the Quebec Superior Court ruled that Canada did not have to reopen the constitution or change its laws for succession reform to be in effect. The case is currently expected to be heard by the Quebec Court of Appeal. In Australia, each state passed its own legislation, and the succession reform finally went into force across the country when the state of Western Australia passed its succession bill in 2015. The process of succession reform began before George was born, and did not come to an end until he was a toddler. The future monarch spent his infancy amid a wider debate concerning gender equality and the role of the monarchy in the Commonwealth.

While the announcement that William and Kate were expecting their first child took place amid a series of international controversies concerning succession reform in the Commonwealth, the announcement that a second child would arrive in the spring of 2015 became part of the debate concerning Scottish independence. The announcement of an impending referendum on Scotland remaining part of the United

Kingdom took place the same week that Kensington Palace announced that William and Kate were expecting a second child. Scotland's plan for independence retained the Queen as constitutional monarch, returning England and Scotland to the relationship of two countries with a single sovereign that existed between 1603 and 1707. Reports that the Queen favoured the continuation of a unified Britain, however, meant that Scottish voters with a positive view of the monarchy seemed more likely to oppose an independent Scotland. Political cartoons imagined England and Scotland as an acrimonious married couple with England declaring "I'm pregnant" in response to Scotland announcing "I'm leaving."[13] When Scotland voted to remain part of the United Kingdom in September 2014, there was press speculation that enthusiasm for the forthcoming royal baby encouraged some voters to favour a continued union between Scotland and England.

There is widespread speculation concerning whether William and Kate will decide to become parents of a third child. Kate is one of three children and is close to her siblings. Across Europe, there is a trend toward larger royal families. King Willem-Alexander and Queen Maxima of the Netherlands are the parents of three daughters, while Crown Prince Frederick and Crown Princess Mary of Denmark have four children, the same number as King Philippe and Queen Matilde of Belgium. Even in an era where the upbringing of royal children is closer to the experiences of other privileged families, the arrival of a royal child continues to have unique political and cultural implications. If William and Kate decide to expand their family, their third child may revive the centuries-old debate about the appropriate role for younger royal children who have little prospect of succeeding to the throne. The wider political events surrounding a subsequent royal birth, including the United Kingdom's place in the European Union and Commonwealth, may also inform the public response to a third child. On June 23, 2016, England and Wales voted to leave the European Union, while Scotland and Northern Ireland favoured remaining integrated with the rest of Europe. Just as the announcement that William and Kate were expecting a second child informed the 2014 Scottish referendum, news of a third child may inform popular attitudes concerning the future cohesion of the United Kingdom. In addition to their place in British, European, and Commonwealth political debates, George, Charlotte, and any younger siblings will grow up amid popular speculation concerning the future of the royal nursery in the twenty-first century.

EPILOGUE

The Future of the Royal Nursery

If Prince George of Cambridge achieves comparable longevity to his great-grandmother the Queen, he may be the king who leads the monarchy into the twenty-second century. The future of the monarchy in the United Kingdom and the Commonwealth, however, is the subject of intense popular speculation. In the spring of 2016, the British press debated whether Prince William was interested in one day becoming king. Queen Elizabeth II was nearly ninety, and his grandfather, Prince Philip, Duke of Edinburgh was ninety-four, and yet they performed far more public engagements than their thirty-three-year-old grandson. By March 1, 2016, William had only performed two public engagements during that calendar year, and he had declined to attend a party for those nominated for the British Academy of Film and Television Awards (BAFTAs), even though he is president of the organization and the celebration was in one of his residences, Kensington Palace.[1] By the fall of 2016, William was being praised for his busy schedule of royal engagements during his Canadian tour with Kate and their children, but comparisons of his schedule to those of his father and grandparents remain a staple of British royal coverage.

Criticism of members of the royal family perceived to be neglecting their duties is a centuries-old theme. Walter Bagehot defended the institution of constitutional monarchy, but wrote that the royal family of his own country, the United Kingdom, consisted of "a retired widow and an unemployed youth," a thinly veiled critique of Queen Victoria and her eldest son, the future King Edward VII, after the death of Prince Albert in 1861.[2] The domestic seclusion of Czar Nicholas II and Empress Alexandra in the early twentieth century alienated them from the imperial Russian elite during the years prior to the Russian Revolution. There are two aspects of the controversy surrounding Prince William, however, that are unique to the twenty-first century. William's current critics expect the current second-in-line to the throne to assume a public profile comparable to past Princes of Wales within a newly streamlined, multigenerational constitutional monarchy. In contrast, William's defenders argue that he is right to keep a comparatively low profile because it allows him to devote time to being an active, involved father to his young children. Both arguments point to the future of the royal nursery.

In the twenty-first century, fewer children than ever before will experience a royal upbringing in the public eye. The last time there was a monarch and three generations of heirs to the throne was during the final years of the reign of Queen Victoria, who had nine children and forty-two grandchildren. At the time of her death in 1901, she had thirty-seven surviving great-grandchildren. The royal pedigree of some of these descendants was questioned in European royal circles, as the queen's youngest daughter, Princess Beatrice, married into the House of Battenberg, which was a morganatic branch of the House of Hesse-Darmstadt. The experiences of the royal children during Queen Victoria's reign, however, from the children and grandchildren of her eldest son to the children of her youngest daughter, were remarkably similar. Victoria took an active interest in the upbringing of all her descendants, and expected to be consulted on everything from their names to their education. Whether Victoria's descendants were raised in the United Kingdom, Germany, Romania, or Russia during her reign, they had English nannies and nursery routines and maintained close ties to their international family of royal cousins. As they grew older, their parents instilled in them the importance of public engagements and philanthropy, and these activities became part of their routine. When Queen Victoria's children and grandchildren grew up and married, they all required the monarch's permission under the Royal Marriages Act of 1772. For the public, which saw Victoria's descendants come together for her Golden Jubilee in 1887, and the elderly queen always in the company of members of her family, all of her descendants were indisputably royal, and their activities were the focus of popular interest.

Queen Elizabeth II's reign has maintained vestiges of the extended royal family in the public eye that was an integral aspect of Queen Victoria's image. The Queen's cousins, the Dukes of Kent and Gloucester, as well as Princess Alexandra (sister to the Duke of Kent) represent her at public events and the annual Trooping the Colour celebrations, and Christmas luncheon at Buckingham Palace brings together numerous children descended from George V. The press eagerly reports on play dates between Prince George and the other children in his extended family, events that bring royal parents together. In February 2016, the actress Sophie Winkleman, who is married to Prince William's second cousin, Lord Frederick Windsor, said in an interview with *Hello!* that her daughter Maud Windsor and Prince George had a play date at Kensington Palace when they were around 20 months old, and that the two toddlers "got on very well."[3] When Princess Madeleine of Sweden, a descendent of Queen Victoria's third son Prince Arthur, Duke of Connaught, and her young family moved to London in 2015, there was immediate press speculation that her daughter Leonore, Duchess of Gotland (born 2014), would become a playmate for Prince George. Compared to the frequent contact between royal cousins among Queen Victoria's grandchildren and great-grandchildren, however, George spends little time with other royal children.

Queen Elizabeth II's Diamond Jubilee celebrations suggested that the current reign will be the last to feature a royal extended family in the public eye. Although all the Queen's children and a number of her grandchildren undertook public engagements in the United Kingdom and Commonwealth during the Jubilee year, the Thames Jubilee Pageant featured only Charles and Camilla, William and Kate, and Harry aboard the royal barge, *The Spirit of Chartwell*, along with the Queen and Prince

Philip. The British press described the royal party as "leading members of the royal family."[4] The "royal mob" of Queen Victoria's reign had been replaced by a streamlined royal family consisting of the monarch and immediate heirs. Recent succession reforms may have increased opportunities for women to become monarchs in the future, but they also emphasize a smaller royal family in the public eye. The concurrent reforms to the Royal Marriages Act mean that only the first six people in the line of succession require the monarch's permission to marry. Since royalty now marry people from a variety of social backgrounds instead of other royalty or aristocracy alone, it is increasingly less likely that minor members of one royal family will become more senior members of another royal family. Fewer connections to Europe's other royal families mean that royal parenting trends from one nation are less likely to influence domestic life in another nation. Beyond the children and grandchildren of monarchs, it is unlikely future descendants of kings and queens will consider themselves "royal parents," obliged to train their children for future public roles. There will be broader political implications to the streamlining of the royal family, including fewer tours of the Commonwealth realms and fewer prominent patrons for charities, but the immediate domestic impact will be that fewer children will receive a distinctly royal upbringing.

For the few remaining royal parents, such as William and Kate, parenting will be a key aspect of their identities, a way of creating common ground with people of all social backgrounds and justifying the need for a private life. In the past, the royal parents who enjoyed the closest relationships with their children were not necessarily the most successful monarchs. The business of ruling took kings and queens far away from their children, and adult heirs were also potential rivals. Royalty who prioritized time with their children often attracted criticism for neglecting their other duties. Deposed monarchs and consorts might find consolation in closer bonds with their children, but reigning sovereigns and their direct heirs rarely invoked childcare as a reason for fewer royal engagements. In contrast, William and Kate have made clear that raising their children is their primary focus while George and Charlotte are young. William responded to criticism of his comparatively small number of public appearances by emphasizing the importance of his presence in the daily lives of his children, stating in an interview with the BBC royal correspondent Nick Witchell, "I am concentrating very much on my role as a father. I'm a new father and I take my duties and my responsibilities to my family very seriously and I want to bring my children up as good people with the idea of service and duty to others as very important."[5] William and Kate's identity as parents is central to the popular debate concerning the appropriate role for royalty in the twenty-first century.

William and Kate's determination to achieve a degree of privacy for their young family and prioritize childrearing reflects wider cultural trends concerning the importance of work-life balance. When George was born, William became the first senior member of the royal family to take a parental leave, spending two weeks away from his position as a Royal Air Force Search and Rescue pilot at full pay. William's leave took place just ten years after parental leave was introduced for new fathers in the United Kingdom. News of William's plans to take a parental leave, a practice that he repeated as an Air Ambulance pilot when Charlotte was born, prompted global debates concerning how different countries approach the balancing of paid work with parenthood. While William and Kate's critics observed their comparatively light schedule of public engagements and questioned their commitment to royal duties, advocates of more flexible workplace conditions for new parents praised the royal couple as trailblazers for a new generation determined to achieve work-life balance. The Institute for Family Studies in the United States even argued that William should not only demonstrate his commitment to balancing work and family by example but actively advocate for workplace policies that acknowledge parental responsibilities, stating, "William has a huge opportunity to help parents everywhere. As a working father with two young children, he knows firsthand how hard it can be to juggle obligations at work and at home…. By speaking out publicly, the prince could shift the discussion on parenting, potentially leading to some concrete changes that would help all parents."[6] Just as William and Kate have successfully raised awareness of children's mental health issues and anti-bullying initiatives, they also have the potential to become the public face of broader debates concerning how parents balance work and family.

The tensions between a public and a private sphere for raising royal children, revealed by the decisions made by royal parents over the past thousand years, will continue in the coming decades. The Queen has famously observed, "I have to be seen to be believed," and the public expects to see the entire royal family on a regular basis. If the royal family retreats into seclusion, there is always the possibility that this will result in declining public support for the institution of monarchy.

The restrictions placed on the domestic lives of royal parents, however, mean that the current level of engagement between the royal family and the public may be critiqued not only by outside observers but also by members of the royal family itself. A recent report released by the University College London Constitution Unit observed that "The Queen, Prince Charles, and Prince William have to abandon freedoms which the rest of us take for granted. Freedom of privacy and family life; freedom of expression; freedom to travel where we like; free choice of careers; freedom of religion; freedom to marry whom we like.... The question is whether future heirs are willing to make the self-sacrifices required of living in a gilded cage."

Among the continental European royal houses, there is more evidence of these freedoms for royal family members and the possibility of retirement at the end of a long reign.[7] The next generation of royalty may decide to adapt centuries-old royal traditions to allow a greater degree of autonomy for themselves and their children. The formative experiences that William and Kate provide for George and Charlotte will help them determine new trends in royal parenting for the twenty-first century and beyond.

ACKNOWLEDGEMENTS

I would like to thank Carrie Gleason at Dundurn Press, who suggested in the summer of 2015 that I write a book about "growing up royal." I am grateful for the opportunity to spend months immersing myself in the history of royal parenting from medieval to modern times.

At Dundurn Press I would like to thank Kirk Howard and Beth Bruder. Thanks to Allison Hirst and Kel Pero, who provided helpful feedback on the manuscript, and Cheryl Hawley and Kathryn Lane, who answered my questions throughout the editing process. I would also like to thank my publicist, Jaclyn Hodsdon, and everyone else at Dundurn Press who has contributed to the success of this book.

Thank you to Len and Suzy Rodness, who first introduced me to Dundurn Press in 2014, for the opportunity to write my first book, *Magna Carta and Its Gifts to Canada*.

Thank you to the Ontario Arts Council for the Writers' Reserve Grant.

At the University of Toronto School of Continuing Studies I would like to thank Gordon Davies, director of Languages, Arts and Sciences. Research that I undertook for School of Continuing Studies courses on Richard III, Peter the Great, and Women in Power informed the writing of this book. I would also like to thank the helpful librarians at Robarts Library, University of Toronto, where I spent a great deal of time during the research and writing of this book.

At Queen's University in Kingston I would like to thank my M.A. and Ph.D. advisers, Andrew Jainchill and Jeffrey Collins. I have been researching royal parenting since my M.A. in history, which focused on motherhood and Marie Antoinette, and my Ph.D., which compared Marie Antoinette and Henrietta Maria as wives, mothers, and heads of royal households.

This book has also been informed by more than five years of providing media commentary about the history of the monarchy. I would like to thank everyone who has provided me with opportunities to engage with the public on royal history, including Dominic Ali, Sandra den Otter, Michael Onesi, and Anne Craig. Special thanks to Kathryn Westcott at the *BBC News Magazine*, who asked me to write an article about the modern "Revolution in the Royal Nursery" in 2013. Thank you to Jonathan Lee for taking the author photograph.

While writing this book, I discussed royal history, politics, and popular culture with a number of other experts in these fields. I would like to thank Richard Berthelsen, Marilyn Braun, Marlene Koenig, Philippe Lagassé, Kelly Mathews, Nicholas Nicholson, Nathan Tidridge, and Patricia Treble for sharing their insights and answering my questions. Thanks to Mark Reid, Amy Licence, and Elena Woodacre for reading the manuscript and sharing their thoughts.

This book is dedicated to my parents, Richard and Sue Harris, and my grandparents, Desmond and Mary Harris and Robert and Ida Hanbidge, who encouraged my interests in history and writing from a young age and shaped the person I am today. My Gran, Ida, passed away in 1997 and my Grandpa, Desmond, died in 2013, and they continue to be missed. I would also like to thank my brother, David, and my aunts, uncles, and cousins.

Finally, I would like to thank my husband, Bruce Harpham, who has been a constant source of love, support, and encouragement throughout my career as a historian and author.

NOTES

Chapter 1: Edgar "the Peaceable" (c. 943–75) and Elfrida of Northampton (c. 945–1001)

1. Harriet O'Brien, *Queen Emma and the Vikings* (New York: Bloomsbury, 2006), 53.

2. J.A. Giles, *Six Old English Chronicles* (London: Henry G. Bohn, 1848), 47.

3. Simon Keynes, "Edgar: *Rex Admirabilis*," in *Edgar, King of the English: New Interpretations*, ed. Donald Scragg (Woodbridge, UK: Boydell Press, 2008), 56.

4. Barbara Yorke, "The Women in King Edgar's Life," in *Edgar*, ed. Scragg, 148.

5. Dorothy Whitelock, *Anglo-Saxon Wills* (Cambridge: Cambridge University Press 1930), 21.

6. Elizabeth Norton, *Elfrida, The First Crowned Queen of England* (Stroud, UK: Amberley, 2013), 150.

7. See Mathew S. Kufler, "'A Wryed Existence:' Attitudes Toward Children in Anglo-Saxon England," *Journal of Social History* 24, no. 4 (Summer 1991): 824.

8. Norton, *Elfrida*, 139.

9. Hilary Powell, "'Once Upon a Time There was a Saint…': Re-Evaluating Folklore in Anglo-Latin Hagiography," *Folklore* 121, no. 2 (July 5, 2010): 171–89.

10. Norton, *Elfrida*, 141.

11. Ibid., 143.

12. Pauline Stafford, *Queen Emma and Queen Edith: Queenship and Women's Power in 11th Century England* (Oxford: Blackwell, 1997), 249.

Chapter 2: William I "the Conqueror" (c. 1028–87) and Matilda of Flanders (c. 1031–83)

1. Marjorie Chibnall, *The Ecclesiastical History of Orderic Vitalis* (Oxford: Clarendon Press, 1983), 3:105.

2. Tracy Borman, *Matilda: Queen of the Conqueror* (London: Jonathan Cape, 2011), 165.

3. Lois L. Huneycutt, *Matilda of Scotland: A Study in English Queenship* (Suffolk: Boydell Press, 2003), 51; and Lisa Hilton, *Queens Consort: England's Medieval Queens* (London: Weidenfeld and Nicolson, 2008), 39.

4. Chibnall, *The Ecclesiastical History*, 103.

5. Ibid., 103, 105.

6. Ibid., 113.

7. William Forbes-Leith, *Life of St. Margaret, Queen of Scotland by Turgot, Bishop of St. Andrews* (Edinburgh: William Patterson, 1884), 33.

8. Ibid., 34.

9. Ibid., 33.

10. Sally N. Vaughn, *Archbishop Anselm: 1093–1109* (London: Routledge, 2016), 12.

Chapter 3: Henry II (1133–89) and Eleanor of Aquitaine (c. 1124–1204)

1. Ralph V. Turner, *Eleanor of Aquitaine: Queen of France, Queen of England* (New Haven, CT: Yale University Press, 2009), 224.

2. Phyllis Gafney, *Constructions of Childhood and Youth in Old French Narrative* (New York: Routledge, 2016), 91.

3. Ibid.

4. Ibid., 92.

5. David C. Douglas and George W. Greenaway, *English Historical Documents 1042–1189*, 2nd ed. (New York: Routledge, 1981), 407.

6. Turner, *Eleanor of Aquitaine*, 207.

7. Frank McLynn, *Lionheart and Lackland: King Richard, King John and the Wars of Conquest* (New York: Vintage, 2007), 115.

8. Michael R. Evans, *Inventing Eleanor: The Medieval and Post-Medieval Image of Eleanor of Aquitaine* (London: Bloomsbury, 2014), 93.

9. Jane Martindale, "Eleanor of Aquitaine and a 'Queenly Court'?" in *Eleanor of Aquitaine: Lord and Lady*, eds. Bonnie Wheeler and John Carmi Parsons (New York: Palgrave Macmillan, 2004), 428.

10. Amy Kelly, *Eleanor of Aquitaine and the Four Kings* (Cambridge, MA: Harvard University Press, 1978), 344.

Chapter 4: Henry III (1207–72) and Eleanor of Provence (c. 1223–91)

1. Matthew of Paris, quoted in Irina Metzler, *Fools and Idiots: Intellectual Disability in the Middle Ages* (Oxford: Oxford University Press, 2016), 70.

2. *Perogativa Regis* 1255, quoted in Metzler, *Fools and Idiots*, 149.

3. Matthew of Paris, quoted in Sally Badham and Sophie Oosterwijk, "The Tomb Monument of Katherine, Daughter of Henry III and Eleanor of Provence (1253–7)," *Antiquaries Journal* 92 (2012), 171.

4. John of Oxnead, quoted in Carenza Lewis, "Indisciplinarity, Archeology and the Study of Medieval Childhood," in *Medieval Childhood: Archeological Approaches*, eds. D.M. Hadley and K.A. Hemer (Oxford: Oxbow Books, 2014), 151.

5. Badham and Oosterwijk, "The Tomb Monument," 175.

6. Magna Carta, 1215, Clause 3, www.bl.uk/collection-items/magna-carta-1215.

7. Ibid., Clause 15.

8. Joseph M. McCarthy, *Humanistic Emphases in the Educational Thought of Vincent of Beauvais* (Leiden: E.J. Brill, 1976), 137.

9. Susan M. Johns, *Noblewomen, Aristocracy and Power in the Twelfth Century Anglo-Norman Realm* (Manchester: Manchester University Press, 2003), 172.

10. Michael Prestwich, *Edward I* (Berkeley: University of California Press, 1988), 82.

Chapter 5: Edward III (1312–77) and Philippa of Hainault (1314–69)

1. John Carmi Parsons, "The Pregnant Queen as Counsellor and the Medieval Construction of Motherhood," in *Medieval Mothering*, eds. John Carmi Parsons and Bonnie Wheeler (New York: Garland, 1996), 40.
2. Hilton, *Queens Consort*, 295.
3. Alison Weir, *Queen Isabella: Treachery, Adultery and Murder in Medieval England* (New York: Ballantine Books, 2007), 197–98.
4. F.C. Hingeston-Randolph, *The Register of Walter de Stapledon, Bishop of Exeter* (London: Bell, 1892), 169.
5. Barbara Tuchman, *A Distant Mirror: The Calamitous 14th Century* (New York: Ballantine Books, 1978), 206.
6. Frederick James Furnivall, *Robert of Brunne's "Handlyng synne"* (London: K. Paul, Trench, Trubner, 1901), 38.
7. Ian Mortimer, *The Time Traveller's Guide to Medieval England: A Handbook for Visitors to the Fourteenth Century* (London: Vintage Books, 2012), 202.
8. Rosemary Horrox, *The Black Death* (Manchester: Manchester University Press, 2004), 250.
9. Corinne Saunders, *A Concise Companion to Chaucer* (Oxford: Blackwell, 2006), 13.
10. Michael Bennett, "Edward III's Entail and the Succession to the Crown, 1376–1471," *English Historical Review* 113, no. 452 (June 1998): 593.
11. Ibid., 586.

Chapter 6: Richard III (1452–85) and Anne Neville (1456–85)

1. Henry T. Riley, *Ingulph's Chronicle of the Abbey of Croyland with Continuations by Peter of Blois and Anonymous Writers* (London: Henry G. Bohn, 1854), 496.

2. Eve Salisbury, ed., *The Trials and Joys of Marriage* (Kalamazoo, MI: Medieval Institute Publications, 2002), http://d.lib.rochester.edu/teams/text/salisbury-trials-and-joys-how-the-goode-wife-taught-hyr-doughter.
3. Riley, *Ingulph's Chronicle*, 496.
4. Alec Reginald Myers, *English Historical Documents* (London: Routledge, 1969), 327.
5. Alexander Vance, ed., *The Book of the Knight of the Tower* (London: Chapman and Hall, 1868), 24.
6. Rosemary Horrox and P.W. Hammond, eds., *British Library Harleian Manuscript 433* (Gloucester, UK: A. Sutton, 1979), 1:83.
7. Caroline Halstead, *Richard III as Duke of Gloucester and King of England* (Philadelphia: Carey and Hart, 1844), 471.
8. Riley, *Ingulph's Chronicle*, 500.
9. Michael A. Hicks, "One Prince or Two? The Family of Richard III," *The Ricardian* 9, no. 122 (1993): 467–68.
10. Stephen Lewis, "Richard III's Son Rests in Sheriff Hutton," *York Press*, February 13, 2013.

Chapter 7: Ferdinand II of Aragon (1452–1516) and Isabella I of Castile (1451–1504)

1. Reprinted in Jon Cowans, *Early Modern Spain: A Documentary History* (Philadelphia: University of Philadelphia Press, 2003), 8.
2. Ibid., 117.
3. Quoted in James Casey, *Early Modern Spain: A Social History* (London: Routledge, 1999), 217.
4. Ibid., 218.
5. Cowans, *Early Modern Spain*, 120.
6. Henry Kamen, *The Spanish Inquisition: A Historical Revision*, 4th ed. (New Haven, CT: Yale University Press, 2014), 354.
7. Peggy Liss, *Isabel the Queen: Life and Times*, rev. ed. (Philadelphia: University of Pennsylvania Press, 2004), 372.

Chapter 8: Henry VIII (1491–1547) and Catherine of Aragon (1485–1536)

1. J.J. Scarisbrick, *Henry VIII* (New Haven, CT: Yale University Press, 2000), 150.
2. Alison Weir, *The Six Wives of Henry VIII* (New York: Random House, 2011), 127.
3. John Leland and Thomas Hearne, *Johannis Lelandi Antiquarii de Rebus Britannicus Collectanea* (London: Impensis Gul and Jo. Richardson, 1770), 4:179.
4. David Starkey, *Henry VIII: Man and Monarch* (London: British Library, 2009), 29.
5. Retha Warnicke, *The Marrying of Anne of Cleves: Royal Protocol in Early Modern England* (Cambridge: Cambridge University Press, 2000), 3–4.
6. Ibid., 3.
7. Juan Luis Vives, *The Education of a Christian Woman: A Sixteenth Century Manual*, ed. and trans. Charles Fantazzi (Chicago: University of Chicago Press, 2000), 71.
8. Weir, *The Six Wives of Henry VIII*, 127.
9. Giles Tremlett, *Catherine of Aragon: Henry's Spanish Queen: A Biography* (London: Faber and Faber, 2010), 306.
10. Ibid., 422.
11. G.B. Adams and H.M. Stephens, eds., *Select Documents of English Constitutional History* (New York: Macmillan, 1914), 264–67.

Chapter 9: Frederick V, Elector Palatine (1596–1632) and Elizabeth of England and Scotland (1596–1662)

1. Ethel Carleton Williams, *Anne of Denmark* (London: Longman, 1970), 4.
2. Leeds Barroll, *Anna of Denmark, Queen of England: A Cultural Biography* (Philadelphia: University of Pennsylvania Press, 2001), 23.
3. James I, quoted in Frances N. Teague, *Bathsua Makin: Woman of Learning* (London: Associated University Presses, 1998), 43.
4. Andrew L. Thomas, *A House Divided: Wittlesbach Confessional Court Cultures in the Holy Roman Empire c. 1550–1650* (Leiden: Brill, 2010), 42.

5. Ibid.

6. Nadine Akkerman, *The Correspondence of Elizabeth Stuart, Queen of Bohemia 1603–1631* (Oxford: Oxford University Press, 2015), 1:13.

7. "Venice: October 1622, 1–15," in *Calendar of State Papers Relating to English Affairs in the Archives of Venice*, vol. 17, *1621–23*, ed. Allen B. Hinds (London, 1911), 466–77, *British History Online*, www.british-history.ac.uk/cal-state-papers/venice/vol17/pp466-477.

8. Akkerman, *The Correspondence of Elizabeth Stuart*, 327.

9. Sophia, Electress of Hanover, *Memoirs of Sophia, Electress of Hanover 1630–1680* (London: Richard Bentley and Son, 1888), 7.

10. Conrad Sam, quoted in Steven Ozment, *When Fathers Ruled: Family Life in Reformation Europe* (Cambridge, MA: Harvard University Press, 1983), 133–34.

11. Sophia, Electress of Hanover, *Memoirs of Sophia*, 8.

12. Mary Anne Everett Green, *Lives of the Princesses of England from the Norman Conquest* (London: Henry Colborn, 1854), 5:513–14.

13. See C.V. Wedgwood, "King Charles's Nephew and the English Throne: The Elector Palatine and the Civil War," *History Today* 4, no. 1 (1954).

14. Elizabeth Benger, *Memoirs of Elizabeth Stuart* (London: Longman, 1825), 324.

15. John Evelyn and John Forster, *Diary and Correspondence of John Evelyn* (London: Bell and Daldy, 1872), 1:384.

Chapter 10: Charles I (1600–49) and Henrietta Maria of France (1609–69)

1. James I, *Basilikon Doron or His Majesty's Instructions to His Dearest Sonne, Henry the Prince* (London: Wertheimer, Lea, 1887), 94.

2. Green, *Lives of the Princesses*, 10–11.

3. *Calendar of State Papers*, 23:501.

4. *Parliament Scout Communicating His Intelligence to the Kingdom*, issue 1, June 20, 1643 (London: G. Bishop and R. White).

5. John Bruce, ed., *Charles I in 1646: Letters of King Charles I to Queen Henrietta Maria* (London: Camden Society, 1856), 69.

6. Ibid.

7. K.J. Kesselring, *The Trial of Charles I* (Peterborough, ON: Broadview Press, 2016), 74.

8. Ibid.

9. Green, *Lives of the Princesses*, 317.

10. Lambeth Palace Library, "Letters Divers of the Royal Family," Mss. 645, 3–4.

11. Samuel Pepys, *The Diary of Samuel Pepys*, eds. Robert Latham and William Matthews (London: Bell and Hyman, 1983), 3:303.

12. Robert K. Massie, *Peter the Great: His Life and World* (New York: Random House, 1980), 14n.

Chapter 11: Peter I "the Great" of Russia (1672–1725) and Catherine I (1684–1727)

1. Translated and reprinted in Massie, *Peter the Great*, 674.

2. Ibid., 675.

3. Ibid., 673.

4. Barbara Alpern Engel, *Women in Russia: 1700–2000* (Cambridge: Cambridge University Press, 2004), 6.

5. Carolyn Johnston Pouncy, *The Domostroi: Rules for Russian Households in the Time of Ivan the Terrible* (Ithaca, NY: Cornell University Press, 1994), 93.

6. Ibid., 104.

7. Translated and reprinted in Arthur L. George with Elena George, *St. Petersburg: Russia's Window to the Future: The First Three Centuries* (Lanham, MD: Taylor, 2003), 82.

8. Engel, *Women in Russia*, 14.

9. Lindsey Hughes, *Russia in the Age of Peter the Great* (New Haven, CT: Yale University Press, 1998), 401.

10. Massie, *Peter the Great*, 608.

Chapter 12: Anne (1665–1714) and George of Denmark (1653–1708)

1. Anne Somerset, *Queen Anne: The Politics of Passion* (London: Harper-Press, 2012), 54.

2. James Anderson Winn, *Queen Anne: Patroness of Arts* (Oxford: Oxford University Press, 2014), 209.

3. Edward Gregg, *Queen Anne* (New Haven, CT: Yale University Press, 2014), 41.

4. Ibid.

5. Charles Beem, "'I Am Her Majesty's Subject': Prince George of Denmark and the Transformation of the English Male Consort," *Canadian Journal of History* 39, no. 3 (December 2004), 457–87.

6. Maureen Waller, *Sovereign Ladies: The Six Reigning Queens of England* (London: John Murray, 2006), 298.

7. Gregg, *Queen Anne*, 47.

8. David Bronte Green, *Queen Anne* (London: Collins, 1970), 114.

9. Jenkin Lewis, *Memoirs of Prince William Henry, Duke of Gloucester* (London: Mess. Payne, 1789), 6.

10. Ibid., 8–9.

11. Ibid., 13.

12. Ibid., 17.

13. Ibid., v.

14. Ibid., 7.

15. Bayle Saint John, *Montaigne the Essayist* (London: Chapman and Hall, 1858), 8.

16. Somerset, *Queen Anne*, 183.

17. Ibid., 182–83.

18. Hugh Noel Williams, *A Rose of Savoy: Marie Adélaïde of Savoy, Duchesse de Bourgogne, Mother of Louis XV* (New York: Charles Scribner's Sons, 1909), 20.

19. Somerset, *Queen Anne*, 183.

20. Anna Whitelock, *Mary Tudor: Princess, Bastard, Queen* (New York: Random House, 2009), 128.

21. Carole Levin, *The Heart and Stomach of a King: Elizabeth I and the Politics of Power*, 2nd ed. (Philadelphia: University of Pennsylvania Press, 2013), 87.

22. Nicholas Seger, "She Will Not Be the Tyrant They Desire: Daniel Defoe and Queen Anne," in *Queen Anne and the Arts*, ed. Cedric D. Reverand II (Lewisburg: Bucknell University Press, 2015), 47.

23. Ibid.

Chapter 13: George II (1683–1760) and Caroline of Ansbach (1683–1737)

1. Mary Beacock Fryer, Arthur Bousfield, and Garry Toffoli, *Lives of the Princesses of Wales* (Toronto: Dundurn Press, 1996), 42.

2. John Hervey and Baron Hervey, *Memoirs of the Reign of George II: From His Accession to the Death of Queen Caroline* (London: John Murray, 1848), 2:365–66.

3. Claudia Gold, *The King's Mistress: The True and Scandalous Story of the Woman Who Stole the Heart of George I* (London: Quercus, 2012), 189.

4. Alan Palmer, *Princes of Wales* (London: Weidenfeld and Nicolson, 1979), 127.

5. Janice Hadlow, *A Royal Experiment: The Private Life of King George III* (New York: Henry Holt, 2014), 71.

6. Ibid., 72.

7. John Locke, *The Works of John Locke* (London: C. and J. Rivington, 1824), 8:44.

8. Flora Fraser, *The Unruly Queen: The Life of Queen Caroline* (London: Macmillan, 1996).

9. Vincent Caretta, *George III and the Satirists from Hogarth to Byron* (Athens, GA: University of Georgia Press, 1990), 179.

10. Justin C. Voyk, *In Destiny's Hands: Five Tragic Rulers; Children of Maria Theresa* (Bloomington, IN: iUniverse, 2010), 240.

Chapter 14: Louis XVI of France (1754–93) and Marie Antoinette of Austria (1755–93)

1. Jeanne Campan, *The Private Life of Marie Antoinette: A Confidante's Account* (New York: 1500 Books, 2006), 144–45.

2. Ibid., 145.

3. British Library, Additional Manuscripts, 39757, folio 2a.

4. Jean-Jacques Rousseau, *Emile, or On Education*, trans. Allan Bloom (New York: Basic Books, 1979), 21.

5. Évelyne Lever, ed., *Marie Antoinette, Correspondance* (Paris: Tallandier, 2005), 331.

6. Georges, Comte de Clam-Martinic, Jean Grasson, and Frans Durif, eds., *Marquis de Bombelles: Journal* (Geneva: Librarie Droz S.A., 1977), 1:326.

7. Antoine-Alexandre Barbier et al., *Dictionnaire des Ouvrages Anonymes* (Paris: Librarie de Fechoz et Letouzey, 1882), 255.

8. *Apologues Modernes du Dauphin, Premieres Leçons du Fils Aine d'un Roi Aux Femmes & Aux Rois. Il Faut Parler par Apologues* (Brussels: 1788), 88–89.

9. Elisabeth Vigée Le Brun, *Memoirs* (New York: Doubleday, Page, 1903), http://digital.library.upenn.edu/women/lebrun/memoirs/memoirs.html#II.

10. Lever, *Marie Antoinette*, 489.

11. Leonard Gallois, *Réimpression de L'Ancien Moniteur Tome Dix-Huitième* (Paris: Au Bureau Centrale, 1841), 146.

12. "Marie Antoinette's Fan," *Royal Collection Trust*, www.royalcollection.org.uk/collection/25092/marie-antoinettes-fan.

Chapter 15: Victoria (1819–1901) and Albert of Saxe-Coburg-Gotha (1819–61)

1. Jehanne Wake, *Princess Louise: Queen Victoria's Unconventional Daughter* (London: HarperCollins, 1988), 172.

2. Robert M. Stamp, *Royal Rebels: Princess Louise and Lord Lorne* (Toronto: Dundurn Press, 1988), 68.

3. Isabella Beeton, *Mrs. Beeton's Guide to Household Management* (London: S.O. Beeton, 1861), 1,013.

4. Hannah Pakula, *An Uncommon Woman: The Empress Frederick, Daughter of Queen Victoria, Wife of the Crown Prince of Prussia, Mother of Kaiser Wilhelm* (New York: Simon and Schuster, 1997), 27.

5. Ibid., 28.

6. Petrina Brown, *Eve: Sex, Childbirth and Motherhood Throughout the Ages* (Chichester, UK: Summersdale, 2004), 160.

7. Alison Plowden, *The Young Victoria* (London: Weidenfeld and Nicolson, 1981), 243.

8. Yvonne Ward, *Censoring Queen Victoria: How Two Gentlemen Edited a Queen and Created an Icon* (London: Oneworld, 2013), 113.

9. *Cassell's Household Guide: Being a Complete Encyclopedia of Domestic and Social Economy* (London: Cassell, Petter and Galpin, 1869), 1:36.

10. Peter Gordon and Denis Lawton, *Royal Education: Past, Present and Future* (London: Frank Cass, 2003), 152.

11. Ibid., 153.

12. Hildi Froese Tiessen and Paul Gerard Tiessen, *After Green Gables: L.M. Montgomery's Letters to Ephraim Weber, 1916–1941* (Toronto: University of Toronto Press, 2006), 112.

13. *The British and Foreign Medical and Chirurgical Review* (London: John Churchill, 1849), 4:507.

14. Helen Rappaport, *Queen Victoria: A Biographical Companion* (Santa Barbara: ABC-CLIO, 2003), 340.

15. Pakula, *An Uncommon Woman*, 67.

16. Rappaport, *Queen Victoria*, 164.

17. Kenneth Rose, *George V* (New York: Alfred A. Knopf, 1984), 1.

18. Ibid., 37.

19. Pakula, *An Uncommon Woman*, 215.

20. Marie Louise of Schleswig-Holstein, *My Memories of Six Reigns* (London: Evans Brothers, 1956), 36–37.

21. Jane Ridley, *Bertie: A Life of Edward VI* (London: Chatto and Windus, 2012), 241.

22. Michael John Sullivan, *A Fatal Passion: The Story of the Last Uncrowned Empress of Russia* (New York: Random House, 1997), 96.

23. Richard Hough, *Advice to My Granddaughter: Letters from Queen Victoria to Princess Victoria of Hesse* (New York: Simon and Schuster, 1975), 124.

Chapter 16: Nicholas II of Russia (1868–1918) and Alexandra of Hesse-Darmstadt (1872–1918)

1. Andrei Maylunas and Sergei Mironenko, *A Lifelong Passion: Nicholas and Alexandra: Their Own Story* (New York: Doubleday, 1997), 151.

2. Robert Massie, *Nicholas and Alexandra* (New York: Athenum Books, 1967), 60.

3. Marie, Grand Duchess of Russia, *The Education of a Princess* (New York: Viking Press, 1930), 34.

4. Hough, *Advice to My Granddaughter*, 138.

5. Margaret Eager, "Six Years at the Russian Court," *Leisure Hour* 4 (1905), 443–57.

6. Helen Rappaport, *The Romanov Sisters: The Lost Lives of the Daughters of Nicholas and Alexandra* (New York: St. Martin's Press, 2014), 80.

7. Grand Duke Gabriel Constantinovich, *Memories in the Marble Palace* (Pickering, ON: Gilbert's Royal Books, 2009), 176–77.

8. Empress Alexandra Feodorovna, "On Marriage and Family Life," www.holy-transfiguration.org/library_en/fam_marriageAlex1.html.

9. "Later Memoirs of Anna Vyrubova," Bob Atchison, *Alexander Palace Time Machine*, www.alexanderpalace.org/palace/2anna1.html.

10. Maylunas and Mironenko, *A Lifelong Passion*, 133.

11. Marie, Grand Duchess of Russia, *The Education of a Princess*, 34.

12. Edvard Radzinsky, *The Rasputin File* (New York: Anchor Books, 2001), 125.

13. Rappaport, *The Romanov Sisters*, 217.

14. Vladimir A. Kozlov and Vladimir M. Krustalev, *The Last Diary of Tsaritsa Alexandra* (New Haven, CT: Yale University Press, 1997), 108.

15. Mark D. Steinburg and Vladimir M. Krustalev, *The Fall of the Romanovs* (New Haven, CT: Yale University Press, 1997), 315.

16. Robert K. Massie, *The Romanovs: The Final Chapter* (New York: Random House, 1995), 17.

17. Rappaport, *The Romanov Sisters*, 369.

Chapter 17: Juliana of the Netherlands (1909–2004) and Bernhard of Lippe-Biesterfeld (1911–2004)

1. Albert VanderMey, *When Canada Was Home: The Story of Dutch Princess Margriet* (Surrey, BC: Vanderheide, 1992), 29.
2. Anne Frank, Otto Frank, and Mirjam Pressler, *The Diary of a Young Girl: The Definitive Edition* (New York: Alfred A. Knopf, 2010), 38.
3. VanderMey, *When Canada Was Home*, 34.
4. Wilhelmina, Queen of the Netherlands, *Lonely But Not Alone* (New York: McGraw-Hill, 1960), 183–84.
5. Ibid., 17.
6. Ibid., 77.
7. VanderMey, *When Canada Was Home*, 17.
8. Alice, Countess of Athlone, *For My Grandchildren* (London: Evans Brothers, 1966), 251.
9. Wilhelmina, *Lonely But Not Alone*, 181.
10. Peter Conradi, *The Great Survivors: How Monarchy Made It into the Twenty-First Century* (London: Alma Books, 2012), 207–08.
11. Janet Davison, "Abdicating Dutch Queen Was a Wartime Ottawa Schoolgirl," *CBC News*, April 29, 2013.
12. "A Speech by the Queen on Her 21st Birthday, 1947," *The Royal Family*, http://www.royal.uk/21st-birthday-speech-21-april-1947.

Chapter 18: Elizabeth II (1926–) and Philip of Greece and Denmark (1921–)

1. *Our Queen at Ninety*, ITV, March 26, 2016.
2. Basil Boothroyd, *Prince Philip: An Informal Biography* (New York: McCall, 1971), 71.
3. While the eldest son of a monarch was heir apparent because he could not be superseded by a younger sibling, the eldest daughter in the absence of sons was heiress presumptive because the arrival of a younger brother would lower her place in the line of succession.
4. Melissa Buis Michaux and Leslie Dunlap, "Baby Lit: Feminist Response to the Cult of New Motherhood," in *You've Come a Long Way Baby:*

Women, Politics and Popular Culture, ed. Lilly Goren (Lexington: University Press of Kentucky, 2009), 139.

5. Ibid.

6. Virginia Nicholson, *Perfect Wives in Ideal Homes: The Story of Women in the 1950s* (London: Viking, 2015), 266.

7. William Shawcross, *Counting One's Blessings: The Selected Letters of the Queen Mother* (New York: Farrar, Strauss and Giroux, 2012), 479.

8. Gyles Brandreth, *Philip and Elizabeth: Portrait of a Marriage* (New York: Norton, 2005), 298.

9. Hugo Vickers, *Alice: Princess Andrew of Greece* (New York: St. Martin's Press, 2002), 345.

10. Anne Edwards, *Royal Sisters: Queen Elizabeth II and Princess Margaret* (New York: William Morrow, 1990), 360.

11. Anthony Holden, *Charles: Prince of Wales* (London: Pan Books, 1980), 91.

12. Robert Jobson, "Prince Philip Turns 95: The Duke Is a Loyal and Lovely Family Patriarch," *Evening Standard*, June 8, 2016.

13. Waller, *Sovereign Ladies*, 478.

14. Nancy McDermott, "Parents Take Parenting Far Too Seriously," review, *Spiked*, July 20, 2007.

15. Robert Hardman, *Our Queen* (London: Arrow, 2012), 396.

Chapter 19: Prince Charles (1948–) and Diana Spencer (1961–97)

1. *Daily Mail*, "Who Gave Prince William His Harry Potter Scar? Royal Reveals Friend Hit Him with Golf Club," *Daily Mail*, March 18, 2009.

2. Louise Lague, "Questions for an Absent Father," *People Magazine*, June 17, 1991, http://people.com/archive/cover-story-questions-for-an-absent-father-vol-35-no-23.

3. *Daily Mail*, "Who Gave Prince William His Harry Potter Scar?"

4. Tim Clayton and Phil Craig, *Diana: Story of a Princess* (New York: Simon and Schuster, 2013), 210.

5. Lague, "Questions for an Absent Father."

6. Holden, *Charles*, 51.

7. Sarah Bradford, *Diana* (London: Viking, 2006), 45.
8. Dimbleby, *The Prince of Wales: A Biography* (New York: Doubleday, 1994), 334.
9. Ibid.
10. Shawcross, *Counting One's Blessings*, 151.
11. Alan Travis, "Revealed: Thatcher Official Planned to Trump CND with Prince William," *Guardian*, July 21, 2016.
12. Clayton and Craig, *Diana*, 211.
13. Jennifer Latson, "The Princess Diana TV Interview That Made History," *Time Magazine*, November 20, 2014.
14. Lucy Clarke-Billings, "Prince Harry Opens Up About Princess Diana Ahead of Invictus Games," *Newsweek*, April 9, 2016.
15. Jean Barnes, *Purposeful Parenting: Six Steps to Bring Out the Best in Your Kids* (Dallas: Destiny Image, 2015), 76.
16. Carolyn Durand, "Princes William and Harry Open Up About Life with Prince Charles," *ABC News*, December 28, 2015.
17. Harry Wallop, "Prince Charles Shows Why Embarrassing Dads Make the Best Dads," *Telegraph*, January 4, 2016.
18. "Prince Edward's Daughter Lady Louise Breaks Arm in Riding Accident," *Hello!*, April 12, 2012.
19. Lague, "Questions for an Absent Father."
20. Allison Pearson, "Kate Middleton: The Commoner Who Could Save the Royal Family," *Newsweek*, April 3, 2011.

Chapter 20: Prince William (1982–) and Catherine Middleton (1982–)

1. "Kate Middleton Shares Adorable George Anecdote," *Hello!*, April 14, 2015.
2. Maria Montessori, *The Absorbent Mind* (Madras: Theosophical, 1949), 1:38–39.
3. Katie Nicholl, *Kate: The Future Queen* (New York: Weinstein Books, 2013), 33.
4. Tina Gaudoin, "How Kate Middleton Imploded the Class System and Gave Rise to a New Kind of Brit," *Town and Country*, July 29, 2015.

5. *BBC News*, "Duke of Cambridge: *Attitude* Magazine Features Royal Cover Star," *BBC News*, June 15, 2016.

6. Richard Palmer, "Kate Middleton Urges Schools to Support Kids in Children's Mental Health Week," *Express*, February 8, 2016.

7. "The Duke of Cambridge on Fatherhood and Mental Health," *Heads Together*, www.headstogether.org.uk/fatherhood-and-mental-health.

8. Carin Pettersson, "Victoria's Father Does Not Want Her as Queen," *Nettavisen*, November 23, 2003.

9. "PM and Palace 'Discussed Reform,'" *BBC News*, March 27, 2009.

10. Randy Boswell, "A Woman First in Line to the Throne? Harper Consults on Succession Changes," *National Post*, October 13, 2011.

11. "Girls Equal in British Throne Succession," *BBC News*, October 28, 2011.

12. Kate McCann, "'Outdated' Peerage Rules Turn Women into 'Non-Persons' Says Downton Creator," *Telegraph*, September 11, 2015.

13. Bree Hocking, "Breaking Up Is Hard to Do," *U.S. News*, September 15, 2014.

Epilogue: The Future of the Royal Nursery

1. Bridget Arsenault, "Kensington Palace Hosts Hollywood Royalty at the BAFTA Nominees Party," *Vanity Fair*, February 14, 2016.

2. Walter Bagehot, *The English Constitution and Other Political Essays* (New York: D. Appleton, 1994), 101.

3. Suzie Bakos, "Prince George 'Is a Very Clever, Articulate Little Boy,' Sophie Winkleman Exclusively Reveals," *Hello!*, February 16, 2016.

4. "Queen's Diamond Jubilee: Royal Family Aboard the *Spirit of Chartwell*," *Telegraph*, June 3, 2012.

5. Carolyn Durand, "Prince William on Fatherhood, His Role as Future King, and What He's Learned from the Queen," *ABC News*, April 20, 2016.

6. Melissa Langstam Braunstein, "Prince William, Father First," *Family Studies*, March 8, 2016, http://family-studies.org/prince-william-father-first.

7. Robert Hazell and Bob Morris, "The Queen at 90: The Changing Role of the Monarchy and Future Challenges," *UCL Constitution Unit*, June 10, 2016.

FURTHER READING

Chapter 1: Edgar "the Peaceable" (c. 943–75) and Elfrida of Northampton (c. 945–1001)

Glasswell, Samantha. *The Earliest English: Living and Dying in Early Anglo-Saxon England.* Stroud, UK: Tempus, 2002.

Lacey, Robert, and Danny Danziger. *The Year 1000: What Life Was Like at the Turn of the First Millennium: An Englishman's World.* London: Abacus, 2000.

Norton, Elizabeth. *Elfrida: The First Crowned Queen of England.* Stroud, UK: Amberley, 2013.

Rex, Peter. *Edgar: King of the English 959–975.* Stroud, UK: Tempus, 2007.

Scragg, Donald, ed. *Edgar, King of the English: New Interpretations.* Woodbridge, UK: Boydell Press, 2008.

Stafford, Pauline. *Queen Emma and Queen Edith: Queenship and Women's Power in 11th Century England.* Oxford: Blackwell, 1997.

Chapter 2: William I "the Conqueror" (c. 1028–87) and Matilda of Flanders (c. 1031–83)

Borman, Tracy. *Matilda: Queen of the Conqueror.* London: Jonathan Cape, 2011.

Gillingham, John. *William II: The Red King.* London: Allen Lane, 2015.

Hagger, Mark. *William: King and Conqueror.* London: I.B. Tauris, 2012.

Herlihy, David. *Medieval Households.* Cambridge, MA: Harvard University Press, 1985.

Huneycutt, Lois L. *Matilda of Scotland: A Study in English Queenship.* Suffolk: Boydell Press, 2003.

Le Patourel, John. "The Norman Succession, 996–1135." *The English Historical Review* 86 (1971): 225–50.

Chapter 3: Henry II (1133–89) and Eleanor of Aquitaine (c. 1124–1204)

Harper-Bill, Christopher, and Vincent Nicholas, eds. *Henry II: New Interpretations.* Suffolk: Boydell Press, 2007.

Johns, Susan M. *Noblewomen, Aristocracy and Power in the Twelfth-Century Anglo-Norman Realm.* Manchester: Manchester University Press, 2003.

McLynn, Frank. *Lionheart and Lackland: King Richard, King John and the Wars of Conquest.* New York: Vintage, 2007.

Turner, Ralph V. *Eleanor of Aquitaine: Queen of France, Queen of England.* New Haven, CT: Yale University Press, 2009.

Turner, Ralph V. "Eleanor of Aquitaine and Her Children: An Inquiry into Medieval Family Attachment." *Journal of Medieval History* 14, no. 4 (1988): 321–35.

Wheeler, Bonnie, and John Carmi Parsons, eds. *Eleanor of Aquitaine: Lord and Lady.* New York: Palgrave Macmillan, 2004.

Chapter 4: Henry III (1207–72) and Eleanor of Provence (c. 1223–91)

Badham, Sally, and Sophie Oosterwijk. "The Tomb Monument of Katherine, Daughter of Henry III and Eleanor of Provence (1253–7)." *Antiquaries Journal* 92 (2012): 169–96.

Davis, John Paul. *The Gothic King: A Biography of Henry III.* London: Peter Owen Publishers, 2013.

Goldstone, Nancy. *Four Queens: The Provençal Sisters Who Ruled Europe.* New York: Penguin Books, 2008.

Harris, Carolyn. *Magna Carta and Its Gifts to Canada.* Toronto: Dundurn Press, 2015.

Howell, Margaret. "The Children of King Henry III and Eleanor of Provence." In *Thirteenth-Century England IV: Proceedings of the Newcastle Upon Tyne Conference, 1991*, edited by Peter R. Ross and Simon D. Lloyd, 57–72. Suffolk: Boydell and Brewer, 1992.

Howell, Margaret. *Eleanor of Provence: Queenship in Thirteenth-Century England.* Hoboken, NJ: Wiley-Blackwell, 2001.

Metzler, Irina. *Fools and Idiots: Intellectual Disability in the Middle Ages.* Oxford: Oxford University Press, 2016.

Chapter 5: Edward III (1312–77) and Philippa of Hainault (1314–69)

Mortimer, Ian. *The Perfect King: The Life of Edward III: Father of the English Nation.* London: Jonathan Cape, 2006.

Orme, Nicholas. *Medieval Children.* New Haven, CT: Yale University Press, 2001.

Ormrod, W. Mark. *Edward III.* New Haven, CT: Yale University Press, 2011.

Parsons, John Carmi, and Bonnie Wheeler, eds. *Medieval Mothering.* New York: Garland, 1996.

Tuchman, Barbara. *A Distant Mirror: The Calamitous 14th Century.* New York: Ballantine Books, 1978.

Weir, Alison. *Mistress of the Monarchy: The Life of Kathryn Swynford, Duchess of Lancaster.* New York: Ballantine Books, 2007.

Chapter 6: Richard III (1452–85) and Anne Neville (1456–85)

Baldwin, David. *Richard III.* Stroud, UK: Amberley, 2012.

Greco, Gina L., and Christine M. Rose. *The Good Wife's Guide: Le Ménagier de Paris; A Medieval Household Book.* Ithaca, NY: Cornell University Press, 2009.

Hicks, Michael. *Anne Neville: Queen to Richard III.* Stroud, UK: Tempus, 2006.

Kendall, Paul Murray. *Richard III.* London: Allen and Unwin, 1995.

License, Amy. *Anne Neville: Richard III's Tragic Queen.* Stroud, UK: Amberley, 2013.

Chapter 7: Ferdinand II of Aragon (1452–1516) and Isabella I of Castile (1451–1504)

Anderson, James F. *Daily Life During the Spanish Inquisition.* Westport, CT: Greenwood Press, 2002.

Boruchoff, David A. *Isabel La Católica, Queen of Castile: Critical Essays*. New York: Palgrave Macmillan, 2003.

Casey, James. *Early Modern Spain: A Social History*. London: Routledge, 1999.

Fox, Julia. *Sister Queens: The Noble, Tragic Lives of Katherine of Aragon and Juana, Queen of Castile*. New York: Ballantine Books, 2011.

Liss, Peggy. *Isabel the Queen: Life and Times*. Rev. ed. Philadelphia: University of Pennsylvania Press, 2004.

Chapter 8: Henry VIII (1491–1547) and Catherine of Aragon (1485–1536)

Starkey, David. *Six Wives: The Queens of Henry VIII*. New York: Harper-Collins, 2003.

Tremlett, Giles. *Catherine of Aragon: Henry's Spanish Queen: A Biography*. London: Faber and Faber, 2010.

Vives, Juan Luis. *The Education of a Christian Woman: A Sixteenth-Century Manual*. Trans. and ed. Charles Fantazzi. Chicago: University of Chicago Press, 2000.

Weir, Alison. *Children of England: The Heirs of Henry VIII*. London: Jonathan Cape, 1996.

Whitelock, Anna. *Mary Tudor: Princess, Bastard, Queen*. New York: Random House, 2009.

Williams, Patrick. *Katharine of Aragon*. Stroud, UK: Amberley, 2010.

Chapter 9: Frederick V, Elector Palatine, (1596–1632) and Elizabeth of England and Scotland (1596–1662)

Akkerman, Nadine. *The Correspondence of Elizabeth Stuart: Queen of Bohemia 1603–1631*. Oxford: Oxford University Press, 2015.

Barroll, Leeds. *Anna of Denmark, Queen of England: A Cultural Biography*. Philadelphia: University of Pennsylvania Press, 2001.

Ozment, Steven. *When Fathers Ruled: Family Life in Reformation Europe*. Cambridge, MA: Harvard University Press, 1983.

Sophia, Electress of Hanover. *Memoirs of Sophia, Electress of Hanover 1630–1680*. London: Richard Bentley and Son, 1888.

Wilson, Peter H. *The Thirty Years War: Europe's Tragedy*. Cambridge, MA: Belknap Press, 2009.

Chapter 10: Charles I (1600–49) and Henrietta Maria of France (1609–69)

Carlton, Charles. *Charles I: The Personal Monarch.* 2nd ed. New York: Routledge, 1995.

Fraser, Antonia. *The Weaker Vessel: Woman's Lot in Seventeenth-Century England.* London: Vintage Books, 1985.

Green, Mary Anne Everett. *Letters of Queen Henrietta Maria Including Her Private Correspondence with Charles I.* London: Richard Bentley, 1857.

Griffey, Erin. *Henrietta Maria: Piety, Politics and Patronage.* Surrey, UK: Ashgate, 2008.

Harris, Carolyn. *Queenship and Revolution in Early Modern Europe: Henrietta Maria and Marie Antoinette.* New York: Palgrave Macmillan, 2015.

Latham, Robert, and William Matthews. *The Diary of Samuel Pepys: A New and Complete Transcription.* Berkeley: University of California Press, 1983.

Porter, Linda. *Royal Renegades: The Children of Charles I and the English Civil Wars.* London: Pan Macmillan, 2016.

White, Michelle Anne. *Henrietta Maria and the English Civil Wars.* Surrey, UK: Ashgate, 2006.

Chapter 11: Peter I "the Great" of Russia (1672–1725) and Catherine I (1684–1727)

Hughes, Lindsey. *The Romanovs: Ruling Russia 1613–1917.* London: Hambledon Continuum, 2008.

_____. *Russia in the Age of Peter the Great.* New Haven, CT: Yale University Press, 1998.

Lincoln, W. Bruce. *The Romanovs: Autocrats of All the Russias.* New York: Anchor Books, 1981.

Massie, Robert. *Peter the Great: His Life and World.* New York: Random House, 1980.

Montefiore, Simon Sebag. *The Romanovs 1613–1918.* New York: Alfred A. Knopf, 2016.

Pouncy, Carolyn Johnston. *The Domostroi: Rules for Russian Households in the Time of Ivan the Terrible.* Ithaca, NY: Cornell University Press, 1994.

Pushkareva, Natalia. *Women in Russian History from the Tenth to the Twentieth Century.* 2nd ed. Trans. and ed. Eve Levin. Phoenix Mill, UK: Sutton, 1999.

Chapter 12: Anne (1665–1714) and George of Denmark (1653–1708)

Gregg, Edward. *Queen Anne.* New Haven, CT: Yale University Press, 2014.

Holmes, Geoffrey. *British Politics in the Age of Anne.* London: Hambledon Press, 1987.

Lewis, Jenkin. *Memoirs of Prince William Henry, Duke of Gloucester.* London: Mess. Payne, 1789.

Somerset, Anne. *Queen Anne: The Politics of Passion.* London: HarperPress, 2012.

Waller, Maureen. *Ungrateful Daughters: The Stuart Princesses Who Stole Their Father's Crown.* London: Hodder and Stoughton, 2002.

Winn, James Anderson. *Queen Anne: Patroness of Arts.* Oxford: Oxford University Press, 2014.

Chapter 13: George II (1683–1760) and Caroline of Ansbach (1683–1737)

Bailey, Joanne. *Parenting in England: 1760–1830.* Oxford: Oxford University Press, 2012.

Hadlow, Janice. *The Strangest Family: The Private Lives of George III, Queen Charlotte and the Hanoverians.* New York: HarperCollins, 2014.

Hervey, John, and Baron Hervey. *Memoirs of the Reign of George II: From His Accession to the Death of Queen Caroline.* 2 vols. London: John Murray, 1848.

Hibbert, Christopher. *George III: A Personal History.* New York: Basic Books, 1998.

Thompson, Andrew C. *George II: King and Elector.* New Haven, CT: Yale University Press, 2011.

Worsley, Lucy. *The Courtiers: Splendour and Intrigue at the Georgian Court at Kensington Palace.* New York: Walker, 2010.

Chapter 14: Louis XVI of France (1754–93) and Marie Antoinette of Austria (1755–93)

Cadbury, Deborah. *The Lost King of France: How DNA Solved the Mystery of the Murdered Son of Louis XVI and Marie Antoinette.* New York: St. Martin's Press, 2002.

Campan, Jeanne. *The Private Life of Marie Antoinette: A Confidante's Account.* New York: 1500 Books, 2006.

Fraser, Antonia. *Marie Antoinette: The Journey.* London: Weidenfeld and Nicholson, 2001.

Goodman, Dena, ed. *Marie Antoinette: Writings of the Body of a Queen.* New York: Routledge, 2003.

Harris, Carolyn. *Queenship and Revolution in Early Modern Europe: Henrietta Maria and Marie Antoinette.* New York: Palgrave Macmillan, 2015.

Chapter 15: Victoria (1819–1901) and Albert of Saxe-Coburg-Gotha (1819–61)

Beeton, Isabella. *Mrs. Beeton's Guide to Household Management.* London: S.O. Beeton, 1861.

Dennison, Matthew. *The Last Princess: The Devoted Life of Queen Victoria's Youngest Daughter.* London: Weidenfeld and Nicholson, 2007.

Hibbert, Christopher. *Queen Victoria: A Personal History.* London: HarperCollins, 2000.

Pakula, Hannah. *An Uncommon Woman: The Empress Frederick, Daughter of Queen Victoria, Wife of the Crown Prince of Prussia, Mother of Kaiser Wilhelm.* New York: Simon and Schuster, 1997.

Rappaport, Helen. *Queen Victoria: A Biographical Companion.* Santa Barbara, CA: ABC-CLIO, 2003.

Ridley, Jane. *Bertie: A Life of Edward VII.* London: Chatto and Windus, 2012.

Chapter 16: Nicholas II of Russia (1868–1918) and Alexandra of Hesse-Darmstadt (1872–1918)

Harris, Carolyn. "The Succession Prospects of Grand Duchess Olga Nikolaevna (1895–1918)." *Canadian Slavonic Papers* 54 (2012): 61–84.

Massie, Robert K. *Nicholas and Alexandra.* New York: Athenum Books, 1967.

Maylunas, Andrei, and Sergei Mironenko. *A Lifelong Passion: Nicholas and Alexandra: Their Own Story*. New York: Doubleday, 1997.

Pitcher, Harvey. *When Miss Emmie Was in Russia: English Governesses Before, During and After the October Revolution*. London: Century, 1977.

Rappaport, Helen. *The Romanov Sisters: The Lost Lives of the Daughters of Nicholas and Alexandra*. New York: St. Martin's Press: 2014.

Smith, Douglas, *Rasputin: Faith, Power, and the Twilight of the Romanovs*. New York: Farrar, Straus and Giroux, 2016.

Steinberg, Mark D., and Vladimir M. Krustalev. *The Fall of the Romanovs*. New Haven, CT: Yale University Press, 1997.

Chapter 17: Juliana of the Netherlands (1909–2004) and Bernhard of Lippe-Biesterfeld (1911–2004)

Alice, Countess of Athlone. *For My Grandchildren*. London: Evans Brothers, 1966.

Conradi, Peter. *The Great Survivors: How Monarchy Made It into the Twenty-First Century*. London: Alma Books, 2012.

Frank, Anne, Otto Frank, and Mirjam Pressler. *The Diary of a Young Girl: The Definitive Edition*. New York: Alfred A. Knopf, 2010.

Hoffman, William. *Queen Juliana: The Story of the Richest Woman in the World*. New York: Harcourt, Brace, Jovanovich, 1979.

Vandermey, Albert. *When Canada Was Home: The Story of Dutch Princess Margriet*. Surrey, BC: Vanderheide, 1992.

Wilhelmina, Queen of the Netherlands. *Lonely But Not Alone*. New York: McGraw-Hill, 1960.

Chapter 18: Elizabeth II (1926–) and Philip of Greece and Denmark (1921–)

Brandreth, Gyles. *Philip and Elizabeth: Portrait of a Marriage*. New York: Norton, 2005.

Eade, Philip. *Young Prince Philip: His Turbulent Early Life*. London: Harper Press, 2011.

Hardman, Robert. *Our Queen*. London: Arrow, 2012.

Nicholson, Virginia. *Perfect Wives in Ideal Homes: The Story of Women in the 1950s*. London: Viking, 2015.

Reynolds, Anne, and Lucy Peter. *Royal Childhood*. London: Royal Collection Trust, 2014.

Shawcross, William. *Counting One's Blessings: The Selected Letters of the Queen Mother*. New York: Farrar, Strauss and Giroux, 2012.

Chapter 19: Prince Charles (1948–) and Diana Spencer (1961–97)

Bradford, Sarah. *Diana*. London: Viking, 2006.

Brown, Tina. *The Diana Chronicles*. New York: Doubleday, 2007.

Davies, Jude. *Diana: A Cultural History*. New York: Palgrave, 2001.

Dimbleby, Jonathan. *The Prince of Wales: A Biography*. New York: Doubleday, 1994.

Holden, Anthony. *Charles: A Biography*. London: Bantam Press, 1998.

Chapter 20: Prince William (1982–) and Catherine Middleton (1982–)

Jobson, Robert. *The New Royal Family: Prince George, William and Kate: The Next Generation*. London: John Blake, 2013.

Junor, Penny. *Prince William: The Man Who Will Be King*. New York: Pegasus Books, 2013.

Lloyd, Ian. *William and Catherine's New Royal Family: Celebrating the Arrival of Princess Charlotte*. London: Carlton Books, 2015.

Montessori, Maria. *The Montessori Method*. New York: Barnes and Noble Books, 2003.

Nicholl, Katie. *Kate: The Future Queen*. New York: Weinstein Books, 2013.

INDEX

Albert, Prince of Saxe-Coburg-Gotha, 149, 150–61, 162, 165, 167, 189, 203, 214

Albert Victor, Prince, Duke of Clarence, 161, 163, 196

Alexandra, Princess of Denmark, 160, 163

Alexandra of Hesse-Darmstadt, Empress of Russia, 163–64, 165–75, 181, 186, 214

Alexei I, Czar of Russia, 112–13

Alexei Nikolaevich, Czarevich of Russia, 166, 167–69, 173

Alexei Petrovich, Czarevich of Russia, 114–22

Alfonso XI, King of Castile, 58–59

Alfred, Duke of Edinburgh, 153, 163

Alfred the Great, King of Wessex, 18, 20, 21, 30

Alice, Countess of Athlone, 179, 180

Alice, Grand Duchess of Hesse-Darmstadt, 153, 160, 162

Alice of Battenberg, 175, 186

Alix, Countess of Blois, 35, 36

Amsberg, Klaus von, 181–82

Anastasia Nikolaevna, Grand Duchess of Russia, 166, 167, 168–69, 173, 174

Andrew, Prince, Duke of York, 187, 190–91, 195, 209–10

Anna of Denmark, 94–95, 96, 107

Anne, Princess Royal, 108, 187, 189, 190

Anne, Queen of Great Britain, 15, 122, 123–31, 154, 187

Arthur, Prince, Duke of Connaught, 153, 160, 163, 215

Arthur, Prince of Wales, 74, 82

Arthur I, Duke of Brittany, 40, 41

Augusta, Duchess of Brunswick, 132–33, 136, 137

Augusta of Saxe-Gotha, 132–33, 136

Bakewell, Joan, 188–89

Balmoral Castle, 157, 159

Beatrice, Duchess of Brittany, 48, 49

Beatrice of Battenberg, 153, 158, 163, 214

Beatrice of Savoy, 47, 48–49

Beatrix, Queen of the Netherlands, 176, 180, 181–82

Beaufort, Margaret, 70, 76, 83, 85–86, 112

Bernhard of Lippe-Biesterfeld, 177, 179

Black Death, The (plague), 58–59

Blanche of Lancaster, 61, 63

Boleyn, Anne, 89, 90, 204

Buckingham Palace, 158–59, 200, 202

Cambridge, Alexander, Earl of Athlone, 176, 180

Cameron, David, 208

Camilla, Duchess of Cornwall, 197, 198, 215

Campbell, John, Duke of Argyll, 150–51, 160

Carol II, King of Romania, 172

Caroline of Ansbach, 130–31, 132–36

Catherine, Duchess of Cambridge, 9–12, 13, 16, 109, 159, 187, 199–200, 201–11, 213, 215, 216–18

Catherine I, Empress of Russia, 115, 120–21

Catherine II, Empress of Russia, 115, 168

Catherine of Aragon, 14, 74, 78, 79, 82–83, 84–90, 198

Cavendish, William, Duke of Newcastle, 107, 109

Celestine III, Pope, 41, 42

Charles, Prince of Wales, 13, 16, 187, 189, 190, 192, 193–99, 205, 208, 215, 218

Charles I, King of England and Scotland, 12, 15, 16, 92, 95, 102, 104–11, 112–13, 127, 152, 187

Charles II, King of England and Scotland, 102, 103, 104, 107, 108–09, 110, 111, 112, 124, 128

Charles V, Holy Roman Emperor, 82, 86, 89, 91

Charles Louis, Elector Palatine, 99, 101, 102

Charles William, Duke of Brunswick, 137–38

Charlotte, Princess of Cambridge, 10, 16, 159, 192, 198, 201–12, 216–18

Charlotte, Princess of Wales, 151, 154, 157,

Charlotte-Christine of Brunswick-Lüneburg, 115, 116, 121

Charlotte of Mecklenburg-Strelitz, 138–40, 158

Chaucer, Geoffrey, 59, 70

Churchill, Sarah, Duchess of Marlborough, 123, 128–29

Churchill, Winston, 190, 205

Constance, Duchess of Brittany, 34, 40

Corfe Castle, 22, 23

Cromwell, Oliver, 109, 113

Despenser, Hugh, 54, 55, 56

Diana, Princess of Wales, 11, 192, 193–99, 204

Dunstan, Archbishop of Canterbury, 17, 20

Eagar, Margaret, 167, 171, 186
Edgar the Peaceable, King of England, 17–22, 23, 184
Edith, Queen, 32, 36
Edith, Saint, 19, 23
Edmund (son of Edgar the Peaceable), 17, 19, 20, 22
Edmund, Earl of Rutland, 66, 68
Edmund of Langley, 1st Duke of York, 57, 61, 67
Edward, Count Palatine of Simmern, 99, 103
Edward, Duke of Kent, 187, 215
Edward, Duke of Kent and Strathearn, 139, 151–52
Edward, Prince, Earl of Wessex, 187, 190, 195, 198
Edward, the Black Prince, 57–58, 60, 61–62, 109
Edward I, King of England, 48, 49, 50, 52, 58, 60, 62, 87
Edward II, King of England, 51, 54–56, 60, 69
Edward III, King of England, 16, 51, 52–64, 74, 87, 109, 185, 209
Edward IV, King of England, 66, 68, 69, 73, 75, 85, 124
Edward V, King of England, 11, 67, 69–70, 85
Edward VII, King of the United Kingdom, 151, 153, 155–56, 159–61, 163, 189, 190, 196
Edward VIII, King of the United Kingdom, 161, 172
Edward of Middleham, 65–67, 69, 71, 72, 73, 128
Edward the Confessor, King of England, 24, 30

Edward the Martyr, King of England, 19–20, 22-23
Eleanor of Aquitaine, 13, 32, 33–37, 40–43, 46, 48, 49, 51, 57, 69, 72
Eleanor of Castile, 49–50
Eleanor of England, Queen of Castile, 36, 42
Eleanor of Provence, 14, 43, 44–45, 47–51, 54, 57, 65, 139
Elfrida of Northampton, 14, 17, 19–24, 27, 29, 184
Elisabeth of the Palatinate, 99, 101
Elizabeth, Princess (daughter of Charles I), 108, 110, 112
Elizabeth, Queen Mother, 186, 189, 196
Elizabeth, Queen of Bohemia, 14, 92, 93–96, 97–99, 101–03, 105, 108, 111, 176
Elizabeth I, Queen of England, 40, 72, 90, 91, 92, 95, 109, 112, 130, 189
Elizabeth II, Queen, 12, 20, 108, 138, 159, 175, 182–83, 184–92, 196, 202, 205, 208, 213, 215–16, 218
Elizabeth de Burgh, Duchess of Clarence, 59, 61
Elizabeth of York, 70, 72, 73, 76, 85–86, 87
Emma of Normandy, 23, 24
Emma of Waldeck and Pyrmont, 178, 179
Enrique IV, King of Castile, 75, 78
Estelle, Princess of Sweden, 202, 207
Ethelred the Unready, King of England, 17, 19–24, 45

Ferdinand, King of Aragon, 14, 15, 74, 75–83

Ferdinand II, Holy Roman Emperor, 93, 97

Frederick, Prince of Wales, 131, 132–38

Frederick V, Elector Palatine, 14, 93, 96–102, 105, 155, 176

Froissart, Jean, 53–54

Geoffrey II, Duke of Brittany, 34, 35, 38–40, 41

George, Duke of Clarence, 66, 68, 73

George, Prince of Cambridge, 9–10, 16, 17, 192, 198, 201–12, 213, 215, 216–18

George, Prince of Denmark, 123, 125–26, 127, 154

George I, King of Great Britain, 13, 129, 130–31, 134–35, 184, 198

George II, King of Great Britain, 13, 20, 130–31, 132–37, 138, 198

George III, King of the United Kingdom, 133, 137–39, 151, 155–56, 158

George IV, King of the United Kingdom, 138, 151, 152, 155, 158

George V, King of the United Kingdom, 161, 163, 168, 175, 187–88, 189–90, 215

George VI, King of the United Kingdom, 172, 186, 187, 196, 207

George William, Prince of Great Britain, 135, 136

Georgy Alexandrovich, Grand Duke of Russia, 165–66, 170

Gerald of Wales, 38, 40

Golitsyn, Darya, 117, 120

Hampton Court Palace, 132, 133–34

Heidelberg Castle, 97, 98

Helena, Princess Christian of Schleswig-Holstein, 153, 162

Henrietta Anne, Duchess d'Orléans, 110, 111, 112, 124, 125, 129

Henrietta Maria of France, 12, 16, 99, 103–12, 124, 125, 152

Henry, Prince of Wales, 95, 105, 108

Henry, Prince of Wales (Harry), 192, 197–98, 205, 215

Henry, the Young King, 34, 35, 37–40, 41, 61

Henry I, King of England, 28, 30, 31–32, 33, 35, 38, 48, 87

Henry II, King of England, 13, 32, 33–41, 42, 46, 48, 49, 50, 51, 57, 61, 69, 72, 87

Henry III, King of England, 43, 44–51, 54, 57, 63, 65, 139

Henry IV, King of England, 59, 63, 67

Henry VI, King of England, 66, 67, 68, 85

Henry VII, King of England, 59, 67, 70, 72, 73, 74, 76, 82, 89, 112

Henry VIII, King of England, 15, 74, 79, 82, 83, 84–87, 89–92, 95, 109, 137, 139, 189, 198

Henry Frederick, Prince of the Palatinate, 99, 102

Henry Stuart, Duke of Gloucester, 110–11, 112

Herbert, William, Earl of Huntingdon, 71–72

Hervey, Lord, 133, 136

Highgrove House, 193, 197

Hudson's Bay Company, 94, 103

Irene, Princess of the Netherlands, 176, 180, 181

Isabel of Aragon, Queen of Portugal, 78, 81

Isabella, Countess of Bedford, 57, 60

Isabella, Queen of Castile, 14, 15, 74, 75–82, 87

Isabella of Austria, Queen of Denmark, 86–87, 91

Isabelle of Angoulême, 42–43, 45, 46, 48

Isabelle of Valois, 54–56, 57, 69

Ivan IV, Czar of Russia, 112, 117, 121

James I, King of England, 92, 94–96, 98, 105, 154, 189

James II, King of England, 107, 111, 112, 124–25, 126, 132, 154, 200

James IV, King of Scotland, 86, 87

James VI, King of Scotland. *See* James I, King of England

James VII, King of Scotland. *See* James II, King of England

Joan of England (daughter of Edward III), 57, 58–59

Joan of Kent, 58, 63

John, King of England, 33–34, 35, 39–40, 41–43, 45, 46, 49

John of Gaunt, Duke of Lancaster, 57, 59, 61–63

John of Pontefract (son of Richard III), 71–72

John Philip of the Palatinate, 99, 103

Juan, Prince of Asturias, 78, 79, 81

Juana, Queen of Castile, 78, 79, 82

Juliana, Queen of the Netherlands, 14, 176–82

Katherine (daughter of Richard III), 71–72

Katherine of England (daughter of Henry III), 44–45, 49, 65

Kensington Palace, 10, 109, 127, 152, 193, 210, 213

Leicester House, 135–36

León, Luis de, 76, 80

Leonore, Duchess of Gotland, 215

Leopold, Prince, Duke of Albany, 153, 158, 178

Leopold I, King of the Belgians, 152, 160

Lewis, Jenkin, 127–28

Lionel of Antwerp, Duke of Clarence, 57, 61

Lopukhina, Yevdokia, 116–17, 118, 119, 120

Louis XIII, King of France, 105, 107, 127

Louis XVI, King of France, 14, 139–40, 141–47, 173

Louis XVII, King of France, 144, 146, 147, 148

Louis-Joseph, Dauphin of France, 144–45, 146

Louise, Duchess of Argyll, 150–51, 153, 160, 190

Louise Hollandine of the Palatinate, 99, 101, 103

Louise Juliana of Orange-Nassau, 97, 101

Louise of Orléans, Queen of the Belgians, 148–49

Louise of Saxe-Gotha-Altenberg, 152, 160

Magna Carta, 34, 39, 45–46, 60

Malcolm III, King of Scotland, 28–30, 32

Manuel I, King of Portugal, 72, 81

Margaret, Princess, 186, 187

Margaret, Saint, Queen of Scotland 28–30, 32, 36

Margaret of Anjou, 67, 68

Margaret of England, Queen of Scotland, 48, 50

Margaret of Hainault, 55–56

Margaret Tudor, Queen of Scotland, 86, 87, 189

Margriet of the Netherlands, 177, 180

Marguerite of Provence, 47, 48–49

Maria II, Queen of Portugal, 154–55

Maria of Aragon, Queen of Portugal, 78, 79

Maria Nikolaevna, Grand Duchess of Russia, 166, 168–69, 171, 173–74

Maria Theresa, Empress of the Habsburg Empire, 142, 143–44, 146

Marie, Countess of Champagne, 35, 36

Marie Antoinette of Austria, Queen of France, 11, 12, 14, 139–40, 141–49, 173

Marie of Edinburgh, Queen of Romania, 163, 172

Marie Pavlovna (the younger), Grand Duchess of Russia, 166, 171

Marie-Thérèse of France, Madame Royale, 141, 144, 146, 148

Mary, Duchess of Burgundy, 76, 79, 81

Mary, Duchess of Suffolk, 86, 87, 160

Mary, Princess Royal, Princess of Orange, 16, 104, 107–08, 109, 112, 124

Mary, Queen of Scots, 92, 94, 154

Mary I, Queen of England, 79, 83, 84–85, 87–92, 109, 130, 198

Mary II, Queen of England, 109, 124–25, 126–27, 129

Mary Beatrice of Modena, 124–25, 126, 132

Mary of Teck, 161, 175, 190

Matilda, Empress, 35, 36, 41, 48

Matilda of Flanders, 13, 24, 25–28, 30–31, 35, 36, 69

Maurice of the Palatinate, 99, 102

Maximilian I, Holy Roman Emperor, 76, 79, 81

Melbourne, Lord William Lamb, 152, 156, 160

Menshikov, Alexander, 119, 120, 121, 122

Middleham Castle, 65, 68

Middleton, Carole, 203–05

Middleton, Kate. *See* Catherine, Duchess of Cambridge

Middleton, Michael, 203–04

Middleton, Philippa, 204

Miguel of Portugal, 81, 82

Montessori, Maria, 202–03,

Montgomery, Lucy Maud, 156–57

Morgan, Mary, 191–92

Mortimer, Edmund, 3rd Earl of March, 61, 63

Mountbatten, Louis, 1st Earl Mountbatten of Burma, 186, 190

Napoleon I, Emperor of France, 148, 160, 207

Neville, Anne, 13, 65–69, 72, 128

Neville, Isabel, Duchess of Clarence, 66, 68

Neville, Richard, Earl of Warwick, 66, 67–68

Nicholas II, Emperor of Russia, 14, 15, 164, 165–75, 186, 214

Olga Nikolaevna, Grand Duchess of Russia, 165–66, 168–69, 170, 172, 173, 174, 196

Parr, Catherine, 90, 91
Patricia of Connaught, 138, 163
Peronne, Madame, 106–07
Peter I, Czar of Russia, 13, 113, 114–22, 129, 134
Peter II, Czar of Russia, 115–16
Philip, Prince, Duke of Edinburgh, 175, 184, 186–92, 205, 213, 216
Philip IV, King of Spain, 105, 107
Philip of Flanders, 79, 82
Philippa, Countess of March, 61, 67
Philippa of Hainault, 52–60, 62, 63, 64, 185
Philippe, King of Belgium, 182, 211
Polastron, Yolande de, Duchess of Polignac, 144, 146
Pole, John de la, Earl of Lincoln, 72, 73–74
Putin, Vladimir, 117

Rasputin, Grigori, 168, 171, 181
Richard, Duke of York (father of Edward IV), 66, 67, 68
Richard, Duke of York (son of Edward IV), 67, 69
Richard I, King of England, 34, 35, 36, 38–40, 41–42
Richard II, King of England, 61–63
Richard III, King of England, 11, 13, 15, 35, 64, 65–74, 75, 124, 128
Richard III Society, 72–73

Robert II, Duke of Normandy, 13, 25–28, 30–31, 35, 36
Rousseau, Jean-Jacques, 143, 147, 188
royal names, 48–49, 99, 139, 160–61
Rupert, Prince of the Rhine, 93–94, 99, 101, 102, 103, 109

Sanchia of Provence, 47, 48
Seymour, Jane, 90, 91
Shakespeare, William, 29, 40, 72, 97, 126
Sophia Dorothea of Celle, 130, 134, 198
Sophia of the Palatinate, Electress of Hanover, 99, 101, 103, 129, 130
Sophie-Beatrix of France, 144, 146
Spanish Inquisition, 80–81
Spock, Benjamin, 188, 191–92
St. James's Palace, 132–33, 158
Stephen, King, 35, 36, 87
Stockmar, Baron Christian von, 155–56, 203

Tatiana Nikolaevna, Grand Duchess of Russia, 166, 168–69, 173, 174
Thatcher, Margaret, 196–97
Thomas of Woodstock, 1st Duke of Gloucester, 57, 61

Victoire of Saxe-Coburg-Saalfeld, 151–52, 157
Victoria, Princess of Wales, 160, 161
Victoria, Princess Royal, Empress of Germany, 153, 154, 155–56, 157, 159–62, 163
Victoria, Queen of the United Kingdom, 148–49, 150–64, 165, 167, 170, 183, 184, 189, 190, 201, 203, 214, 216

Victoria Eugenia of Battenberg, Queen of Spain, 163, 167

Victoria of Battenberg, Marchioness of Milford Haven, 161, 164, 166, 175, 186

Vitalis, Orderic, 26–27

Westminster Abbey, 26, 45, 103

Wilhelmina, Queen of the Netherlands, 176, 177–81

Willem-Alexander, King of the Netherlands, 182, 212

William, Duke of Gloucester (son of Queen Anne), 123–24, 126–29, 187

William, Prince, Duke of Cambridge, 9–12, 13, 16, 109, 159, 184, 185, 187, 192, 193–200, 201–11, 213–14, 215, 216–18

William I, King of England, 13, 24, 25–28, 30–32, 34–35, 36, 48, 50, 69

William II, King of England, 28, 31–32

William III, King of England, 109, 122, 123, 125, 126–27, 129

William III, King of the Netherlands, 178, 179

William IV, King of the United Kingdom, 139, 152, 155, 158, 159

William of Malmesbury, 21, 23

Winchester Castle, 47, 109

Windsor, Lady Louise, 192, 198–99

Windsor Castle, 45, 50, 157–58, 197

Woodville, Elizabeth, 68, 69, 85, 124, 204